This is an account of an engineer who stumbled into loss control and safety that was in the fullness of time to exceed four decades that the author never had an inkling of upon joining the army apprentices college direct from school at the age of 15. Serving both home and on active service overseas with the British Army, as an artisan, was subsequently invalided out. Immediately following discharge gained employment with Ford Motor Company where ultimately a career in loss control and safety followed attaining a senior engineering appointment due to additional qualifications and experience, all within a few years.

  The Ford experience led to far more challenging posts in the financial sector employed by international insurers that entailed surveying, appraising and investigating claims related accidents, across the five continents, visiting in all seventy-six countries. Reaching executive status with two major insurers was the sole author of seven risk management manuals and in excess, one hundred guidance standards. By virtue of being considered as an authority in loss control and risk management, he was an invited guest speaker at a number of international risk management conferences during his days in insurance. *Mundane Insurance* is a chronicle of some of the most invigorating and illuminating cases and experiences from a largely unknown profession.

D. Stuart McCreadie

MUNDANE INSURANCE

AUSTIN MACAULEY PUBLISHERS™
LONDON * CAMBRIDGE * NEW YORK * SHARJAH

Copyright © D. Stuart McCreadie (2020)

The right of D. Stuart McCreadie to be identified as the author of this work has been asserted by the author in accordance with section 77 and 78 of the Copyright, Designs and Patents Act 1988.

All rights reserved. No part of this publication may be reproduced, stored in a retrieval system, or transmitted in any form or by any means, electronic, mechanical, photocopying, recording, or otherwise, without the prior permission of the publishers.

Any person who commits any unauthorised act in relation to this publication may be liable to criminal prosecution and civil claims for damages.

Austin Macauley is committed to publishing works of quality and integrity. In this spirit, we are proud to offer this book to our readers; however, the story, the experiences, and the words are the author's alone.

A CIP catalogue record for this title is available from the British Library.

ISBN 9781528909143 (Paperback)
ISBN 9781528988612 (Hardback)
ISBN 9781528923330 (ePub e-book)

www.austinmacauley.com

First Published (2020)
Austin Macauley Publishers Ltd
25 Canada Square
Canary Wharf
London
E14 5LQ

Table of Contents

Introduction	7
Early Days – Ford Motor Company	10
Boring, Boring Insurance?	28
Expansive Insurance Surveying	42
Post Loss Surveying	56
Surveying for Non-Negligence	71
Surveying Services	83
Brokerages	99
The Unexpected – Be Prepared	122
Routine Surveying with a Twist	159
Up Market Surveying	173
State Securities and Enforcement	188
Related Challenges	200
Legacies	205
Taking My Leave	211

Introduction

'First things first' as the saying goes. I claim no credit for embarking on this account of my 4 decades in loss control engineering. The credit goes to a mixed group of young insurance delegates at a Middle East seminar, some of whom had very limited knowledge of insurance or manufacturing industries, let alone loss control, prior to my presentation. Citing a few of my most diverse and interesting experiences during the session seemed to capture the imagination of the majority of those present, to the extent that a significant number suggested that my accounts would make an extremely interesting read; hence this personal record of my involvement and points of view regarding insurance surveying and industrial loss control as a whole.

Just prior to leaving full-time education, at the age of fifteen, I was offered a place at Gravesend Art College with the intention of pursuing a career as a commercial artist. This came about as a result of my submission being runner-up in a county art competition. My father, a marine engineer, had other ideas, and told me to forget art and get myself a trade, telling me that the army was the best available source. No one could argue with my father so my school informed Gravesend College of my parents' decision and I subsequently sat the entrance examination for the Army Apprentices College. Passing the examination, I left home at the age of fifteen years and four months and joined the college where my indentured apprenticeship commenced. I passed out some three years later to join the British Army as an artisan. I served home and abroad, even celebrating the night of my nineteenth birthday on guard duty in Yemen, which was an experience in itself. During my tour of service, I suffered injuries and, after hospitalisation and treatment for nearly two years, I subsequently failed to meet army medical requirements and therefore was medically discharged.

Just how bizarre is that when, within three years, I would embark on a career involving consultations and advice so as to avoid losses including personal injuries? At the time of my discharge, I wasn't too bothered, although being medically downgraded to home only postings I lost military seniority. However, there were positives in the form of being in possession of excellent engineering and educational qualifications. Within two months of my discharge, I was lucky enough to have joined Ford Motor Company where ambitious employees are provided with every opportunity to develop, which I would like to think I did. Reflecting on my father's stance upon my career path, I am still uncertain whether he was right or not.

I have tried many, many times to establish a connection between these beginnings and what came next, trying to pinpoint something that ultimately led me to embark on a long career in loss control, but without any success. Looking back, since leaving full-time education I have continually drawn a blank as to where and why I ended up in a profession I never had any inkling of until I was actually employed in it. It was as if loss control simply crept up on me unexpectedly and, before I knew it, I was fully engrossed in a role I carried out with a passion for a little over forty-four years. I just wonder how many other people remain in jobs where there never seems to be a dull moment or a time where they begin to look elsewhere for fresh challenges. Well, I relished all of my time in the profession, regardless of one of my employers ceasing to exist leaving me without employment for a short while. As far-fetched as it may seem, just like a good romance, almost every day out of the office, for that matter during my Ford loss control days, smacked of new beginnings.

This is my account of my time spent in loss control. While essentially being about my period in the insurance industry, I could not overlook those years spent in manufacturing at Ford where it all started for me. I learnt so much from my days employed by Ford that I felt it was only right to include some of those interesting times and incidents from which I gained so much knowledge. For the record, all the accounts and incidents to follow are my experiences, or those where I was involved to a significant degree, usually from the outset to the closing of the file. There are, therefore, no hearsay or second-hand versions, descriptions or stories in this account. However, safety engineering and insurance surveying more often than not entails investigations and interviews, where some intimate details were obtained. In such cases, some were completed with the understanding that names, dates and places would remain strictly Private and Confidential. In those few cases, only intimate details are withheld.

Manufacturing industries are common knowledge as the likes of the motor car, television, foodstuffs and power supply services are about us every day and forcefully advertised. The same applies to banking, but it is only true to a lesser degree for insurance. I would guess that if the average person in the street were asked about insurance, they would immediately think about their life insurance policies, health insurance, motor cover, house and contents, pet plan insurance and so on. Put like that, it is all very boring and therefore hardly a subject worth writing about, or is it? That was certainly my impression of insurance even up to the point where I was about to move into the financial sector from the manufacturing industry.

Taking matters on a step further, I would again hazard a guess that if those same people were quizzed about the types of people employed in the insurance industry, they would probably describe their own insurance person who deals with their insurance needs or simply a voice at a call centre. When I was a child, I can recall a middle-aged insurance man calling weekly, in all weathers, dressed in a shabby gabardine raincoat and trilby hat, carrying a note pad. Like me, the middle-aged and elderly will probably have similar thoughts and memories. Imagine trying to conjure up something to get the pulse racing about that gentleman save him nervously looking about him when a certain dog of ours was about, who seemed not to like him.

Again, this lack of knowledge or awareness is hardly surprising because all we see nowadays are the television advertisements. Just occasionally, we have the odd movie involving highly skilled specialist claims investigators investigating or dealing with a multi-million-dollar theft or those secretive types in ransom negotiations with kidnappers. Having touched upon the world of make believe, it is difficult just knowing where to begin an account of a career where there were times when, had I been forewarned about what I would encounter, I would never have believed it. These experiences entailed having had business consultations with and surveying the property of two heads of state, one of whom was infamous, along with a prominent foreign minister plus observing a number of household names from the cinema performance both on film set and in side studios. It was a privilege, in some cases and something to reflect on later; however, at the time, my mind was fully focussed on the job at hand because getting things wrong with such people would have cost my employers dear.

So, why write a book at all if there is little to no interest or knowledge inside the industry, let alone the wide world outside? Part of the reason is that there is a great deal more to insurance than Mr and Mrs Average know, including many people employed in insurance, who have little knowledge of that which goes on beyond their own workstation and their own accounts. I hope to reveal some of that.

To me, the two most important phases in my loss control career, which converted me from a stereotypical engineer and surveyor, were the ones at Ford Motor Company and a little later at Cornhill Insurance, where I was described on a number of occasions as being a loss control specialist, while at Ford they had some referring to me as being a 'drum banger'. Regarding both organisations and my work colleagues employed there I owe a debt of gratitude as it was Ford's policies and procedures that provided adequate scope for me to express myself while Cornhill's ethics and training, which involved many brokers and policy holders from a variety of industries, were simply irreplaceable. Consequently, I just cannot say enough about the safety teams in Ford because they were largely responsible for spurring me on to me seeking additional qualifications that coupled with everyday experiences went so far as to transform me from a naive engineer to a first-rate sceptic. With Cornhill their underwriters and claims staff along with the policy holders and associated brokers kept me on that very steep upward learning curve, completing my conversion from by now a sceptical safety engineer into a five-star super cynic!

Early Days – Ford Motor Company

I have to start at the very beginning where loss control and health and safety are concerned. Ford has systems for promoting from within, or certainly they did in my former days, and having got to grips with their way of thinking and work ethic I became aware of both managers' and supervisors' roles at the outset and importantly the standing and status of workers and trades unions. The most difficult period was certainly moving from hourly paid to staff which involved me beginning a supervisor in Parts, Planning, Production and Control (PPPC) and then literally swapping my coat to Safety Engineering which was part of the Industrial Relations department. In those days, it was possible to identify the department and the status of the staff member by the length of their coat and collar colour. In general, industrial relations staff were left to their own devices which in my case was a suit, collar and tie.

Getting known in the plant was easy: just upset a few production people and the hourly paid staff and you were established. You could be forgiven for believing that endearing yourself to production staff would be easier than going head to head with the hourly paid and the trades unions, but you would be sadly misguided. In the natural progression of things, staff expected that they would stick together while the hourly paid assumed a person in a suit would be management. Seeking to make myself popular or otherwise never once occurred to me. I acted without fear or contradiction, never took my role or responsibilities lightly and, as for siding one against the other, the question of workers and staff, never came into the decisions I made regardless of my staff status.

People could be forgiven for thinking otherwise regarding where my loyalties lay but I can dispel that theory by sharing an early Ford workplace experience that I could never forget. This one experience stood me in good stead in my profession and was one where due to the actions of a Ford shop steward, I survived so where loss control and safety is concerned for me there is no them and us. We are all guilty of making mistakes and in the workplace some take believing and my biggest was in my first year of employment at Ford's Metal & Stamping Division where I began my employment in die try-out and repair as a toolmaker, my task being to ensure that the metal stampings emerging from the presses were of high quality. Just occasionally, some pressed steel panels were split or the surface had an impairment meaning the power press required adjustment or the draw die reworking. To deal with the die that usually entailed entering this extremely powerful machine, to make good more often than not lying prostrate investigating the cause of the defect lay. When defect panels were identified, it naturally brought the production line to a halt so there was urgency placed on the toolmaker to resolve the problem. In a situation like that, being totally inexperienced, I acted first with the priority being to fulfil my duties which tended to push other issues to the back of my mind. Being informed by the production supervisor of the defect on the draw die, with the press operators standing back, I leapt into the die to investigate the problem only to be physically dragged out by my ankles by a passing shop steward who screamed all manner of profanities at me that caused great embarrassment so much so that it had me blushing profusely.

Continuing with his tirade, but now with an audience, he asked me what I thought I was doing which I tried to explain not understanding at that point where I had transgressed. The shop steward turned around and hit the run button on the press operator's panel and of course the press *turned over*, meaning the ram crashed down under the power of the flywheel and the bottom of the stroke returned to the top once again. Still totally at a loss, the steward requested from one of those workers at the scene for a matchstick and upon receiving one, threw it onto the bed of the die and hit the press run button again. When the press cycle was complete the steward retrieved the matchstick that now resembled a thin piece of paper which finally made his point. "That," he said holding the remains of the matchstick aloft, "could have been you." Not wishing to labour the point, the shop steward strode off leaving me both embarrassed and speechless. Recognising my shame my supervisor, who by this time had arrived on the scene, went on to explain that if the clutch on the press was to slip or someone accidentally hit the run button, I would have been crushed to death. Being old school, my supervisor went on to suggest that I should speak with my father who was employed there some few years back when one of his colleagues did, without thinking, what I had just done except he was not so lucky when the press inadvertently operated killing the toolmaker. My supervisor went on to paint a vivid picture describing how a member of the janitorial staff was assigned the grey task, water hosing out the toolmaker's remains from the die and press save the lower limbs that had fallen to the floor.

There obviously was a safe system of work that had been explained to me during my certificated training course but under self-imposed pressure I had a lapse in thinking that could so easily have proved fatal as a 100-ton power press has, simply put, a mind of its own. Having experienced such a near miss is something that stays with you for the rest of your life and to reiterate, it went a long way to shape my way of thinking where loss control and safety is concerned.

As difficult as it was for many to understand, being part of the industrial relations team meant that you could never take sides if you wanted to avoid problems a little further down the line. To illustrate this point, I recall during a 13-week long strike senior management decided that, to avoid salaried staff sitting on their hands, safety engineering should conduct a series of training sessions. Making matters worse, it seemed that I had drawn the short straw and I was to conduct the sessions. Imagine entering a conference room and facing in excess of 100 hardened staff members drawn from production, my old departments of quality control and PPPC, not forgetting engineering; it seemed that the vast majority of those present looked upon me as the opposition.

Taking the fight to them I couldn't help myself when I addressed the assembly with the opening line, "Well, good morning cynics!" You can imagine the response, almost uproar, but most of it was good humoured, thankfully. I continued with my opening address, "Like you, the safety department has a job to do, and again like you, it is no easy task knowing that by doing nothing and failing to act even-handedly you would be courting disaster. Further, I make no apologies for trying to do my job with the knowledge I have of accident prevention and the legal jungle that exists outside and beyond these walls." At that point, everyone realised I had turned my attention to one of their number who with me had recently attended a coroner's court. As if by magic silence fell across the room.

I mentioned earlier that Ford encouraged people to better themselves and so, assessing my new working colleagues I noted that there was a vast difference between the top and the bottom, in terms of experience and dedication. Some simply went through the motions whereas others worked diligently to make the difference. Simply reading a safety audit form that seemed to repeat month after month listing the same shortcomings never spurred on the responsible engineer to do something positive to change things. To many, the job's responsibilities involved accident investigation, whereas I enquired as to why accident prevention was not on their list of priorities. I began to look at the accident statistics in my area and previous safety audits, which showed that, prior to an accident, a problem, albeit not directly related, was identified. I suppose my staff' accident training sessions still stuck with me because, after all, if one of your team was injured the direct supervisor was the first person called. Now, the situation is a reversal of this, where the supervisor, while being interviewed, will turn to the safety department requesting action leading to one of the only occasions where I saw union and production supervision holding hands.

Now, once again, acting anything other than subservient where the shop floor and trades unions were concerned, I would resort to politics, asking the union representatives on occasion to join me in pursuing malpractice. I endeavoured to secure their support because without it I sensed that we were simply going round in circles. During a night shift, sitting in the safety office, I found myself looking at the annual accident returns for my area, which happened to be engine assemblies. I had two years of accident and incident statistics before me and measuring my returns against other plant operations, I began questioning where I was going wrong. The reason being accident statistics for my area were unusually high according to my way of thinking, differing only from other areas of the plant by having the lowest severity ratings. Time and again I quizzed myself as to why there were so many accidents in such low hazard operations, in so short a period of time, and particularly since the employees were generally fresh from a full safety induction. New starters at Ford Engine Plant were usually assigned work in engine assemblies which entailed simple light repetitive operations, little to no machining or heavy manual work. The safety induction took place on the new employees' first day, right after the lunch break which was preceded in the morning by medical, union briefing, salaries, pensions and personnel sessions.

Just maybe I reasoned, it was possible that these new starters' attention levels were very low following an intense programme of briefings and a full lunch, so that much regarding the safety issues was lost on them. I looked at my presentation as to what would hold their attention better and ran it past my colleagues for their take, which was positive. It was true that the majority of these hourly paid workers were largely unskilled labour, and consequently, minor injuries such as cuts, abrasions, foreign bodies in the eyes and the odd back injury were very much the order of the day and could be expected. Naturally, I made out the accident reports following the interview of the injured person, obtaining a prognosis from the medical team, employment details and work assignment instructions from the line supervisor to complete the file, and all the while hoping to elicit something to work with.

Without realising it, I was thoroughly enthralled in the exercise and I seemed to work as diligently as I had ever done in either QC or PPPC. During the quieter periods, as occasionally occurs when shift working, I reflected on the job requirements of an efficient safety engineer, which I felt were considerably more than I possessed. Recognising that I didn't really possess the necessary skill set and qualifications for a top or senior position, I decided that I needed to do something to address the shortfall. With some determination, deciding this was a job requiring far wider knowledge and understanding, I enrolled on a course at night college for health, safety, legal and loss prevention. After two years of study and examinations, and through my thesis, I was awarded my diploma.

As the thesis needed to be original, I thought what better way than to use those accident details at my fingertips? After all, there were over three hundred incidents where I had been the investigating engineer. So now being motivated, I began looking into those statistics deeper in an effort to understand where I and the supervision were failing. In those preceding 12 months there were 370 accidents, nearly seven percent of which involved employees losing three or more days off work. I then took it upon myself to look into the individuals, and I discovered that very few accidents involved employees who had worked in assemblies for six or more months. Further research led me to establish that almost 92% of the injured employees were under the age of 25 and of those they had fewer than four weeks' service. With the valuable assistance of two shift supervisors, we identified those tasks that turned up the most accidents. Regardless of this latest initiative and my determination to justify my opinion and belief that those tasks were the root problem I drew a complete blank.

Out of nowhere, however, I struck gold when I witnessed an employee attempting to load a cylinder head casting onto a conveyor. It evaded his grip and the casting dropped to the floor. Fortunately, the employee suffered no physical injury. I knew the job very well as it was a stage one operation where loaded timber pallets were placed at the head of the line, with employees using a hoist to lift the heads onto a mechanical conveyor. Needless to say, I asked why the employee was not using the hoist to which he told me it was quicker to do it manually. He added that all the other employees adopted the same practice so he naturally followed suit, particularly as his supervisor made no adverse comment. Now things were becoming so much clearer when, during the latter part of the week, an employee suffered a facial injury whilst using a ratchet spanner, which allegedly flew off as a bolt was being tightened and struck him in the face. Again, in the individual's absence, I watched the operation where I observed the practice of 'spinning' the spanner, learning that it was commonplace regardless of the fact that in unskilled hands it was hazardous.

Witnessing so many malpractices persuaded me to study the twelve operations that accounted for most accidents and, without exception, malpractices existed in them. It became clearer still that the new, uninitiated employees had adopted bad working practices by watching the more established employees, the most adept of whom had become more skilled at avoiding injury. Subsequently, I presented my findings to senior management with a strong recommendation that all new starters were given a refresher induction session before or in about one month. In addition, I recommended that all supervisors should look out for these malpractices where new starters were concerned, plus all new employees involved in an accident were interviewed and reminded that they were still in their probationary periods. There were concerns expressed by some members of production management regarding downtime, at least until my figures showed that medical attendance and time lost away from workstations, accident reviews and the like all took up precious labour time, often including their own. Adopting the recommendations, the accident returns fell by over 60% in the following half-year with the Ford Engine Plant adopting the recommendations long after I moved on. There were some interesting and rather bizarre incidents and accidents whilst in the power train before I moved on to my time in the Foundry Division that I would make sense of the statement I made at the safety conference concerning 'beyond these walls'.

My most uncomfortable time was following an accident that occurred during an annual shut-down. During the three-week shutdown at Ford, production ceased to allow for model change, major engineering, planned maintenance, etc. Those employees who hadn't accrued sufficient holiday were offered paid work. We had some fourteen employees for assigned work with one of those tasks involving the clearing of the Engine Plant's roof area of all manner of redundant materials and some equipment left by contractors and maintenance staff during the preceding year. This was an annual ritual, and had been going on for years, so the routine was well established. The group assembled and safety inducted regarding the task and the safety aspects, which included access only by tied ladders and staying within the edge protection installed by contractors. The assembled workers were instructed to walk the roof valleys between the sloping asbestos cement sheeted roof, which was occasionally interrupted by glazed roof lights. The instructions were to walk the roof valleys from one end of the extensive plant roof to the other, noting, by the roof lettering, the location and description of the materials or articles seen.

At no time were there instructions given to move or touch what they saw, just simply identify the location with the emphasis in my mind that under no circumstances should the workers walk on the roof slopes. The gang was dispersed leaving safety engineering to assign and induct other workers to other duties in and about the plant. Within some 30 minutes we received a call from the top end of the building that someone had fallen through the roof. Rushing to the scene we found one of the workers slumped across a transfer machine some five metres or so beneath the roof. The roof area directly above was holed and roof debris littered the area below. Unfortunately, the worker was, following examination by a doctor, pronounced dead at the scene and, because neither foul play nor breach of health and safety statutes were suspected the enforcing authorities left the site leaving safety engineering to follow our own protocol and preparing ourselves for the inevitable enquiry and subsequent coroner's court.

We established that the worker had climbed on the roof slope, since his footprints were seen clearly on the glass roof light which obviously gave way due to the worker's weight. We also felt that the safety induction was complete and revisited those other workers to recite what had been disclosed during their induction, which clearly established that the roof slopes were a *no go* area. Believing that we had acted with due diligence we prepared ourselves for the coroner's court which is where the travesty, to our mind, lay. While the HSE were not critical of the arrangements, the coroner held another view in his remarks. The Health and Safety Executive is a UK government agency responsible for the encouragement, regulation and enforcement of health, safety and welfare in the workplace. While the court found the death tragic and accidental it did question the depth and level of the induction where he used the phrase 'glib'. Further he suggested, it would have been prudent to ask the gang if any of them had worked at height before. The criticism was, I felt, entirely unjust because all of the workers making up the gang were well informed; all understood English, as was a Ford requirement, bearing in mind that many workers came from ethnic groups. However, you do start to have doubts regarding the part you played when you are sitting across the court facing the family of the deceased looking directly at you when questioned and with the coroner's barbed comments, all of which left me with memories I shall never forget.

Following my time in the assemblies, I became more senior, and I took up other duties within the plant. On the night shift, there was a skeleton safety staff only, whose responsibilities extended beyond the plant covering the rail sidings, road transport, the jetty and the power station. However, in reality, the engineer would simply act as a safety advisor, accident investigator and recorder. During these times, I learnt a valuable lesson in loss control engineering: that what first appears is not always the case where people in the workplace are concerned. Consequently, keeping an open mind is absolutely crucial in the role. I believe it was here that I learned most quickly as it was rare that there was anyone senior and experienced enough on hand to provide guidance. I did learn during this stage that you should never underestimate the extent of opposition, which in Ford usually came from all: production, engineering, shop-floor workers, and not necessarily belligerent supervision or militant unionists either. These parties usually became concerned following an accident or a near-miss resulting in production downtime.

Cooperation, it has to be said, was normally found in senior management or those engaged in non-production roles such as personnel, training, quality control and engineering because quite simply they hardly, if ever, worried too much about productivity. Whenever there was a serious accident, accusations were rife, with either management or the workers allegedly being at fault, which is why safety or loss control had to appear impartial, keeping an open mind. It was certainly not beyond a line supervisor to ignore faulty production equipment and work around it until the end of shift. Alternatively, work equipment with a minor defect could be ignored by all until ultimately it involved long-term production downtime.

The worst deception I encountered was while I was on the night shift as duty engineer. Sitting up in the safety office after the shift had started, I received a summons on the radio from the medical centre to attend quickly as there was a casualty. Using an electric buggy, I arrived at the medical centre in less than five minutes where I located the duty doctor and nurses, who informed me an operative had lost the ring finger of his left hand. It was a clean cut that was good fortune insofar as, if we could recover the severed piece, it could possibly be sewn back. Consequently, I needed to get to the scene of the amputation and find the missing digit. Regardless of the employee groaning in pain, I informed him I needed to know how his finger was damaged; in which department and on what machine? I managed to get the information, all the time with the doctor leaning on my shoulder requesting I make all haste as the ambulance from the nearest A & E was en route, plus the casualty was in shock.

Arriving at the piston line, I met up with the supervisor and manager plus two employees who worked on the same section. Ascertaining where the employee was working, I stressed that we needed to find the missing finger to minimise the severity of the loss. The pistons were produced in aluminium and were being machined by a milling machine where the top was shaved leaving off-cuts that fell into a small waste skip beneath. Believing that the cutters had severed the finger, I naturally looked carefully in the vicinity. One of the workers, though, claimed that the injured man had been trying to clear aluminium off-cuts from the conveyor. This threw a whole different light on the matter because I had satisfied myself that the mill cutters were fully guarded so we started looking about the ten-metre long mechanical conveyor. We had stopped the process so the power to the machine was isolated as I didn't want a repeat if the machine was faulty. We took out the waste skip and I suggested that the others sift through the waste to see if they could locate the digit while I would look at the conveyor. We had hardly begun, some five minutes since I arrived on the scene, when the medical department radioed through asking if I had found the finger yet. Harassed and irate I said, "No, and there are four of us searching!"

The conveyor was clear, without sight of the finger, tissue or blood that I assumed would be present. I suggested that, because the finger would probably be colourless by now, we should get a canvas sheet on the floor and sift gradually through the swarf as the missing part might have fallen through. We laid out the canvas and I was gingerly searching the waste with my pen, not really knowing what a severed finger looked like, when the radio interrupted us again. Now being not so polite I told the nurse that we were diligently searching all possible areas. Having gone through the entire contents of the skip and the complete parts of the machine, we drew a complete blank. Frustrated and tired, I returned to the medical centre and informed the staff there that perhaps the finger was so gnarled up in the conveyor or the cutters that it was unrecognisable. The doctors replied that it was possibly so and that now it was possibly too late to repair the hand.

Back in the office, I made out a full accident report, knowing that it would have to be reported to the enforcing authority; therefore, I took photographs, witness statements, drew up a plan of the layout, floor condition, lighting and machine details. I had already, as was the norm for me, noted the injured employee's attire; particularly the footwear. The night shift had been over for some time, therefore I handed over to the day shift's senior engineer with my report and findings. I drove home thinking all the while about where the mysterious finger had gone. At home, I had my usual tea and was too tired to eat, so I showered and fell into bed. It seemed I had just closed my eyes when my wife came and woke me up telling me Ford was on the line and wanted to talk. In those days there were no mobile phones so I had to tramp downstairs in a somewhat irritated state wondering what I had overlooked.

The engineer on the other end of the line apologised and informed me that they had found the finger. Before he had the time to continue my response was unprintable but it went along the lines of, "We searched high and low for that finger for hours, looked everywhere without luck, so if you have found it, good for you!" Laughing, the engineer told me to calm down and he would explain all. A security officer had been walking the fence line, as was the norm in the early morning, when he spotted something glittering on the top of the two-metre high security fence. Taking a closer look, they found a gold wedding ring attached to half a finger.

The enquiry that followed revealed that the three operatives had been working a scam with the supervisor allegedly looking the other way. Every night shift the three operatives would turn up early at the plant, clock in and make their way to their section. They would start the shift but when the supervisor moved on to another area two employees would slip away, exiting the plant with stragglers from the previous shift or, as in this case, climbing the security fence to get to the external car park and drive home for a night's rest. The remaining employee would attend the three workstations until the shift's end and clock out his two workmates. They had apparently only been working this for a few weeks, and on this night, one of those climbing had caught his finger, not in the machine, but on the fence. The three were dismissed and the supervisor disciplined. As I previously stated, things are not always as they first seem and that was, for me, one of the most telling experiences I had ever encountered. It was astonishing to think that in such a short time the three workers managed to concoct such a story, particularly given that one or both would have been in a state of shock.

Certainly there were some weird happenings at Ford, some tragic, others almost laughable, but one I remember vividly was one involving attempted theft and quite surprising health and safety, at least a safety-cum-accident report! Trying to steal a car might, to some, appear a worthwhile risk but the theft of something so small and petty as a spark plug seems incomprehensible, but why then during this attempted theft would the perpetrator risk his life for a few pounds? The account starts and finishes on the service road between two of Ford's major plants at Dagenham, the Engine Plant and Thames Foundry, as they were then known. This was a long, straight road, security fenced on either side and floodlit during the hours of darkness. The route was used extensively by tractor tow-trains supplying engine castings from the foundry direct to the Engine Plant, with a midpoint security lodge that had the usual retractable road barrier. The security person, stationed in the lodge, would check the loads passing through and the accompanying paperwork. They would also be viewing other traffic on legitimate business, all of which could be observed the second they entered the stretch of road in either direction for at least 300 metres. There was also a paved footpath, not that it was used much.

My investigation and report cited a security man observing a pedestrian walking from the direction of the Engine Plant, which was a little unusual as there was quite a distance to walk from the plant to the main road where public services ran. As the man approached his gait appeared uncertain, which made the security man even more curious. As the distance to the lodge got shorter, the pedestrian started to stagger unceremoniously which resulted in the security man emerging from his lodge to see if he could offer assistance. At the lodge the man collapsed with, as my accident report stated, an odd facial expression and colour. In an attempt to offer first aid, as it was thought the man was suffering a heart condition, the security man tried to loosen the man's buttoned collar and in doing so made a startling discovery. Around the neck was a noose of electrical flex that was clearly choking him as the knot had slipped. The flex was taut so in an effort to loosen the noose the security man tried to pull up the other end to relieve the tension. To his surprise, it was tied to a camshaft that the man was trying to steal! We retained the evidence when the man was taken to the hospital for treatment, after which he was released. The camshaft's weight was sufficient to pull the flex tight when it became dislodged from the worker's waistband, luckily he only lost his job.

The most contentious issue that I was required to deal with as a safety engineer involved a forklift truck driver who previously, as his supervisor, I found him indolent and reckless to the point of being dangerous. My transfer from PPPC to safety was at a time where there never seemed to be a day that went by without industrial action of one type or another largely in the Dagenham plants or up in Halewood, Liverpool. One thing for certain, as far as management controls and safety related incidents went, it provided me with invaluable insight where the workplace was concerned where attitudes, ethics, peer pressure and lastly the environment were concerned. For example, internal transport in the Engine Plant entailed a largely militant workforce that appeared to hold sway over an over-accommodating management brought about by virtue of the fact that the plant would quickly come to a halt without internal transport. Those driver operators were vital as they were the means to mechanically handle all materials and parts within the plant.

To put things into perspective, employed in the Engine Plant were 6,500 operatives whose productivity was entirely reliant on some 100 or so internal transport operatives. These employees' existence being vital to help maintain production of internal combustion engines that were, on completion, shipped to the likes of Langley, Southampton, Basildon, Köln and the main car assembly plant on the Dagenham estate, in all employing in excess of 50,000 staff. Should there have been a withdrawal of labour, go-slow or a work to rule, those plant's productivity would be sorely affected. Consequently, there was always a cautious approach to any driver regardless of their existing a clear justification for disciplinary action. It got to the stage where once even the Joint Works Committee (JWC) agreed to permit PPPC staff to operate the internal transport to keep the plant in full production. PPPC staff supervision and management, all being competent transport operatives, myself included, kept production supplied with all necessary materials and parts regardless of operating with less than 30% of the normal compliment of PPPC drivers, 24 hours per day 7 days per week. In less than 8 days the transport drivers sheepishly returned to work with their grievances unresolved that involved undisciplined drivers serving their suspensions.

One of the most militant drivers was a former Trades Union shop steward who openly boasted to me following a stoppage, for alleged safety failings of a few hours, that his duties would only be complete when the entire plant was at a standstill. As illogical as that seemed, it served to show the mentality of the individual with some of his workmates suggesting as to the reason why he was no longer their shop steward. The incident that led up to disciplinary action and ultimately, suspension, was the final action following on from a series of near misses involving this individual. The first incident involved this driver feeding a production line with a cage of castings ready for machining. The driver crashed his loaded forklift truck into a quality control workstation that only avoided injuring a QC inspector due to the inspector's swift reaction, as an overturned cage of casting toppled about him. Conducting the near miss safety investigation everyone was at fault save the driver, according to him, where clearly there was no excuse for the alleged congested work area that resulted in impaired manoeuvrability. The driver failed to keep the area clear that comprised ten large empty cages that he should have loaded onto a waiting train of six empty trailers.

My submission was, of course, momentarily challenged a week later at the enquiry as the unions unwittingly were unaware that I had taken photographs of the area at the time, much to their embarrassment. The upshot, however, was limited to yet another verbal warning much to the dismay of safety and production departments. On completion of his verbal warning period, this same driver was challenged by a production supervisor for speeding and without slowing down the driver took both hands off the steering wheel and made improper hand gestures while continuing on his way. As good fortune would have it this reckless action was witnessed by a senior PPPC supervisor which again gave rise to further disciplinary action resulting once again limited only to a verbal warning, the justification being that the demand for engines was at its height consequently plant senior management was determined to do all in its power to avoid any stoppages. In my estimation, with the driver being dealt with so lightly, I wrote that with this latest slap on the wrist he must have gained the impression that he was now untouchable. Further in my report on the individual to senior management, I suggested that should there be a serious accident, perhaps resulting in a fatality, I wonder how, if questioned, would the management justify their lack of positive action against the individual. For certain I added that those other incidents involving this cavalier driver would certainly be investigated by the HSE who could then bring Ford's approach to driver safety and disciplinary codes into question.

It was this report that made it appear that I had foretold the future because within a few months' safety was informed of a serious collision on the very same production line where the QC inspector had escaped unscathed from accidental impact by a forklift truck. Due to my period in PPPC I was assigned to deal with the incident. Arriving at the location, that area of the plant and production was at a standstill due to a lack of electrical power. The reason being a transformer had been struck violently by a loaded forklift truck that bowled over the transformer severing the three-phase cable. Local supervision and electrical maintenance had immediately isolated the supply and then proceeded to douse the heated cable by using suitable hand held fire extinguishers. There to my surprise sitting motionless, head in hands, on a stack of timber pallets was the driver operator. Probably not thinking, I commented when the production supervisor pointed an accusing finger at the driver, I remarked, "Now why I am not surprised." For there was the very same driver.

As this was a major incident, there was a hive of activity with the electrical engineers already in attendance trying to rectify the damage so as to get production back on line. The driver upon seeing me remarked to another driver operator that regardless of not being entirely to blame for the incident this safety engineer would find fault as we 'have a history'. One thing for certain, I was now fully in control of my senses and ignoring his remarks, as if not heard, I requested of him for his account of the incident. Once again congestion was allegedly the root cause and looking around I took my camera requesting exactly where the area was congested as there was nothing in the immediate vicinity of the transformer that suffered considerable impact so much so the safety crash barrier, designed and positioned solely to protect the transformer, had been torn from the floor. I took some witness statements and satisfied that the electrical supply no longer posed a threat to staff, I returned to the safety office to complete my report.

Recording what I had seen and those that had actually witnessed the incident it was clear that there had been a case of speed with little regard for the plant about the area. The JWC was called as was the transport supervisor where my previous report and opinion was read out to those present. There was an alarm at my assertions and conclusion regarding the driver's accident history that largely involved a lack of safety awareness that could be life threatening. All agreed to immediate suspension, now a written warning and an external driver re-test at a proper training centre. Thinking that this was the least management could do in the interest of safety a course and re-test was arranged.

Regardless of this being a safety matter, on the very first day of the driver training and assessment course the training centre's doctor-cum-examiner made contact with our medical team informing them of the driver's impaired vision. The medial report listed a detached retina in one eye suggesting the driver was, to all intents and purposes, blind in that eye and to compound matters he had limited vision in the other eye and should be wearing spectacles. As were the requirements of the registered test centre, on the first day it entails a mandatory medical including an eye test which obviously resulted in a failure even before the individual got up behind the wheel, let alone the actual driving tests. It was during this driver's period of suspension, subsequent eye surgery and eye test that I was reassigned to European Foundry Operation so I never got to hear of the driver again.

Following two fatal accidents in the Foundry Division, Ford reorganised the safety operations, which resulted in me being promoted to a newly created position known as Senior Safety Development Engineer, Ford European Foundry Operations. The role involved deputising for the chief engineer when required and taking sole responsibility for any new processes, machinery, or working practices, including approving safe systems of work, signing off on and inducting contractors. I liked the responsibilities simply because I was initially able to sign off, or not, on projects, new plant and equipment. This seemed far better than chasing my tail once the equipment was installed and in production. This was forward thinking by Ford, but I had many a run-in with both the engineering and production departments, who didn't like what they considered to be others stepping on their toes. Imagine the misgivings of the foundry when they learnt of my appointment and promotion as it was those very same staff who labelled me the 'drum banger'.

Given my reputation I was, upon arrival, called to the Chief Safety Engineer's office. As opposed to a courtesy welcome I was read the riot act. There was to be no 'maverick' approach to the task at hand, before entering into any controversial issues I was to consult the chief engineer, there would be no safety memorandums and no consultation with union representatives without prior approval. I didn't feel in the least put out by these restraints because I knew my job and why I had been assigned to the foundry by the Head of Group and European Operations. However, like the best laid plans, the unexpected turned up in the first 30 minutes. I was being given a quick guided tour of the foundry by one of the engineers when a few metres in front of us an aged employee tripped and fell on a piece of scrap casting. He struck his head on the corner of a conveyor system with his hard hat rolling down the aisle. It was quite an unnerving scene. Not stirring, the man had obviously lost consciousness. As we were close by the medical centre, a nurse ran out and was with the employee within possibly two or three minutes.

The employee lay motionless and the attending nurse, who knew the man well, knelt down and examined him before bursting into tears, cradling his head in her arms and informing those present that he had gone. Now the heat was clearly on and safety were now being looked at as nothing more than a lame excuse for an essential and critical activity. As I was not active officially, the enquiry did not require my presence but the Chief Safety Engineer was now clearly under pressure. This resulted in a meeting between the Head of Safety, industrial relations and me. I was asked for my take on the situation we found ourselves in and concluded that without going over old reports, audits and inspections I had to start with a clean sheet of paper. There was little the chief engineer could do but agree with my proposal and so the work commenced in earnest.

My audit identified shortcomings in almost every department. I found contractors to be the most troublesome as they seemed to have the run of the foundry, being engaged in unsafe working practices, non-compliance with safety apparel and equipment. The two aforementioned deaths were both contractors employed on the same contract. I went on to cost the improvements, which, as I recall, amounted to some $300,000, a tidy sum even by Ford's standards. There were so many omissions that I found it difficult, when asked to prioritise my findings, to identify the high risk and lower hazard situations. The findings and related costs meant the foundry would need to budget for the improvements over the next two years. I countered that if we were to introduce stricter working practices, we could look again and prioritise as requested. Probably true to form, I audited again after some three months and found that nothing of any consequence had occurred. I resubmitted a fresh audit and a new estimate, the new estimate coming out at $425,000, simply because of the deterioration of those areas formerly considered acceptable when they were not maintained.

Making savings through shortcuts is not smart and in fact, is dangerous, more often than not. Just to illustrate the point regarding contractor problems, there was one particular glaring omission that resulted in a work stoppage, and that went some considerable way to convince plant engineering that they needed to understand that with every project there had to entail loss control input. The project that was a wakeup call to me regarding both contractors and engineers was one I was required to sign off that involved, on paper at least, a straightforward contract for the dismantling of a 120 foot chute used to convey redundant sand cores down to a waste skip sited over 100 feet below in the yard. The tower was an angle iron frame clad with corrugated asbestos cement sheets, the cladding designed in the main to prevent dust from polluting the external areas of the plant. Discussing the issue with the project engineer, I agreed that the cladding should be removed and lowered within the confines of the elevations of the chute, thus ensuring that all the debris would be contained.

As my subsequent report involving the sequence and scheme of works stated, the contractor would contain the debris by commencing at the top of the chute. However, despite the permit to work, the contractors found they could not access the cladding externally as they had not planned or budgeted for access scaffolding. So like most contractors, they opted for the quickest and least expensive option. The method of work decided involved men working from scaffold boards resting on the exposed angle iron framework within the chute. The contractors, now balanced on insecure boards, set about smashing the cladding with sledgehammers from within the frame, resulting in these sheets floating down uncontrolled, some 120 feet. Needless to say, there were unsuspecting Ford employees walking below and, while a small area was cordoned off, it didn't stop several sheets striking against the wall of the pattern shop over a hundred feet away.

The shop stewards were immediately alerted as those employed there withdrew their labour until the problem was resolved. Orders came through direct from the plant manager to resolve the situation and, upon arriving at the scene, I was appalled to learn of the malpractices. I asked the contract manager if he had heard anything I had said, and I showed him the scheme and system of work we both signed off on. With a full-time stoppage now I had little option but to remove the work permits and called security to usher the contractors off site. This was shortly followed by a call from the engineer, who had miraculously turned up, asking me what I thought I was doing. I told him to visit the scene or better still contact the plant manager, or if he really felt brave speak with the JWC.

Hanging up the phone I spoke with a member of the JWC who arrived on the scene giving assurances concerning arrangements previously signed off being fully observed. The hourly paid staff were at first unwilling to return to work but the intervention of myself and the JWC member we convinced them the crisis was over and that they should return to work. From there, I went directly to the head of engineering and informed him of the event, pulling no punches where his own staff was concerned. I also took the time to remind him of the two fatalities just six months before and less than 50 metres from the debris chute, suggesting the likely outcome if HSE were to be called in again. It was not beyond the unions to call the HSE who had on occasions responded immediately and sided on most cases with the unions. With that in mind, the agreed safety precautions were introduced and the engineer was cautioned regarding unsafe working practices.

Without doubt, in those early Ford days I looked upon my position and purpose as being to contribute as best I could to the prevention of accidents. This wasn't just confined to personal injuries but also damage to plant and equipment. It was my job, and because it was my job, I took it seriously; this meant that I gained a bit of a reputation. One reason was that, to my way of thinking time wasn't important. Consequently, I never clock watched and during quiet spells, I even pursued near-miss situations that were not treated with the level of attention I felt the subject demanded. To say I was fanatical about my approach would be an exaggeration but investigation and reporting as such gave me only limited satisfaction, as in almost every case I found that the incident could have so easily been avoided.

Although I found myself faced with a certain amount of apathy regarding my approach at the lower levels I, fortunately, found I had sympathetic ears in the upper echelons of management at both plant and group level, as they saw the effects of any shortcomings. My path was clear and with the role's objectives I never felt the need to seek compromise. My enthusiasm for the task never hit home until a visit to a hospital following up on an incident at the plant. It was during one of the quiet spells in the early hours that I was following up on an incident involving an employee and I found myself in conversation concerning industrial accidents, with a middle-aged nurse at the A&E department of a general hospital. The topic was incidental but observing the dedication of this seriously single-minded sister totally engrossed in patient care as if nothing else mattered, was laudable. The department was particularly busy and in spite of being on duty nearly two hours after her shift end, she was tireless in pursuit of patient welfare during which time she asked of me what I was doing at the hospital as she had never met a loss control or safety engineer before. I explained that the Ford employee had an unidentifiable injury or illness and was found semiconscious on his forklift truck without apparent witnesses. Being in such a condition, we needed to be aware of exactly how he sustained any injury so I needed to be there when and if he was able to communicate, since he hadn't been able to do so in our medical centre. I took it on myself as a duty engineer to wait until he was able to speak at the hospital.

Reflecting on this nurse's dedication I suggested tactlessly that, given her working hours and remuneration, working in the likes of Bahrain and Oman would offer greater rewards. At that time certain states in the Middle East were advertising for qualified and experienced British medical staff. The sister reacted strongly by stating that nursing was a vocation and she had never considered another career, least of all one motivated by money. Dwelling on the role she played she intimated that we were alike, which stumped me momentarily as I never saw it the way she did; I had never considered my role to be a vocation. I had to stop her there explaining that I was paid to prevent accidents and so performed to the best of my ability within the time allocated that certainly didn't run some two hours or so over my shift. On reflection, I admitted that I never saw myself as the vocational type although I felt that prevention of accidents was certainly my main objective.

Not forgetting the hospitalised employee, to everyone's utter amazement he had suffered an acute slipped disc in his lower lumbar area while climbing onto his forklift truck, which caused him to momentarily lose consciousness. The cause never entered anyone's thinking at the plant yet the A&E duty consultant established this in minutes of examining the patient resulting, thankfully, in us not having to take preventative measures. As for the employee, his treatment entailed traction sessions for six-weeks and, while at work, he wore a surgical corset. Regarding the vocation issue, my belief was that the nursing sister was the epitome of her profession, tending to the needs of the sick and infirm, while the likes of me weren't the same, regardless of showing more than a modicum of interest in people's health and safety.

While there were many accidents and incidents to complete my education where the workplace was concern one of the final situations which many colleagues found amusing directly involved me. During my time "on the tools," a term used to describe labouring in a non-managerial position, I witnessed and heard of a number of injuries being experienced through horseplay. These involved toolmaker's toolboxes being nailed to the floor and in an effort to lift the immovable box the individual strained his shoulder and back, initially to his workmate's amusement. Another painful experience was caused by workmates filling an employee's mitts with a form of superglue that took some careful treatment by medical staff to remove the glove and a minimum amount of skin. There were more serious cases where, while an apprentice was stooping over a millwright, pushed a high-pressure hose down the individual's overalls resulting in internal injuries via the anus. Another serious incident caused eye damage where the eye protection left unattended had the seal laced with marking paste that entered the employee's eyes when slipping his goggles on unsuspectedly.

Turning to my own experience this occurred during my latter days in Ford Foundry. While to many there is always room for good humour in the workplace there are limitations as if misguided, on occasions in the most challenging of circumstances, it could result in serious repercussions. Having settled into my new role in the foundry where the duties more often than not required my presence in the production areas I soon became known not least of all by way of my attire. Hard hat, face and eye protection and safety footwear were very much order of the day, rightly so and only to be expected from the senior safety development engineer. However, apart from my personal safety protection I always wore a two-piece suit, collar, and tie. My chosen dress code to some senior production staff, in their Ford overalls, was found to be amusing with rarely a day going by when one Irish hot metal house superintendent, a close work colleague by this time, was never lost for a word about my appearance.

Ford Foundry, the largest manufacturing foundry in Europe at that time, boasted of four blast furnaces and a single arc furnace in a straight line. These furnaces were fed by Ford rail conveying thousands of tonnes of pig iron, limestone and solid fuel used in producing tens of thousands of grey iron castings per year with a workforce close to 5,600 working multi-shift systems. The demand for castings was at its height therefore, the furnaces were worked relentlessly so that any stoppage required speedy attention. The structure of these high-rise cupola furnaces comprised steel case bodies each lined with refractory material into which air was blasted through water-jacket twyers. It was a leaking twyer that caused a furnace to be shut down and subsequent discharge of the entire contents into the drop area some fifteen metres below. This emergency drill because of a serious threat of explosion due to violent boiling or flashing of water into steam.

The crisis was almost immediately brought under control by the swift action of the hot metal house superintendent, safety engineering and maintenance personnel who dropped the furnace contents into the drop area below. The escaping water had however cooled layers of the slag above the molten metal that had subsequently been dropped leaving a honeycomb of slag trapped against the furnace walls. The task was then to water cool the slag and other internal areas of the furnace, which took several hours, that would then permit workers suspended from safety harnesses, equipped with pneumatic drills, to climb into the furnace and set about the arduous task of breaking up the slag. However, this manual and hazardous time-consuming method was short-lived with it decided to remove the offending slag by way of controlled explosive charges, the work to be carried out by certified contractors.

Following a meeting between safety engineering and hot metal house management, we worked out a safe scheme that required manned control points at either end of the drop area, charging platforms and the furnace area itself at ground level. All personnel were issued with siren whistles and both the superintendent and myself also equipped with two-way radios, me being positioned at one entrance of the drop area and the superintendent way above me on the charging platform. When the explosives were ready, I was notified by the superintendent which triggered the whistle blasts indicating the respective areas were clear. For obvious reasons, each of us, save the superintendent, was positioned behind substantial brick elevations shielded from the intended blast. Following the desired whistle responses, I was to call the superintendent that they could proceed and satisfied all was in order I did so. The response was inaudible for some unknown reason so I tried again which resulted in the same negative response to my confirmation.

Shouting from the charging platform the superintendent requested my response which meant I had to come from behind my safe area to make contact as the radio seemed to have gained no response. As soon as I came into view in the centre of the drop area entrance the explosives were fired thus hitting me with grit, coal dust, sand, water from I don't know where and not least of all hot air. I was covered from head to my toes, save my nose, mouth, eyes and hair so much so resembling someone auditioning for the Black and White Minstrels. By way of the laughter and a camera being produced suggested the event was all very well pre-planned thus resulting in only my pride dented and my clothing being impregnate with the grit and water. As for the comments that followed those who orchestrated the farce were certain my eyes, head and other exposed area would be covered. It took a while for me to live it down especially with the Polaroid shot never being out of the superintendent's possession and as for my dress code, it never changed even after experiencing an extreme taste of British workplace humour.

So given everything was progressing so well for me at Ford, apart from the blast, did I decide to move on and look for fresh challenges. Just prior to reaching this decision Ford had recently built a new Engine Plant in Bridgend that I believed I was the ideal candidate for the new Chief Safety Engineer's position. Applying through group my applications were brought to the attention of Ford of Europe Chief Safety Engineer who allegedly remarked that being a completely new plant he would feel secure in putting a monkey in there overseeing safety and that he had other plans for me. The plans involved me being appointed the senior safety engineer at the Ford vehicle research establishment at Dunton. The two establishments were chalk and cheese with the latter workplace hazards including wind tunnels, material testing and destruction, test track and so on therefore a deal of experimentation on new models, designs and materials. Bearing in mind I had gained experience in arguably two of the Ford's toughest plants, certainly the most hazardous in Thames Foundry, so I guess being honest, in a fit of pique and in the middle of a thirteen-week strike, I decided to move on.

So as far as Ford Motor Company was concerned those experiences and my management induction courses set me on a path I never once strayed from. Recalling my first management course at Dagenham, sitting anxiously amidst a group of about twenty staff and waiting for the session to commence, the door burst open and a very large gentleman strode in. I am sure the idea was to grab our attention and, without pausing to introduce himself, he asked the group, in a strong American accent, "What do we make here in Dagenham?"

Now in every group, you will always get someone who likes to be noticed, either a brave person or a stupid one.

"Ford Capri and Ford Cortina," one opined emphasising the *Ford*.

Another delegate offered, "Ford Prefect." Clearly, these were not the responses this tutor was seeking so, silence followed.

"You buddy," he said looking straight at me, "What do we make here in sunny Dagenham?" he drawled.

I too, paused then simply said, "Automotive parts and assemblies." Even though I knew I was wrong I didn't want to offer nothing.

He thumped his hand hard on the lectern, "No, goddamit, we make money! If there was more money in manufacturing chamber pots, we would be into those instead!" Those words struck home and I carried them with me until my final working day insofar as maintaining a healthy balance in business dealings.

Boring, Boring Insurance?

The title of this book is just about as far from reality as it could be from my standpoint and while being tempted to use the word 'semi-autobiography' this would imply fictitious events. Everything here is the truth, and nothing here is hearsay. Some of the cited situations felt like fiction at the time though, because they were so removed from anything I was informed the job of work would entail. Many of my colleagues even found them difficult to accept, despite being employed within the industry for a considerable number of years. Of course, to put things into perspective, I did complete in excess of 14,000 surveys, large, medium and small, including claims investigation, desk-top analysis, situations involving casualties, products, public liability, contractors all risk, financial including professional indemnity, property fire and perils, business interruption and appraisals for high net worth clients and K & R (Kidnap and Ransom). Whether by good fortune or professionalism I avoided any major losses save on three occasions where I had recommended declining a policy or imposing strict policy conditions but underwriters opted to ignore my opinion. They proceeded to provide cover based in the business' interests or perhaps out of stupidity, as was certainly the instance in one of those cases.

Having perused many insurance publications I have never come upon one that revealed the actual day-to-day events that go on behind the scenes, and by that I mean in the field, to capture my interest. It was just maybe that all the works I picked up on were based on theoretical studies detailing the usual practices and procedures; an ideal training material for many of those who saw their futures in the industry. However, not all insurers embrace the same policies and procedures which is why there are successes and failures in the insurance industry. One marked difference that I experienced during my time was with some insurers who were primarily bent on profit from investment income while others sought profit through prudent underwriting. Without fear of contradiction, they all spoke of not wishing to rely on investment income, as opposed to underwriting profitability, but in practice, I witnessed both. Prudent underwriting and claims management to me were clearly the critical factors in the interest of increasing and managing the existing book of business. It always puzzled me how a major insurer could hope to achieve that desired profitable book when it failed to fully utilise the likes of its underwriters and risk management teams. For example, it might fail to conduct post-loss surveys, or rely on the limited expertise of loss adjusters or claims inspectors to somehow reveal the quality of the insured, more often than not based on a single loss.

When moving onto another insurer I asked to see the liability claims history only to be told it was not the policy to release those details, just the total claims experience. Why the secrecy, when we had a large team that could so obviously have benefited from such information? As one surveyor remarked to me, while at a loss control seminar, why was it that when there was a wildfire, earthquake, tsunami or a product recall the details were extremely well covered in the press yet access to employers' liability claims and settlements proved so difficult to come by? Some of the post-loss surveys that I was assigned resulted in a large number of declines simply because the insured believed that their risk management was in the form of their insurance policies and did nothing else. However, I was aware that some underwriters never trusted all the surveyors available to them who they perceived as ranging from poor to average, with the surveyor's impact matching the quality of the individual. Added to which I often heard the phrase 'added value' where surveying was involved but rarely witnessed it being provided; yet another golden opportunity lost by field staff.

Understandably, being a highly qualified civil engineer did not necessarily make someone a good risk surveyor simply because that individual had previously never been assigned those duties in their industry before joining the ranks of an insurer. I always felt that it was a case of the blind leading the blind, as proved to be the case with all three insurers I was involved with. At Cornhill I attended underwriting courses where I began to understand what an underwriter's needs were and yet there was no such policy adopted by the other two insurers. If an individual does not recognise what their customers want, how can their customers best be served? Investment in training is vital yet it was not common practice, resulting in newly recruited surveyors and engineers being assigned risk surveys, involving considerable sums, of high hazard trades and contracts. These risk surveys often extended to include product liability, environmental pollution, professional indemnity and just occasionally financial loss, yet all the while the surveyor possessed little to no knowledge of where the potential for loss existed which, to put it bluntly, is the reason why so many risk management services were and still remain ineffective.

Even now, I wonder why my loss ratio was so low given that I worked with some outstanding surveyors who would assess an unsatisfactory risk just as soon as they walked through the door of the premises and once inside would spot an unsafe condition, situation or act without batting an eye-lid. Some were so quick they often caught the insured's representative off guard, which enabled them to conduct the survey leading from the front as opposed to being subservient, which is where many surveyors found themselves. For a considerable number of surveyors, my adopted approach did not sit too well but they could be forgiven for that because a majority had never experienced working in what I described as *the real world.* Try meeting production targets within a strict, almost impossible, budget, or managing a team of workers where only 80% turned up to work on time or working for a director who wouldn't spend money on such niceties as personal protective clothing or maintaining firefighting equipment. Well, in industry, the surveyor meets labour under those severe constraints and just to add to their woes an insurance surveyor arriving on site gives the representative more worries so they appear to go along with whatever the surveyor recommends 'just to get him out of my hair' as an insured party once told me.

If I am to be critical of those employed in the insurance industry, neither underwriting nor claims would be included simply because in both of these disciplines I came across some of the most imaginative people I ever had the privilege to work alongside. I always maintained that if I had the choice to employ or engage people to conduct surveys I would, against tradition, recruit those with either an underwriting or claims background and experience. Of course, I would include loss adjusters, as opposed to loss assessors, on my wish list as I found they have similar qualities. My record perhaps would show that, while employed in a senior surveying role, it was from industry or the enforcing authorities where we recruited the majority of our surveyors. The reason behind this was simply that, as the hierarchy in both underwriting and claims made it clear, it was *hands-off* their quality staff. It is true that there are many in the industry who believe that surveyors should possess a technical background; however, this is overplayed, as it tends to push profitability back somewhat. Insurance is about financial gain, and consequently, those employed should be focussed firstly on safeguarding the account, as opposed to producing lengthy technical reports that are of little to no value. Their customers, the underwriters, are basically non-technical people. I just could not accept this technical bias in reporting because of the impression made on me by the gentleman's comment at that Ford seminar: we are in business to make a profit.

My arrival at Cornhill's office was a pleasant surprise with almost everyone being extremely courteous, well dressed and with offices or workplaces fit for royalty, well probably not quite but certainly a far cry from my office in Thames Foundry, Dagenham. Being so impressed I wondered what else was in store for me, particularly work wise. I didn't have long to wait as I was provided with a number of liability survey reports to peruse, which contained information I had no understanding of, including why certain details were even included. As best I can recall there was a section headed *numbers employed* which in the completed report before me listed *skilled, unskilled, young persons, female, supervisory numbers, disabled* etc. all of which had me questioning why such detail was so important. I have to confess I had absolutely no idea why such information was an underwriting necessity and why these details were prominently displayed on the cover page of the report form. On the same leading page, there was a section requiring the listing of statutory provisions that I was comfortable with; consequently, I was not totally mystified as to the report's contents.

With mixed feelings, I continued to read the remainder of the report culminating in the final page which summed up the surveyor's opinion of the risk. A little befuddled I just assumed that they the underwriter and the small team of existing surveyors making up the team were happy and so, when undertaking my first surveys, I attempted to adopt the same approach. This was a tremendous mistake because other than the policy number, the site, contact details, reason for the survey, numbers employed and previous loss history the front page was just padding, like most of the detail contained within. For example one of the first risks I recall surveying was an innocuous piece of business that should never have been looked at as workplace statutes for the most part never applied, without claims experience, that it must have cost the company more in survey expenses than the insured's total premium. Selection, I concluded, was of paramount importance but my opinion in the instance fell upon deaf ears. Of course, Cornhill was not reputed to take on the heavier liability risks hence their loss ratios were probably the best in the industry at the time, which I would suggest was more to do with prudent underwriting than any survey input. There are, of course, exceptions to the rule and I was at the scene when an accident occurred which ultimately resulted in a public liability claim.

The risk was a large commercial laundry, catering in the main for the needs of hotel businesses based around London and the Southeast. I had met with the proprietor and had a half-hour discussion in his office where I learned of nothing untoward that had occurred in the past 15 years of trading, most of which while insured with Cornhill. As we passed through the access door leading from the office to the laundry there was a redundant steam boiler measuring three metres high by six metres long. Leaning against the boiler was a timber ladder and at the top was an elderly man dressed in an anorak wearing a beret. The man was taking details off the boiler's plate when suddenly the ladder slipped and the man came crashing down, at our feet, to the concrete floor of the laundry, with his beret rolling away and his clipboard contents scattered. Realising the man was injured, I went to assist while the proprietor, to my astonishment, simply stepped over the ladder and prostrate body exclaiming, *"It's OK, he is not an employee,"* and simply walked on.

Even while having experienced insurance for a limited period I remarked that if the man was injured there could be consequences. The owner simply shrugged and walked on, informing me that the man was an assessor for a potential buyer of the boiler and it was they who should be concerned and worried, if anyone! Ultimately a claim was settled for a small sum under the public liability cover. For the record, I visited the same laundry some eight years on and they were still claims-free under their other policies.

It was during my first three years at Cornhill that I received a call from a law partnership in London who were requesting I contact them at my earliest convenience. I have to say that it brightened up one of my routine days with Cornhill. It all sounded very official and had it not been for the fact that a meeting was requested at my earliest convenience I would have been concerned. My mind did however race; had I been caught speeding again, did I overlook a payment of some description, was I somehow being implicated in a court case and so on as my mind jumped about searching for a clue as to what it involved. I made the call and enquired as to the purpose of the request. An extremely well-spoken lady told me that she was not obliged to discuss the matters over the phone but that it concerned my previous employer. That gave a choice of two: The British Army or Ford. The army and MoD did not request when they could order so it had to be down to Ford, much to my relief.

I turned up promptly at the prearranged date and time at the barrister's chambers learning that those involved were the legal counsel representing Ford Motor Company's insurers. I knew how it worked as I had meetings with their like before following serious but questionable accidents in both Dagenham plants so I wasn't too perturbed. Apparently, all this resulted from Ford being at odds with the plaintiffs who were now proposing to up the ante and battle things out in the courts. My first comment to the barrister was, "Excuse me for asking but why do you keep referring in plurals; 'plaintiffs' and 'courts'?"

"Sorry," came the reply. "But, yes, we had difficulty tracking you down since the first case and now you are here. Perhaps you can shed some light on another of our cases?"

As I have already intimated, I have only fond memories of Ford and the thought of being of use to them excited me a little, plus of course the relief that I believed that I was not facing anything that left my actions questionable. One thing for certain was that all of my accident reports included an opinion based on the facts as I saw them at the time so of course, this was the reason I believed legal counsel was seeking my assistance. Requesting my presence was anything other than an inconvenience as it broke my routine and being forthright with lawyers seeking my input it did intrigue me somewhat. Once in their presence sitting around a large circular table it would have been impossible not to have caught sight of two files with the Ford Motor Company blazoned across the cover and the Ford logo on one corner. Not even when momentarily catching sight of the somewhat bulging folders did it in any way phases me least of all filling my head with negative thoughts because I recall just how single-minded I was where accident investigations were concerned. Opening up one folder the barrister asked if the name Kellati meant anything to me which drew a shrug and a shake of the head from me followed by me suggesting that he should reveal the circumstances as names I initially would struggle with. I knew immediately by the uncomfortable shifting of those around the table that this was not the response they were looking for. I don't know why but momentarily at least I enjoyed the reaction followed swiftly by me suggesting that they would probably be best cutting to the chase by presenting me with a description of the incident and what is being alleged. The barrister began by setting the scene, dates, places and finally the circumstances at which point I remarked, "So that was his name, I am not good with names but circumstances I recall very well?" Consequently, I gave a detailed account of the accident so much so that the barrister and those about the table expressed their surprise that in almost an instant I was providing such detail yet couldn't recall a name or a date.

In an attempt to explain my ability to recall detail regarding so many accidents was unquestionable I explained in the first instance down to the severity and extent of the injuries or the magnitude of the material loss. Consequently, such vital issues thus determined my level of investigation, which in some cases knew few boundaries. Secondly, which was more of a personal motivator, I have yet to meet a person who likes to be hoodwinked consequently if the circumstances or accounts appeared questionable or I suspected collusion my investigation was thorough to the nth degree, such as in the Kellati case. As was my way when meetings become too sombre and stern I explained that my adopted approach when recalling accidents or incidents was akin to listening to someone humming or singing an old tune or song where the tune is immediately recognisable with only the lyrics being a little vague. Well, accident circumstances for me are cognisant of the music while the names, dates and the like just take a little more time coming to mind. Adding for the record that neither demeture nor senility had not yet set in so of course I recall the circumstances. Plus, for the record any acts or omissions on the part of those involved such as in the Kellati case which while sympathising with his injury I opined he was very much the victim of his own failings.

The barrister went on, referring to my report and to comments made at the time by the operative just before he was taken off to hospital. Although he was somewhat bloodied and a little shocked, I believe I obtained and clearly established his account of the accident. The operative alleged that while he was tightening up a bolt on an engine block with a ratchet spanner the spanner slipped off the bolt striking him in the face and causing his nose to be shattered. All of this was witnessed by another operative, Mr Burni. I went on to explain that I investigated the accident, and there were some serious discrepancies in the allegations which had those present sitting up. Firstly, Mr Kellati was not tightening a bolt or nut but an air filter unit fitted on engines bound for Australia, due to their strict exhaust emission limits. Now all those present were really attentive so I added that the ratchet spanner was, in fact, a strap ratchet that grips the irregular piece to be tightened and should not be confused with a spanner with a socket head that fits on a hexagonal bolt head or nut. I was asked to describe in layman's terms what exactly was involved.

Continuing with my description of the air filter and operation I explained that it was an irregular-shaped aluminium valve with a threaded end that screwed into the engine's cylinder head. The strap ratchet employed to tighten the valve comprised a self-tightening noose strap of flexible metal that is looped over the valve once the operative has engaged the threaded components. The lever action causes the valve to turn until the ratchet at the desire pressure slips indicating the valve is tight. During this levering action, the operator is required to have the palm of one hand ensuring that the loop stays over the valve while the other hand simply levers the handle back and forward, in short, a two-handed operation. Mr Kellati, however, was *spinning* the ratchet, which, if not held firmly, could more often disengage. This happened, and the spanner flew off the filter into his face. This was a malpractice that the experienced assemblers were extremely proficient at whereas Mr Kellati was not. He was neither trained nor instructed to operate using that method and as for the condition of the ratchet it was examined and being found serviceable was put back into service that very shift.

As for Mr Burni, his witness, I interviewed him a day or so later, as it became clear Mr Kellati would not be returning to work in the immediate future and I knew it would involve me completing a lost time accident report as required by law. As I indicated in my report, we were in my office where I asked him to describe the incident. His account was sketchy, to say the least. In fact, he simply told me he saw the spanner slip off the nut and it hit Mr Kellati in the face. I did my homework at that time and learned from others and the supervisor that both the injured employee and the witness were friends having started together, and were from the same town in Pakistan. As for Mr Burni's position, he was unloading pistons from plastic trays some 25-feet or so away from the injured Kellati's work station and given the work in hand I doubted that he had observed the incident as he claimed because he would have had his back to Mr Kellati's work station.

I put all this to Mr Burni at the time, suggesting that if it was established he was fabricating an account he could be dismissed which I suggested was foolhardy given if it did go any further it would be out of our hands. I recalled suggesting that his friend at worst had a broken nose and would be back working in a few days or so. I told the barristers that I continued counselling Mr Burni informing him that my job was simply to avoid the repetition of accidents and I could only do that if I knew what had really gone on. Not believing for one minute that I would several years hence the situation would come to this, I asked him, "Do you think I am a competent investigator, Mr Burni? Because if you believe that to be the case, just wait until you have to take the stand in a court of law. These barrister guys are the real deal and being thoroughly proficient at their trade would have you believing night was day. So as to avoid seriously damaging your friend's case, if they establish you have lied, as it could well prejudice, Mr Kellati, your friend's situation. So I suggest you give what I have said careful thought a few minutes before I submit your witness statement." After a few moments, I handed Burni his statement. "Here is your statement, would you like it to stand or amend it? Or you can tear it up and that will be the end of your involvement." Mr Burni hesitated a moment then proceeded to tear up the statement and left my office.

Now one of the barristers present asked how could I recall in such detail the accident given that I had previously suggested there were so many. My reply was quite simple informing him that if he wished I could provide him with a plan of the area, a sketch of the spanner and my findings regarding the malpractice of *spinning* the ratchet as these were clearly recorded in my thesis, dating back to the year of the incident.

"So I think we can put this to bed and I am sure, given your clear recollection, you would never be called, well certainly not by the plaintiff's counsel," said the barrister.

Following lunch, we reconvened and another accident report was offered, which I refused simply asking again for the barrister to briefly detail the accident. The name again meant nothing to me but the incident did, involving a worker slipping adjacent a carousel wash. Mr Bhakti had allegedly slipped on a wet surface outside the bund of an engine cylinder head carousel wash and had suffered hip and pelvic injuries, leaving the plaintiff with a permanent disability. My first comments went somewhere along the lines of, "My God, these are Engine Plant accidents, haven't you got anything later? Give me something from the Foundry at least." Ignoring my comment, the barrister returned to the accident with me suggesting this was certainly more cut and dried than the Kellati case, which seemed to wake up one or two of those present. Naturally, I was asked why I could be so sure given my comments regarding the Engine Plant and this being sometime in the past?

"I will tell you all about the accident but could you brief me on what is being alleged please?" I enquired.

Apparently, the plaintiff was walking with one of his colleagues from his work place to the canteen when he slipped on some fluid in the aisle way immediately adjacent the carousel wash resulting in him falling into the bund area. The carousel, I had to explain, resembled a large box constructed in sheet metal on a steel frame through which passed an overhead conveyor. The conveyor carried the machined castings through what was effectively a high-pressure wash. The spray from the wash obviously was not completely contained but splashed out onto the immediate floor area. This area was bunded, capturing any splashes, spray and drips. The bund comprised a raised kerb, painted yellow as all hazardous surfaces are, the smooth surface within sloping into a drain and sump.

This second case was another where, upon learning the date of the accident and the date the claim was initiated, I cynically suggested one or two obvious reasons for the delay. Clearly, the statute of limitation was my first thought as the three-year grace period had just about past. Secondly, and more pertinent, the plant layout most certainly had changed during that time and as for the supervisor for the area he, like me, had parted the scene. As my report listed no witnesses and with me no longer seen about the plant it left the employee with his account of the accident and of course his obvious injuries. What, however, had been overlooked was that at the time I hotly disputed the employee's account of the accident and retained details that were not entered in the accident report.

From my point of view, I was called to the scene as the medical staff intimated that the injuries to the casualty were serious. So with camera and report form I attended the area and observed foot and other skid marks within the bund area. Photographs inside the barrier-cum-fence were not possible so I made do with external shots, including the aisle way, but I did sketch the scene including all dimensions, skid marks and position of warning notices. I followed this up by visiting the medical centre but was too late to speak with the injured employee as he had been transported to the hospital. However, his work apparel, such as overalls and footwear, had been removed so I was able to see these items, which were both wet from the fluid from the carousel wash and that on the surface within the bund. The employee's footwear was in good, serviceable condition. Some two weeks later, I obtained a statement from the employee, who was at that time an outpatient at Romford Hospital, and had returned to the plant for personnel reasons: sick pay and the like. He told me that he had slipped on the aisle outside the wash and fell into the bund area. Unable to find a witness, even though he earlier reported he was walking with a work colleague, there were no witness statements.

It has to be understood that the Ford accident report forms were restrictive where details regarding the circumstances and, as in this case, too would be the claimant's account which were at the time non-existent as a result of the injuries sustained being severe and hospitalisation. Unfortunately, for me, the claimant's account was without foundation as simply there was no evidence to support his assertions. At this point, the barrister said that this was the very reason for my attendance as they were struggling with this case. Responding to this, I requested being permitted to read the insurance claims form completed by the claim's inspector and the employee's account, clearly I would suspect was prepared by his legal advisors at a much later date.

Reading through the documents, it was a complete fabrication on the part of the claimant which did take a moment to sink in for it was as if we were looking into two accidents. The detail in the employer's account was so far adrift from my findings and I just wondered about the individual's state of mind insofar as believing that his account would hold sway. The discrepancies were considerable, in fact, at the meeting, I suggested that he was in fantasyland if he was holding Ford responsible for his injuries. At this point, I gave those present the precise findings of my investigation down to the accessibility into the bund, footmarks inside the bund itself, the employee's footwear, fluid marks on his overalls, lighting, layout, warning notices, malpractices in relationship to the carousel wash, accident history and Ford Safety Engineering's measures taken to prevent recurrence. It never ceased to amaze me that people who make statements do not realise that if not true and remotely questionable, it could seriously damage their case.

At that point, I went on to explain to those present, again in some detail, my findings, including the extensive corrective action that followed to prevent recurrence. There were details in the claimant's account that by and large were true insofar as the carousel wash made floor conditions treacherous adding that was however within the bund and not beyond the kerb. The details that were, as I suspected, purposely overlooked were firstly the surface areas beyond the kerb were dry and free from fluid and secondly, conveniently, there was no mention of the metre high steel-framed fence, mounted on the kerb, completely enclosing the wash save one area where a lockable gate was positioned for ease of maintenance. The fence during my time had been modified by way of an intermediate rail welded into place and the gate padlocked as we experienced workers were still stooping below the top rail as opposed to climbing over the upper rail. The reason for this malpractice being that the wash was directly at the end of a wide aisle from assemblies en route to the canteen resulting in there being a rush that resulted in some taking the shortcut as opposed to walking round a further fifty or so metres.

The barrier and kerb were a deterrent certainly but to some the walk around the production line and the carousel wash was more daunting and time consuming than climbing the two barriers and negotiating the slippery surface of the wash. The claim, however, told a different story where the employee slipped on the surface outside the wash and fell into the bunded area. After a quiet chuckle to myself, I asked the lawyer if they had met Mr Bhakti and as they had not, I explained that Bhakti was about 16-stone, five feet six inches tall and rotund, and that for him to have fallen through the barrier, he would have needed to have either been a gymnast or contortionist to have managed it.

Now, without pausing, I went on to explain our medical centre treated a number of injuries through employee's slipping and falling while attempting the short-cut, so initially a single rail barrier was erected and further warning notices posted. Subsequent falls and a serious head injury resulted in the intermediate rail being introduced to stop employees ducking below the top rail that was in position at the time of the Bhakti accident. Looking somewhat bemused, one of the lawyers asked about the head injury who he surmised had resulted in another slip, trip and fall. With a knowing smile I continued with my explanation regarding the circumstances of the head injury which was not as they imagined but involved one employee carefully watching his footing while negotiating the tricky wash surface and was struck on the head by an engine block passing overhead on the conveyor which knocked him unconscious. Again, further preventative measures were taken which resulted in the barrier being raised a further metre and enclosed with chain link fencing making now the barrier insurmountable.

Sensing that while the photographs taken at the time were of little help, my drawings with dimensions would show the scene quite clearly as these, along with my observations, were still in my possession and within my thesis much to the amazement of those present. The lawyer accepted my offer of providing my drawings and the detail of the accident was also accepted which again proved damaging and damning evidence that resulted in a minor settlement. Subsequently my drawings were provided and the details noted that resulted in a letter of gratitude from the lawyers who further informed me that a settlement had been reached, well below the reserve, out of court.

Returning to my early days at Cornhill I was, on one occasion, surprisingly called to attend a claims meeting, not believing for one minute that I was being viewed as the ogre of the piece. I was shown a liability report of mine and had my attention drawn to the accident section where an alleged 'foreign body' entered the eye of an employee. I was asked to explain what was discussed with the insured at the time of the survey, particularly in relation to the eye injury. Fortunately, I have an awfully good memory, which was prompted by those present handing me a copy of my report. I went on to explain that there were, in fact, two eye injuries, and enquired as to which injury they were referring to.

Apparently, the incident those present were referring to involved an injury sustained by an employee during a welding training session where the managing director was demonstrating a new technique, to a small group of trainee welders including the injured worker. All the trainees were provided with eye protection and so ensuring all were protected the director proceeded with the demonstration. It was alleged that the injured employee, for some unknown reason, removed his eye protection as the demonstration continued. On completion of the demonstration, the employee was seen rubbing his eye as if he had something in it. The director could hardly be criticised as he would have been concentrating all the while on fusing the two pieces of metal together. The employee was nonetheless treated and the accident details entered in the accident book. Following up on the incident, the employee allegedly admitted removing his glasses while the welding was taking place believing the demonstration was at an end. As the accident had occurred just one week or so before the survey and up to that point in time the employee had not taken time off work, thus suggesting that he had suffered no long-term after effects, it was treated as a non-notifiable accident or minor injury.

Subsequently, I was now being informed, the eye deteriorated to a degree that resulted in surgery, which apparently proved unsuccessful resulting in the loss of the eye. Hence a claim was submitted, all of which was unknown to me and certainly the director would not have been qualified to assess the condition of the eye up to and about the time of the survey. However, the incident took a turn as while being interviewed by a claims inspector the employee stated that it was the end of the welding rod, being handled by the director, that had struck him in the eye and not a 'foreign body'! I sat still without comment because I was at a loss as to why in fact I had ever been called to attend this meeting. The head of underwriting, realising I was not adding anything, asked me for my opinion on the lack of reporting and the sketchiness of the entry in the accident book?

Feeling rather peeved I asked how much detail they believed was missing given the number of minor injuries recorded in the accident book, which dated back two years and was all entered in my report? There were in fact just two entries involving the eyes, one suspected fractured finger, one cut to the face, five cuts to the hands and three burns. Another employee reported to work feeling dizzy, who was sent home, while another had a grazed knee when he slipped on an oil spill in the car park. I then asked those present which would they have expected me to investigate further, given that all the employees returned to their duties, save the dizzy spell. It was a rhetorical question and I added that as the employee did not inform his employer about subsequent treatments until a short while later, what would you have expected the director to have done save reporting the injury and proposed surgery?

Now on my 'high horse,' I said, "I am tempted to speak of contributory negligence," adding, "We surveyors are expected to spend two to three hours at most on the site, anything longer and the insured would probably object. To discuss each accident as detailed as you here are intimating is impossible and given my experience, where accidents are concerned, I rightly target those where working days have been lost or the employee is absent or the severity of the injuries are of concern. Other than that, you are asking something I and other surveyors cannot deliver so before I leave this meeting please tell me what you want."

Without waiting for an answer from either I stated that I was not inexperienced and hated the fact that I should be classed as such. I could see I had both shifting uneasily in their seats. Detecting the meeting was not going as the senior managers planned, I decided to add to their discomfort by way of continuing with my take on surveying insofar as I did not see myself as just a professional person, there to report on policyholders or those seeking insurance cover. My role, I added, was far more expansive than that insofar as not simply leaving an insured to rectify any noted failings, as they themselves see fit, but by me providing cost effective solutions and ultimately delivering the underwriter with an accurate risk rating.

Having now spoken for a full ten minutes without a reply, I asked that I might continue as I should like to be corrected where those present feel I was missing out on my objectives, as I held a senior surveying position and was present on all underwriting training courses. With a simple hand gesture, the head of underwriting invited me to continue which led me to speak of conducting a survey in such a way and manner that it was likely to result in positive long-term risk management and not just at the time of the visit, all of which I submitted would create a worthwhile business partnership. I just couldn't help myself at this juncture by stating that each surveyor should surely be judged on their merits and occasions such as this with underwriting and claims management reaction to a single loss could result in surveyors becoming ultra-cautious, which is exactly why many brokers and insured look upon a survey as being an imposition.

Accepting totally that a major loss should be reviewed my contention was that first, as opposed to calling for heads to roll, the circumstances that led to the loss should be looked at subjectively, taking into account the situation at the time of the survey and not at the time of the loss. Secondly, we had to ask if the existing conditions were identified at the time of the visit as having the potential to lead to the loss. Finally, there was the question of if the loss circumstances were common to the trade or property. In all three areas, I argued that I could not be found wanting as my report contained those details.

As a parting shot, I said that my attendance at underwriting courses made me think like an underwriter and that part of my initial training was to underwrite risks myself. I gained so much from that experience that I believe that I could under any circumstances, given the limited time on site, make the right choices regarding my lines of enquiry. Given that in the case here, there was little to no indication about the severity of the injury with only the injured employee being aware of it at the time of my visit. Consequently, we had to move on and target what appeared significant and relevant. The head of underwriting was of course at a loss, as was the head of claims so they simply thanked me for my time and I walked out never hearing about the incident again. Hindsight, in this case, would have made no difference as the worker had at the outset claimed something in his eye only to later change his story when the severity of the injury was realised.

A culture of blame was, to my way of thinking, counter-productive simply because it led to surveyors always looking over their shoulders, resulting in them being almost pedantic during the survey or appraisal. At one point during another senior management review, I suggested that provided the surveyor covered the common trade hazards, in order of priority and severity then that should be sufficient provided the underwriter was made aware of the insured's overall rating, of which there were five ranging from decline to excellent. During all my years of surveying, I only ever encountered three risks that merited excellent but did, however, rate a number of risks well above average, many of which were given a clean bill of health at the time. What differentiates the excellent over the other ratings is simply that risk management is fundamental to those businesses' way of thinking and that they were, more importantly, proactive.

People's perception of risk can be a major challenge, particularly when the person or organisation you are dealing with has little to no experience regarding losses. I am not sure which is the more dangerous group, those that operate in ignorance or those who function accepting the dangerous elements of their trade or profession. An example of the latter concerned a steeplejack insured who was put on cover. However, the underwriter recognised that this was a high hazard trade and wanted a liability survey conducted within a 30-day period of inception. Making the necessary arrangements, as was the norm through a broker, I arranged to meet up with the insured's principal at a cathedral where the insured had won a contracted to make repairs to one of the spires, including the lightning conductor. The classification for the steeplejack trade then was where work was in excess of 30 metres or 100 feet.

There were two areas that required detailed comments: the prevention of falls of persons and avoiding falling materials. In the majority of cases, steeplejacks labour from bosun's chairs, ladders and rope access systems. This is in contrast to other building contractors, such as roofers, who work from fixed working platforms or scaffold. The reasons for this are obviously the excessive heights involved and the question of exactly what would you tie the scaffold onto when working several hundred feet above the ground on say the likes of a tapering steeple? Arriving on site I found the insured sitting in his slightly battered Ford Transit van drinking tea. He opened the passenger door and beckoned me to take a seat while he finished his refreshment. He informed me that the contract was for a southwest diocese with a contract period of six weeks; however, due to the height, the location and the time of the year it was more of a guesstimate as high winds, visibility, and precipitation all have to be taken into consideration and therefore could result in delays. Well, that was the theory in this case as the wind I guessed was gusting up to 30 mph at the time at ground level, so I raised the question as to their means of measuring wind speed, which the insured answered by sarcastically wetting his forefinger and sticking it in the air. *We were obviously not going to get on*, I thought.

Needless to comment we got off on the wrong foot, so I tried a different line remarking on how clear the weather had been and it being good for their business. Yet I was wrong again because, full of bravado, the insured stuck out his chest and suggested that the weather conditions were largely ignored otherwise they would never get any work done. By the insured's tone and remarks this I assessed that this was an individual who found insurance surveyors in their suits, collars and ties to be an imposition he could well do without. When he finished his tea, we got out of his vehicle and crossed the car park towards the cathedral. I couldn't help noticing that he had a pronounced limp. Tactfully I ignored the insured's condition believing perhaps it was a football injury or something unrelated to his profession; given his responses thus far I thought I should steer away from it.

We entered the cathedral and reached the first landing stage via a very long spiral stair. The landing was some twenty or so metres above the choir. Stepping out of the building, onto a parapet that ran its length, we could observe the spires, which extended nearly 80-metres or so. I could feel the wind and, in the interest of safety, I left my clipboard and camera inside the parapet. The work involved some roof covering and repairing the lightning conductor, all working from the parapets or tied ladders and ropes on the spires. "The wind isn't too bad," the insured remarked. "It always seems worse at height than below." Well, with this off-hand remark I asked about how if the wind were gusting, it wasn't possible that the speed could increase down a narrow passage such as the parapet or around the steeple. That gained another of the insured's now trademarked shrugs.

My question obviously hit home and, as the insured obviously had no intention of answering me, I had to comment on the rope harnesses that were on the parapet but not being used by the workers. The response put everything into context for me, and went along the lines of, "If you have ever tried working with a rope about you, you wouldn't have asked that question," the insured said.

"Ropes can be cumbersome and I think more of a hindrance than being useful; you drop tools and materials if you swing around and I know you people don't want us to be dropping hammers from height, now do you?"

It got to the point where I suggested that the job was perceived as highly dangerous and so asked why he didn't do all he could to avoid deaths from falls?

"Look, that is the job, people fall just as I did and that is why my hip and leg are no good." Now I knew the reason for the limp. "These guys are on good wages because of the risk," the insured added, "so they take the rough with the smooth, if not then they should find a job sitting behind a desk, like yours." There was little else to be said so I thanked him for the informative chat and visit, adding that he would be hearing from his broker in due course. This was one of those businesses where those employed accepted the consequences as being an occupational hazard and would not change. Following my detailed report and assessment, the policy was cancelled.

Expansive Insurance Surveying

The time came when I could see that, while I seemed to understand the role we surveyors should play in the grand scheme of things, others seemed to want the quiet life, and were simply just going through the motions. As a team, I believe we were guilty of simply treading water. At this juncture, with over a decade and a half at Cornhill, I was approached indirectly by what was described as a new, progressive insurer. Following my take on things, it appeared to be the challenge I had been waiting for, as the business had not, at that point in time, fully established liability surveying. In reality, it was non-existent. To date the insurer had simply relied on their property surveyors to look over liability exposures, bearing in mind that all but a very limited number of insured had stand-alone policies; combined policies were the order of the day and only through brokers. This appeared to me to be the sort of opportunity I had been longing for so I attended an informal meeting where I was impressed by the liability underwriting manager, who clearly was old school, and was one of the reasons I decided that if offered a position I would accept. Following a couple of interviews that I thought were almost perfunctory, I was offered the vacant senior liability surveyor position. Following my resignation at Cornhill, I was informed by the head of personnel that if things did not work out for me with my new employer, they would keep my old position open for me to return; it was a typical nice gesture by a classy employer.

    This new appointment, however, took me to new unforgettable levels in loss control and surveying. For the next decade, I felt I was on a switchback. The CEO and MD at Independent Insurance were the like I had never encountered before and were on top of everything that moved, or not, as it happened, in the company. On my very first day, I was provided with a pile of completed liability reports, produced by property surveyors while they were on site, looking at the associated fire risks and perils. Scanning through these reports, I just wondered about the level of their expertise as very few of these reports would have been of benefit to any underwriters I was used to dealing with. In fact, when looking at the trades, very few identified high hazard processes and, as for recommendations, they always seemed to include bland statutory requirements such as safety policy statements. As for accident history and severity ratings, they were rarely given a mention. All of this left me with the feeling I would need to begin over and rehash report formats, putting together some documentation that would actually be of some benefit to the underwriter.

At this point, I know that being a little controversial didn't sit well with some of my former surveyor colleagues, some of whom I, in turn, looked upon as being bland, with little to no appreciation of the golden opportunity they had to make a significant difference when involved in risk surveying. Why, given the chance, did so many surveyors fail to grasp the moment to promote the insurer, their profession and themselves? The age-old cliché was *being the ears and eyes of the underwriter*, but with many, it never really sunk in regardless of it being so true. Consider that essentially an underwriter is akin to a bookmaker or turf accountant, where they attempt to make a profit based on expert opinion regarding the quality of the risk in management terms. It follows that the underwriter is seeking assurances about possible losses, whether they be property damage, employee accidents or perhaps the business being disrupted.

Never once did I give a clean bill of health to a risk where it was not merited, in fact, I would go as far as to say the opposite was my policy. However, if the insured responded positively at the time a comment was passed and made good then it would only be necessary to record the issue in the report. I would, however, draw a line if during the survey I witnessed a serious malpractice or a number of loss control omissions, irrespective of the insured taking appropriate steps at the time to make the situation acceptable. The details regarding those omissions would, of course, be in my report, would influence my overall assessment and would result either in a general or a specific comment in the letter to the insured.

Standard wordings were often seen in property reports, which were encouraged due to a desire for quantity over quality. However, for me, they lacked something of a personal and individual touch where the risk and persons seen were concerned. I once had an insured say to me during a post-loss survey, where the failure had more or less been predicted by a previous visiting surveyor, that he had received a word for word recommendation but thought it was just a general observation.

Clearly, no debriefing took place at the end of the visit where this particular issue should have been discussed in earnest and a loss possibly avoided. My policy was to list the issues and cite exactly who they were agreed with or not. Where the recommendation involved expenditure and the contact was unable to commit then this would be for the underwriter to follow up on, but effectively from the surveying point of view, the matter was closed. Being true to these principles and policies I never believed I would ever have problems as the aims and objectives were so clear and simple, yet my early days with a new employer proved otherwise.

At Independent's Technical Head Office, located at Edenbridge, I trawled through property reports with liability comments waiting for the time for me to be assigned liability survey work. This seemed an age in coming but it came in a manner I never envisaged when the CEO, almost a daily visitor to the technical head office, made sarcastic remarks about me being seated in the office as opposed to being out surveying. I finally couldn't take this badgering any longer and turning to the CEO, I made it clear that I was entirely opposed to 'sitting in the office day after day', and that I would only be too pleased to get out. It was as if I had lit the proverbial 'blue touch paper' as there was utter silence across the entire office followed by a flurry of activity. My GM asked me afterwards, and when I related what had gone on I was told that nobody talked back to the CEO, and that they were right now finding me survey work. The personalities at Independent were poles apart from those I had become accustomed to and if either the GM at Cornhill or the Plant Manager at Ford had a complaint about an employee, they would go through the supervisor first, so I was finding things altogether strange.

Obviously, I had ruffled feathers, which some translated as my employment quickly coming to an end, not that I cared too much as I would simply take up Cornhill's re-employment offer. Nonetheless, the survey requests piled in and had me scurrying from my West Surrey home to the four corners of the UK. My very first survey turned out to be one of the most telling, visiting a boilermaker in the West Midlands. It had in the past been surveyed by a fire surveyor who unsurprisingly overlooked what I thought were both minor and major hazardous situations, which I simply could not let go. The quality of the risk was, to say the very least, poor and probably would have merited a decline at my previous employers. Nonetheless, I started with a clean sheet of paper and worked my way through the disorganised factory. I discussed the hazardous piles of steel heat exchanger tubes with the foreman, with me intimating that the stack of these four-metre-long steel tubes, that had spilled out onto the factory floor, was hazardous and required tidying up.

The response was to inform me that the workers would use up the loose tubes by the end of the shift, as was the norm every day. The supervisor simply walked away to continue his duties as if I had not been there. I was struggling with this obvious hazardous risk when I noticed an old newspaper beneath some of the tubes at the back of the pile. The newspaper bore the headlines of the Falklands War and the sinking of the battleship Belgrano, in 1982. As this survey was taking place some eight years later, I took the paper to the supervisor and asked him to take note of the date as I had taken it from beneath the pile of steel tubes that he had earlier claimed was cleared almost daily. It certainly left the supervisor with egg on his face and without waiting for his response I continued my walk down the main aisle, where I saw an operator opening up a three-phase electrical box; I asked him why and was the power on or not? The operator told me not to worry myself as he only kept his pile of two-penny pieces in there, which he used for the tea machine nearby! All this added to the fact that the bottom bank of fuses was burnt out while the upper tiers were alive and what is more the pennies were stacked close by. I was starting to enjoy myself again at last.

Warming to the task I was starting to wonder what I would find next as these were not trivial issues but high hazards. Continuing my walk down the aisle I came across a forklift truck with a loose bundle of insecure steel tubes balanced across the forks. Sounding the horn, the driver manoeuvred his truck avoiding pedestrians, stanchions and the partially built boilers. Witnessing this malpractice and other conditions and acts I made my way back to the office and the factory manager. I reported that there were some issues that needed urgent attention and listed about eight including electrical safety, mechanical handling, systems of storage, stock rotations, machinery guarding and noise. The manager agreed to look at the list, suggesting he would attend to what he could, provided they were achievable within his budget. I commented that housekeeping needed no expenditure, nor did safe handling of materials, while admitting electrical matters did require urgent attention. I then asked if he would mind me taking a few photographs to go with the report. Offering his hand, he politely suggested that I put my camera away, so I took the hint and left.

Returning to the office I wrote up the report and suggested it merited decline given management's attitude and the indiscipline of the workforce. Unbeknown to me, my reports were being filtered through to the very top and the MD was instructed by the CEO to go take a look at the risk in question without delay. The point of the exercise was supposed to confirm that I was unsuitable for employment as this was during my probationary period and they could terminate my employment without any serious problems. Some of this I was made aware of later by some people who believed in me so I was prepared to soldier on until my fate was decided by those at the top. I was not so full of confidence, I recall, when informing my wife that my days were numbered and I would soon be rejoining Cornhill.

My survey work in the few weeks to follow involved some harmless risks, I believe because it meant that they wouldn't have any complaints from their brokers about me identifying more substandard hazardous risks. However; one risk did slip through, which involved the manufacture of motor parts close to one of my old Ford plants. The business was principally about machining flywheels, crankshafts, camshafts, housings and so on for the likes of Ford, GM and Volvo. Some of the machinery and tooling were supplied by their customers and to meet demand they worked a three-shift system out of four separate factories. There were problems but in general, I found the MD and his son, also a director, very appreciative of the guidance and suggestions I gave and made. One of the issues that was subject of debate was a milling machine that skimmed the face of a flywheel casting. This casting was placed into the machine, at which point the clamps energised, holding the piece firm and leaving the cutters to skim the face. The problem was that the clamps were not sequential; in fact, the two-button control had been tampered with so that the operator could have both hands free, which left them exposed to both the clamps and cutters.

Following discussions, I informed the director that the operator had rigged the controls and consequently these needed urgent upgrading as the machine would have been protected while at Ford. This surprised the director and he informed me he would see to it by sounding out Ford safety who visited occasionally. In the meantime, they would change the system of work to ensure the operator's hands did not get near either the clamps or the cutters. This was all set out in writing on my newly devised letter to the insured that came with an introductory note at the head. I had already prepared a new report format, letter heading and guidance notes at Independent, as there was nothing to speak of in existence at the time of my appointment. One evening with not much on my mind I received a call from the technical head office requesting I come in early the next morning as the MD would be present. Anticipating the outcome of the summons I made arrangements with my wife to come to Edenbridge the next morning to collect me, as Independent would surely be repossessing the car.

Early next morning I drove up to the office and on arrival noticed that there were only the liability manager's and the MD's vehicles in the large car park. I now believed they wanted to get my termination over without others being present. I walked into the liability manager's office and the MD stood with his back to me looking out of the window, so no niceties. The atmosphere was cold but I wasn't at all taken aback, just simply waiting for the decision. The liability manager produced one of my reports: and like an interrogator asked if it was mine? Looking at the report and recognising it, I replied, "It's got my name and signature on it so of course, it is mine." At this point the MD joined in from his position by the window literally pushing the liability manager aside he pointed at the report asking me if I had discussed the recommendations with the insured. Now I too was being belligerent and, without waiting for further response I read very slowly and purposefully from the introductory letter I had devised, and I quoted, "Thank you for the courtesy extended to me and for your time and patience during the survey. I have, as agreed, set out below those issues that were discussed and agreed with *Mr Smith* I made the name up, in the interest of health, safety and welfare of you and your employees. Should you need further guidance or assistance regarding the aforementioned or indeed any other matters regarding safety in the workplace please do not hesitate to contact me on this number."

This was met with complete silence as clearly neither the MD nor the liability manager had read the introductory paragraph because I suspected they had never seen the like before. They were totally in the dark regarding the steps I had taken to confirm my findings and agreements, and more importantly, provide the underwriter with a hint as to how the relationship with the insured stood. This silence suited me because my Ford days had hardened me in such situations that screamed out for me to let others suffer in silence. I had quickly ascertained this was not going to plan for those present. The MD finally broke the silence by informing me that an operator had lost the digits on both hands when he became trapped in the machine I had now clearly identified as dangerous and discussed with the insured. Now given time to think and having taken in all that had been said the MD remarked to the liability manager that we should repudiate the claim, much to the surprise of both the liability manager and me. We remarked in unison, 'We can't do that.' Now completely flustered the MD turned his attention back to me asking if I had any work to do. I nodded. 'Well, get out and do it.'

I left the office and informed my wife that I was still employed, for now. What was to follow was even more surprising because following a few months of uneasy silences my presence was this time required at the head office in Minster Court, London. I hadn't been at the head office since the very first day of my appointment, so I again thought it was for real this time, and my days were finally numbered. Again, being prepared like any good boy scout, I told my wife not to worry about me getting home because I could catch the train on this occasion. My only concern was that the six months' grace period offered by Cornhill was fast evaporating so maybe I should take the initiative. However, I had got everything wrong so far and true to form what happened at head office I was again totally unprepared for.

Before that though, we should first return to the hand injuries discussed with the MD. Apparently within just two days following the survey I was to learn later that a loss occurred, more or less as I had predicted, with the insured allegedly waiting for my detailed recommendation before implementing the necessary and agreed risk improvements. The delivery had apparently been delayed as the broker who handled the case was on leave. The company was also now being asked by the insured and the broker that the surveyor should revisit the risk and assist in the design of appropriate guarding on the flywheel machine, along with those other machines identified as requiring additional safety features. The requested visit and my planned involvement apparently again found its way all to the top which I am sure rankled with one or two members of senior management.

As it happened, within the next month the West Midlands boiler manufacturing risk had also experienced a serious loss where an employee suffered severe brain damage during a work process which I had identified and reported as being dangerous. Presumably, the process continued unabated without my recommendations ever being sent, let alone adopted, as the insured had been previously been given a clean bill of health by our property surveyor. Again, I later learned that the MD had been sent to look at the risk and in conclusion simply described it, warts and all, as a typical 'Black Country' engineering concern. In both the aforementioned cases the settlements involved six-figure sums; a costly experience for an emerging commercial underwriting company.

Now I was being summoned at short notice to report to head office, where again I anticipated that my days of employment were all but over as I was to see the director of personnel and training. It has to be borne in mind that I had no idea what had gone on at either of those aforementioned risks where these serious, costly losses had taken place. The early days in Independent were so unpredictable and, true to form, those misgivings I held were completely wrong for I was shown to an office and there was warmly greeted by a director who I had met up with on a few previous occasions and found him always to have a spirit of friendliness about him. He requested I should be seated, offered refreshment and handed me a sealed letter. Sitting with the letter unopened in my lap, as I anticipated what was within, I was prompted to open it. The letter, signed by the chairman and CEO, was in short concerning my promotion to liability survey manager and that I was no longer on a six-month probation.

Now perplexed, yet relaxed, I thanked the director expressing my surprised and relief that things seemed at long last to have worked out. The director said that he was also very pleased but the niceties were over because there was a downside to all this. My first objectives concerned, without undue delay, to go out and employ four other casualty surveyors of my ilk. Secondly, I was charged with the responsibility of training up the existing property surveyors to a level where they could at least identify the difference between a good risk and a substandard one. The director's final comments were as he left me somewhat bemused, sitting alone in that office, "Well done. Congratulations and my, my how in such a short time the worm had turned!"

The ten years that followed were more like a rollercoaster ride, where risk management changed year in year out with the survey teams getting larger, more experienced and sophisticated. All the while, the risks being underwritten were becoming decidedly heavier by any stretch of the imagination, which meant we needed more specialists, plus we introduced a health and safety hot line that provided our insured and brokers with a 24-hour risk management service. In addition, we introduced bespoke risk management manuals, free audits, guidance notes and on-site risk management presentations. The size of the team increased to the extent that we had approximately 26 liability surveyors including a number of specialists drawn from mining, construction, nuclear, occupational health, ex-scenes of crimes officers and quality contractors. This meant a total of 180 surveyors and assessors in the field.

As the numbers of surveyors increased, to meet the survey demands, so my role changed but only as far as I dealt principally with the corporate and multinational risks, which entailed considerable travel and which is where the adventures really began. I believe that the overseas accounts grew out of all proportion which resulted in me visiting and surveying in some 76 countries including South America, the Caribbean, US, New Zealand, China, Russia, the Indian sub-continent, the Middle East, Africa and so on. My overseas surveying, I had to admit, did not always sit well with my CEO who was not enamoured with my periods of 'absence' from the UK book. The overseas accounts, as the CEO was at pains to point out, amounted to approximately 30-million GBP as opposed to one billion GBP in the UK and Europe principally Spain and France. Avoiding debating the matter I held my peace even though I was heavily involved in very nearly every one of those UK corporate accounts.

It was about this time, some five years on from when I totally committed to Independent, that I received a general manager's invitation to a retirement luncheon for one of those underwriters to whom I was so indebted at Cornhill, who was to retire following over thirty years of service with them. When I arrived at Cornhill some twenty years before Geoff was a senior superintendent underwriter, then in the head office, and was one to whom everyone seemed to look up to. Rightly, in the interim, he had moved on up the ladder to very near the top. Without hesitation, I accepted the invitation and arriving at Cornhill's head office and entering the GM's suite I immediately recognised some old faces and of course the retiree himself. Lunch was a very pleasant affair going over past times with some and meeting other prominent people from the likes of the FSA (Financial Services Agency), the institute and the like, so it made a very impressive gathering for a highly respected person. There was more to come when during Geoff's farewell speech he turned his attention to me saying, 'Thank you for coming as it would not have felt right not to have had the very best surveyor in the industry amongst so many distinguished guests at my retirement.' Embarrassed would have been an understatement but it was nonetheless one of the most rewarding compliments that I have ever received.

Returning to Independent and despite my best efforts, we failed to attract the right calibre of surveyors, who we felt could competently tackle the unexpected and uphold the good name of the company, regardless of a considerable sum spent on a recruitment drive. However, as fortune would have it, a PhD engineer from the nuclear industry contacted one of our directors, informing him of his interest in joining Independent in a loss control capacity. This application was allegedly unconnected to the recruitment consultancies we used from time to time. To this end the PhD candidate impressed the regional liability survey manager, so, after being hired, he was coached as to our now adopted general approach to surveying, policies, documents and so on. After he suggested to the regional manager that he was comfortable with our surveying policies and procedures I dispatched him to Australia to look at some risks we insured there. His briefing included being informed that he would be dealing with the most reputable international brokerages in the insurance world and, therefore, needed to act with tact and diplomacy with both them and our insured.

The best laid plans as the saying goes failed miserably for, following just one trip down under we almost lost one of our biggest risks plus an international broker's goodwill. All this was due to what I was informed involved a host of issues with the new person: a total lack of diplomacy, promoting himself bordering on self-importance, being someone who spoke as if lecturing, who talked but never listened, and worst of all imposing risk recommendations based on UK statutes and approved codes of practice. It seemed not to have occurred to him that, rightly so, many Australians take umbrage at having UK and European standards forced on them. Further, many of the risk recommendations required our insured being obligated to spend considerable sums and worst of all overlooked the fact that the underwriters impose conditions, not the surveyors, all of which did, I fear, serious damage to the company's image in Australia.

What this meant was that after a very short sabbatical I was back on international surveying once again. My first single and priority task was to try and repair relationships with insured and brokers in Australia, with whom the surveyor had dealings and who he had upset to an amazing degree. Regarding the surveyor, before I departed for Australia, it was left with me to deal with the individual, which given the surveyor's standing in the field of loss control engineering I could have done without. The problem was that I had never met the surveyor as his grade merited the regional manager conducting the interview prior to his appointment. Upon arrival at head office from his branch, I briefed the surveyor on the reasons for me seeing him and for me to understand what had caused our business partners in Sydney being so furious. We sat for a full ten minutes with only the surveyor talking until I asked him to sit and listen. I then had to insist he listen as my initial request was totally ignored. Recognising the problems, I decided to extend his probationary period and for him to conduct home only surveys, all of which resulted in his welcomed resignation shortly afterwards.

Returning back to the home front one of the major insured I was assigned was Swan Hunter, the shipyard on the River Tyne, Newcastle. The business was in mothballs and all items of plant were being offered for sale along with the waterside frontages and structures. There was machinery such as power guillotines, with a beam or blade measuring some five metres, the same with box-formers of equal size, 1500ton powered presses, radial arm drills, welding machinery, generators, pumps, tanking... it was all very much standard size equipment for a shipyard plus quay cranes, mobile cranes and lifting equipment some on the river's edge, others in the yard with some of the lifting equipment being amongst the largest in the UK if not Europe. My task initially was just to observe that the standard precautions were being taken for clerical staff and authorised visitors interested in purchasing the machinery so that consequently employer's and public liability cover were in place. The arrangements were all very much standard with the main players at that time being the security who ushered the prospective buyers around and the administration staff. Following one or two routine visits I was instructed to revisit the yard again as a Dutch owner, Mr Jaap Kroese, apparently purchased the entire facility with the intention of resurrecting the shipyard ready to convert the *Solitaire*, a super tanker, into a pipe-laying vessel.

Whether it was simply prudent underwriting due to Independent Insurance already carrying the liabilities or not, the insured decided to stay with us. From the insurer's point of view, the fact that shipbuilding and shipyards are 'heavy' risks doesn't always mean that they are poor risks. No two businesses, even those of a similar trade are ever the same. We had two other major shipyards of note on the books at the time and both cases were considered 'high hazard' in every sense of the occupancy rating. The risk had changed obviously having now won a major contract insofar as the facility was functioning as before, only under a different management. A 100-metre centre section of the hull of the *Solitaire* had been removed in Santander, Spain and was now being readied for conversion into a mega pipe-laying vessel. To compete the contract, the yard recruited 1,500 staff, many of whom possessed shipyard experience at the very yard until its forced enclosure some years previously. The insured was clearly aware of the employment difficulties and working practices involved in such an undertaking so I was assigned to provide assistance where health and safety were concerned given that the ownership and management were now in Dutch hands.

Being now very familiar with the yard gave me from the outset an advantage as it was unnecessary to tour the facility or to identify the types of equipment and machinery, their condition and the necessary safeguards required to be maintained whilst in everyday use. While not directly designated the safety engineer I was assigned the task of providing risk management. Subsequently, I met with the Dutch owner and his senior managers, who were a breath of fresh air, not looking to cut corners but to make a once successful shipyard into a bigger success; consequently, we established a great working relationship along with the brokers. Shipbuilding establishments in the UK were not the best for worker relationships and I made the insured aware of the likely obstacles that lay ahead unless there were firm management controls. The insured were extremely interested in my dealings at Ford and wanted to ensure that they or we, as the insurers, were not about to inherit the lax years of management that preceded their ownership. Types of industrial diseases and injuries were our main concern so we set up pre-employment medicals and examinations of all would-be employees, all in their very own excellent medical facility. It seemed that we would, with careful planning, avoid claims later for the likes of vibration white finger, noise-induced deafness, welder's lung, stress related problems and so on.

Swan Hunter became a prized possession in underwriting terms, so much so the Dutch brokers attempted to deal with Independent Insurance directly, thereby cutting out the London brokerage. Independent's head of underwriting made it clear that they would only deal through the existing broker; therefore, we would cease to be Swan Hunter's insurer. As I understand things, the MD asked who would then be the risk manager insofar as would my services still be available. Apparently, he was informed that Independent's head of loss control was only assigned insured policyholders' work and I was not available on a contract basis. Following this, the MD instructed the Dutch brokers to leave the business through the London Market brokers and of course Independent.

It went without saying that the relationship between all parties blossomed and the claims experienced were outstanding simply because I was always accompanied on my audits by the MD and their Head of Safety. Anything untoward observed was swiftly actioned and as I was to learn the reason for the supervisor cooperation was that two habitually offending supervisors whose reputations were seen to be cavalier were demoted. It went without saying I was described as the yard's safety inspector. Upon reflection, I am sure many supervisors and managers were unaware I was simply an insurance surveyor with a keen eye for malpractices and unsafe equipment. Being involved at the outset I was known to have been in place before all of the current workforce's employment, which gave me an edge.

All was running smoothly with Swan Hunter until the day I received a call from our senior underwriter in the city bristling with sarcasm.

"So this excellent risk is one we should make certain we secure eh? Well, how does this sit with you: one fatal fall and another as yet unconfirmed death in the workplace through unknown causes? *Brighty* is not going to be best pleased."

Brighty, as he was known, certainly out of earshot, was of course our CEO. "I would suggest you get yourself up to Tyneside as quickly as possible," was the underwriter's forthcoming suggestion. Rather perplexed, I booked a flight immediately after a call to Swan Hunter confirming a meeting the very next day, not mentioning the urgency or need. Having such an excellent relationship with the insured they asked for my flight details as they usually sent their limousine to collect me from Newcastle airport. I arrived at about 9 am in Newcastle and was met by the chauffeur who, I must say, was as perky as ever and asked about the flight and how things were in general with me.

Arriving at the shipyard I was shown to the offices where the PA to the MD apologised for him not being there to greet me but suggested I take in the shipyard with their security officer and he would catch me up. The MD, to reiterate, always accompanied me. I thought that they were all taking things very well for having experienced two fatalities, so much so I began having serious doubts. The yard and operations all appeared normal and given the Ford experiences where even serious accidents were concerned, let alone fatalities, the atmosphere was, to say the least, intense. Some of the supervisors I had previous reasons to speak with regarding certain conditions gave me a cursory glance and nothing more while others were their usual courteous selves. I wanted to get to the bottom of things as I felt I was missing something so I suggested the medical centre was as good a place as any to start.

At the medical centre, we found the senior nurse sitting on the wall outside smoking her usual cigarette, and she seemed surprised to see me but nonetheless ushered me inside. By this time, we were joined by the newly appointed safety manager, yard supervisor and machine shop supervisor. It was really weird and to break the ice I asked to see the accident book, where I fully expected to see the details. While I had been perusing the accident register the MD had slipped into the medical centre and I felt so awkward and even a little tongue-tied by the apparent lack of concern amongst those present. After acknowledging the MD, I turned to the safety officer, enquiring, "Any F 2508 or F 2509?" These are reportable statutory accident documents. "What on earth for, nothing reportable has occurred?" came an emphatic response.

Now totally at a loss, I came clean. "Look, I have to tell you that yesterday afternoon I received a phone call from the underwriting room in London telling me about two fatalities here at the shipyard."

These remarks seemed falling on deaf ears until the nurse said, "Two bodies eh, we must keep a lookout lads for those." The nurse broke the ice with her remark and now the mood changed with obviously all present save me enjoying what they obviously saw as some kind of hoax.

I spoke up, "Okay, your humour is appreciated but in short I was told that a man fell from a scaffold and died through his injuries." That last statement was met with howls of laughter with the nurse as usual at centre stage. I still had to ask about the other fatality. "All I know is that another worker died on the premises, and I can't add more," I said. The safety officer then stepped in and told me scaffold supervisor had slipped off a pile of scaffold boards and fell some two or so metres, injuring his leg and all the while accepting he was entirely to blame. He wrote up the injury himself as being self-inflicted.

The nurse, never one to not to be heard, quipped, "Hell, if we had cremated him, he would have been awfully mad as he is out there somewhere now limping about working." These remarks followed by yet another chorus of laughter.

At this point another of the managers cut in, "You must be referring to old Eugene who suffered a heart attack on his way to work and passed away in hospital yesterday?" So there ended the mystery.

"Well," I said, "I am glad I brightened your day but rest assured, I will get to the bottom of the matter regarding how some things so comparatively simple, save the employee's passing, could get blown out of all proportion, and I will let you know." To a degree feeling back in control, I felt that the safety officer had something to say so I asked that he share his thoughts as something was clearly bothering him. I asked, "Do you know how these fatality rumours possibly came about? My interest is, I assure you, to protect our standing as leading liability insurers in the London insurance market."

As I suspected he had the answer as apparently he had been speaking with the Dutch brokers based in the Netherlands about events in general. His update to the brokers, probably through poor translation and not least of all his strong Geordie accent, got the message completely wrong. The brokers, in turn, went on to inform our London Market brokerage. The brokers immediately got through to our underwriters who by this time imagined that there were bodies lying everywhere! The upshot was that there were no claims and normal relationships with the insured were resumed.

It goes without saying that my surveying took in all manner of occupancies and trades but the challenges, as such, rarely came from the workplace or the work processes but from people's perception of risk, and a lack of understanding that ranged from incompetence to crass stupidity. In such a case our underwriters were so nearly caught out when underwriting an abattoir, that was reportedly a good piece of business, as described by a broker, but was cancelled through the coordinated efforts of surveillance and underwriting. In all the years in the industry, this was in my experience the best example of teamwork that proved wholly beneficial to the insurer. As was the norm, the underwriter suggested that they were holding cover for thirty days on the abattoir asking if I could fit it into my already busy survey schedule, when next in the vicinity. As a result of our findings with this reportedly good piece of business we adopted a whole new strategy when dealing with suspect or substandard risks. An abattoir is not the best of risks to underwrite at any time, so imagine where there is such a business, and totally unbeknown to us, the management pays no heed to health and safety, largely by permitting the workforce to do what they please. In spite of promises to turn the risk around to the acceptable they metaphorically speaking hung themselves by believing the insurer and the brokers were as lackadaisical in our business as they were in theirs.

The broker attended this new client, visiting their business premises for the first time, but clearly couldn't differentiate between a well-managed and a poorly run abattoir. In addition to this, the broker was unaware that the abattoir's management had a workforce primarily made up of self-employed staff who were rewarded on a piece-rate basis; hence the high wage role, which they believed made it even more attractive as no claims for injuries or other losses were made. Attending the business premises for the first time, I found the insured to be wholly engaged in the slaughter of cattle from as far away as France, despite being based in Kent. The lairage was full on my arrival and there were even more heads of cattle in a line of waiting vehicles, all of which indicated just how busy the facility was. That business was reflected in the work process, which, along with the labour force, simply put, placed quantity ahead of safety, health, or animal welfare, in fact almost anything else. The only thing the abattoir apparently did was to satisfy the Health Ministry's meat inspections regulations.

Entering the stun area from the office, I could feel my feet sliding in the gore, akin to a tallow works, which you will not often find in even the average run abattoir. Simply, the 24-hour killing contributed to the appalling housekeeping but with a little care it could have been improved upon. The principals of the business were father and son, with the former being the head while the son permitted the appointed slaughterhouse manager to handle the day-to-day operations in and around the facility. Unfortunately, I had brought along with me a junior surveyor as these types of risks are ideal for training, as the risk exposures are, while gory, also all too obvious. I could see from the surveyor's expression he was somewhat taken aback by the smell and noise that is all part and parcel of the processes; the noise from mechanical handling plant, pneumatic tools, lowing cattle who, many claim, know what is in store for them, and the smell from droppings, blood, hide, etc. All makes for a unique environment and so the surveyor, being somewhat new could be forgiven for his sensitivity.

The business operated a single stun bin, non-halal, where I estimated the kill rate was less than five or six minutes, which was very fast given the operating procedure of the captive bolt stun gun. The gun, after firing, requires putting to safety, re-cocking, the loading of the cartridge, safety off and the gun placed to the animal's head and fired. Should the slaughterhouse man fail at the first attempt to deliver the fatal shot, the animal perhaps shifting its head suddenly or the gun slipping in the grip of the operator, it would require another preloaded weapon to hand to complete the kill. All this takes time and should, as was the case here with us watching, the slaughterhouse man be blasé, it could result in some serious self-inflicted injuries in the trade.

Once stunned the slaughtered animal is dropped out of the stun bin onto the floor surface adjacent where it can still kick; therefore, the shackling operative is in turn vulnerable from the risk of kicking. The animal being hung is then suspended over the blood bath and the throat cut, thus bleeding the animal. Such was the casual approach, I witnessed two animals being bled before the carcass was correctly positioned over the bath and therefore blood spilled on the floor. The next few operations were probably the cleanest of all until we reached the offal. Having been cut from the sides, the worker cast these cuts several metres across the work area towards the offal bins. Unfortunately, most of the offal was hitting the wall behind the bins, sliding down the wall and further adding to the already treacherous floor surface. One bin was so full at one point that even when the odd piece found its way to the bin it slipped out onto the floor surface.

My list of faults was growing by the minute like I had never before experienced, so much so it rated as the worst abattoir I had ever surveyed, having seen some pretty gruesome scenes in India, the Middle East and Africa. Returning to the office and thanking the director, I informed him I would complete my report immediately before passing it on to the underwriters. Leaving the premises, my colleague uttered his first words since we arrived enquiring as to why there was no debrief. I had, prior to the survey, briefed him on the standard procedure so he was rightly questioning why there was no final consultation. I explained that firstly there was absolutely no way the insured could ever reach the level we would require and if they did the culture within the workplace would never allow any changes to be maintained. Such was my confidence, I said, that I would be strongly recommending decline and cancellation.

Following the submission of my report, I was requested to attend a meeting with the head of underwriting who asked if there was anything that could be done, as the father had now handed the day to day business dealings over to his son and that he was now asking for my guidance, as he was frankly at a loss as to where to start. Well, it was a first but I thought that it was a tall order and unlikely to succeed, but nonetheless, I would give it a try. Returning to the abattoir and sitting with the director, I ran through those issues I identified as being priorities. We spent a considerable time in the workplace and, on each issue, the director took the time to correct the malpractice. Thoroughly satisfied I had done all I could, and as the director appeared totally committed, I informed him that I would set out all the issues and send him the list to work with. I also suggested a weekly audit to maintain standards.

With the insured's agreement, I proposed that I should return within the month to witness the promised improvements, with one proviso: my visit would be unannounced. Both the broker and the underwriter remarked they had never heard the like of such an approach before. Explaining my take on it, I said that if the insured were aware I would be returning at a particular time and date, they would simply make every effort to have the facility shipshape ready for the visit. The broker was far from happy but I suggested that his misgivings were borne out of fear of the standards not being maintained. Working on that basis, the underwriter submitted that without the condition they would come off cover, leaving the broker with effectively nowhere to go. Days dragged by and I received two calls from the underwriter saying time was running out. On the second occasion, I responded by explaining that as anxious as he was, so too would be the insured and broker, until they ultimately believed we had forgotten.

That is the subtlety of it all, where if the insured let things slip, we would see that their long-term commitment wasn't there. If they were half-hearted and with me turning up on the last day we would see the standard for the future. On the morning of the very last day, I arrived at the abattoir and I have to say the director was caught in a state of shock seeing me. Believing that I would not return he suggested he remained in his office and I should complete the visit myself. *Skating* through the first few metres, I knew exactly what I would find: the place was in the same state as I had found it one month earlier. Returning to the office I apologised to the director and informed him that I would have nothing positive to report back to the underwriter, but that the decision ultimately was his alone. The upshot was a cancellation of the policy and my strategy was adopted regarding unannounced visits.

Post Loss Surveying

The principal objective of post-loss surveying is to establish the quality of the risk exploring the likelihood of there being further losses, either under similar circumstances or perhaps in other areas. From some misguided surveyors and underwriters, I gained the impression that the purpose was to recognise if any circumstances could result in a repudiation of the policy or reducing the size of the reserve. I always felt that these were issues for the loss adjusters, or perhaps legal counsel. Admittedly I did provide an opinion where it was to be clear that there was a legitimate case for doing so, or where there were serious flaws in the claimant's assertions.

Usually, however, there were serious failings that could, if not rectified, lead to further losses, and which ultimately suggested the management was substandard. Of course, there were cases where the insured took a closer look at their endeavours following a loss and took positive steps to prevent a recurrence, without the likes of the enforcing authorities or insurers introducing or proposing appropriate measures. As rare as these cases were, though, they were exactly what the insurer desired and also made the post-loss survey an almost non-event. However, sadly I found on several occasions that despite experiencing a large loss the insured never looked beyond that process or item of plant or equipment in the interest of loss control. Without external coercion or forces, the business limited their investigations to the loss in hand rather than taking a wider view of matters to prevent further losses. On an occasion, in Pakistan, a commercial printer experienced a major loss due to a chemical explosion and fire that destroyed a multi-colour offset printing machine valued at USD 145,000.

Arriving on site the insured had assembled all their senior managers including their engineering director consequently, the insured felt that those present could provide answers to my questions, which they knew only too well would be forthcoming. I requested their take on the loss, exactly what had caused the explosion and what steps they had taken to prevent a recurrence. The engineering director was the first to speak followed by the Production Manager and the maintenance manager who all, in turn, spoke of the failings and the root cause and as if to satisfy me the change of materials and in the process to ensure there was no repeat. At the appropriate time, I requested their approach to the cleaning process when the machine first arrived on site and as to whether that or the cleaning materials had changed, after all the machine had been installed for at least two years.

When you pose a question that the assembly was not prepared for, there is always a period of silence with each of those present looking around for another to speak. I could also predict that a stock answer would entail a request to elaborate on the question as if it was I was speaking in a foreign tongue. I too had a stock answer insofar as I repeated word for word as to the difference between the former process and the new one. Now given time to think the director informed me that the cause was both the process and the cleaning materials used both of which had been changed further a passive fire damping system being installed. It was as if the director was patting himself on the back which had a morale-boosting effect on all those present. The mood in the room changed as if the solution and steps taken had in a stroke put the insured back in a favourable light.

My response again took all by surprise when I added, "You run five offset printing lines, do you not?" Without waiting for an answer, I continued, "And the measures you have taken on the newly reinstated line have been adopted and incorporated on the other four lines?" I had, as anticipated, caught all off guard, easily recognised by the frantic exchange of glances about the room. Again, the director broke the silence by suggesting that maintenance had the matter in hand and that it be dealt with shortly. Now I knew I was being fed a line when I asked the maintenance manager an update on the process and progress and he informed that his team had met to discuss the matter. "Just so I can satisfy both the underwriter and myself that you have been proactive, may I see the minutes of the meetings and the proposed design of the fire and explosion protection?"

Of course, there were no plans or minutes, so as to save further embarrassment I suggested that they prepare themselves from a backlash in the form of draconian conditions and requirements because my report would not be complimentary given you have experienced a six-figure loss and have not taken a closer look at your failings. "You cannot expect the underwriter to simply carry on providing cover when you are not exercising forward thinking. Consequently, I would suggest some swift action on your part and trust this will satisfy those in London."

One of my very first post-loss surveys was one revealed that, while the management laid the failings at the door of their employee, they should have been the ones shouldering the blame. The insured was a crane hire company whose fleet of road cranes ranged from machines with lifting capacities of as little as 20 tonnes up to 100 tonnes. Their static tower cranes could reach heights over 150 feet using additional mast, slewing and jib sections. The mobile road unit would travel independently while both rigid and articulated vehicles would carry the mast and jib sections, themselves weighing several tonnes. There was a fatality where, while a mast section was being lifted from the back of a truck, the rope sling broke, resulting in the section falling onto the banksman and narrowly missing the slinger.

The rope sling was neither certificated nor tested and was in fact used exclusively by the truck driver to secure his loads on the back of his truck. The enquiry and coroner found that the death was accidental, while our insured faced prosecution by the HSE for using uncertified equipment and subsequently found guilty by the courts. Their employee, the slinger, was also subject to criticism for failing to sling the load safely. While the truck driver was allegedly disciplined by the insured for being in possession of unsafe rope slings, regular audits were introduced in compliance with the improvement notice imposed by the HSE.

The insured had some ten road cranes, five-tower cranes and several block and tackle hoists, along with numerous chains, wire slings, shackles and rope slings. The training and qualifications involved newly appointed employees being in possession of various recognised certificates, while the insured sent non-trained personnel on approved courses in compliance with statutory requirements and their ISO certification.

At my initial meeting, all the management team were present from the workshop manager, who maintained the records and certification documents plus service records of all the vehicles and equipment, through to the yard foreman. The interview unfortunately continually switched back to the circumstances that led to the accident as it was still very much on the insured's mind. All seemed in order regarding their policies and procedures so I requested a tour of the compound and workshops. Within the vehicle compound were three road cranes and three trucks with the remainder of their plant and vehicles out on their sites. I attempted to open the locker bins on the cranes and the vehicles but they were all locked; I did this in an attempt to establish what equipment was generally available on these vehicles, ready for everyday use.

The insured, in a clear attempt to side track me, informed me that some of the bins contained some personal possessions of the operators such as high-visibility clothing, foul weather gear, protective footwear, gloves and hard hats, so they were kept locked. This raised the question concerning their ISO accreditation, 9002 and 14000, of exactly what their audits covered and what their frequency was. Finding the keys, we opened the first bin on a crane and found the contents in order, including rope slings and shackles, all with identification tags. Some of the personal protective equipment had seen better days but at least it was present. I think that the manager was as relieved as me; in fact, it was as if he was seeing the inside of these bins for the very first time.

Moving onto the trucks the padlock keys could not be found so I asked how the auditors could possibly complete their checks. The manager changed tack, in an attempt to avoid answering my question, and claimed that since the accident they had issued instructions and that a new code of practice was now in existence. In yet another obvious attempt to side-track me, the manager then suggested that they would sometimes introduce relief drivers and that realistically there were no dedicated vehicles. 'And the padlock keys?' I asked. 'Don't bother to answer.'

Now determined not to move from the spot I told the manager that if they wouldn't at least satisfy the underwriters, by letting me view the truck's equipment, that was telling when it came to the insured's new approach to health and safety. Far from happy now, the manager summoned their vehicle mechanic from the workshop to break the padlock allowing me to view the contents of at least one of those trucks' storage bins. The lock was removed and the contents of the locker laid bare. It was a shambles, full of contraband equipment and with little evidence of safety apparel. The contraband included untagged rope, some in poor condition, wire slings that had never been inspected and tested and some shackles that were damaged by being distorted and that could never have been secured.

Now, with the manager completely at a loss to explain the situation, I again commented that failing to access the other bins would result in the insured failing to follow their own policies, which, I added could result in other injuries. Duly complying with my demands the other bins were forced open and it seemed that the root cause of the fatality had been wasted on the vehicle drivers and management alike as the bins were the proverbial Aladdin's Cave full of unsafe, unregistered equipment. This resulted in some very harsh conditions being imposed on the insured, which included criticism of the management as opposed to the employees as it was they who should have taken disciplinary action against the offending employees. It was also required of me to visit all seven of their listed sites within the following two weeks, where it was pleasing to report that the survey had surprisingly a greater effect on them than the fatality and the legal action.

Another post-loss survey that proved an eye-opener to the underwriters at Cornhill was one where an ex-loss control engineer from the manufacturing industry had a great deal more to offer than they ever imagined where product liability was concerned. The post-loss involved questionable products resulting in the tragic death of a child, where a baby bath stand collapsed and the child suffered neck and head injuries. Thinking of the circumstances I attended the manufacturers, who specialised in childcare products such as carrycots, beds, baths and some buggies. The insured were very well established and were quality accredited so the survey should have proceeded without anything untoward being established. Nonetheless, I was able to view first-hand the defective item and those still being manufactured, which basically comprised two horseshoe-shaped frames formed out stainless-steel tubes, one frame slightly smaller than the other, which both were drilled and riveted in the centre to form a scissor action. There was a metal brace affixed to one frame that locked into the other designed to support a baby bath or carrycot. The stainless steel was considered ideal by virtue of being lightweight, capable of avoiding surface rust and easily cleaned.

Having seen the assembled stand and, following a review of the defective product, I enquired as to the insured's response to avoid repetition of the unfortunate incident. Their response came as a surprise to me because they didn't seem to want to change anything. There was supposedly no criticism levelled at them following the death; in fact, the verdict appeared to be one of misadventure or accident. Nonetheless, while there was no negligence or intended harm there was room for improvement in the product, either by additional engineering or user guidance. My question was initially about the life expectancy of the stand, which had been used by the family for a decade without incident. The axis pins on the defective stand showed serious signs of rust, which had also eaten into the inner metal tube over the years; consequently, it was not readily visible but the structure weakened. Being in a predominantly Catholic country, and seeing extensive wear, I openly asked how many children the insured thought would have used the product. They informed me that the bereaved family had five children and the youngest died and that they believed the family had bought the stand new for their firstborn.

I enquired of the insured if they understood where my line of questioning was leading? To ensure that they did understand, I submitted that they might consider putting a life expectancy on their products, which I quickly added was impractical, which they agreed. Secondly, I asked what weight limit they put in their brochure or user instructions regarding the approximate weight of the water? How would it be if the family put more than one child in the bath, which I suggested would be common if there were multiple births? Again, I answered my own question by suggesting that while some users would use a minimum amount of water others might fill the bath up. By this time, the insured was sure he knew where my questions were leading and requested some guidance as obviously, I had some in mind.

In response, I conjured up a picture of a very large lady, with twins in the bath and this mother leaning on the bath's edge supporting the children, adding that the bath had been in use with the family for a number of years. Submitting this as a worst-case scenario I recommended that the axis point pins should also be manufactured in stainless steel while at the axis joint there should also be an inner tube of steel to give added strength, while in their brochure some weight and a user guide should be provided. Surprisingly, the insured complied with the recommendations within two weeks of the post-loss survey and only a small settlement was made to the bereaved family. The survey resulted in post-loss surveying every product's risk where a loss had occurred and the risk solution submission was used on future underwriting training courses as an example of a survey's added value.

Being assigned post-loss survey work more often than not came with specific instructions, accompanied by requests to establish the circumstances that led to the loss and exactly where it left us as the insurer. Roughly translated, I was to go in and tell all. The underwriter was looking for something that justified underwriting the business in the first instance and whether or not they could feel confident in continuing providing cover or offering renewal terms. In defence of the underwriter, I should comment that the initial proposal was usually backed up a by a glowing report from the broker or, just occasionally, where the business was direct, by the business completing the proposal form. It goes without saying that I found many provincial brokers would adopt that policy consequently, and there was on many occasions the need to almost contradict the content of the proposal details regarding the occupancy or trade, the business standing, the accident history or indeed the numbers employed. One such risk that was being surveyed following a loss involved a business that was simply a front for what was the real money earner and the reason that it came to our knowledge was by accident during an innocuous post-loss survey.

On this occasion, the loss involved a slip and fall of a customer on the icy steps of the shop premises located in London, where the trade description was as an importer, retailer and wholesaler of water systems. It had a wage roll suggesting fifteen people, including administration staff, sales and management. Visiting the shop premises, I was led to believe that the company imported plastic components from some overseas manufacturers where these items were unpacked and displayed on shelves within the shop. The insured also had galvanised metal products available that again were obtained through a UK supplier. All in all, the insured looked quite harmless from a risk viewpoint so I began wondering why I was surveying something that was little more than a shop where a customer had fallen.

Regardless of my first impressions and feelings, I continued with the survey, obtaining details of the business, the processes and the risk management. I viewed the accident book and found it blank; not even the slip and fall of the customer had been recorded. The premises, in good order, comprised ground and first floor with the latter taken up with storage and an office. However, while I was on the wooden staircase, I felt vibrations and as I moved to the rear area I heard the familiar sound of metal stamping. Once having worked in a metal stamping shop you never forget the sound of power presses. Out of earshot of the manager who had been showing me around, I asked a lady engaged in wrapping some products, if the noise bothered her at all. She informed me that part of her job was to go to the press shop behind to collect finished metal stampings, replenishing the stock in the store, so it didn't bother her at all.

I approached the manager and asked how long they had been operating the press shop. Unwittingly, he told me they had as long as he could recall. I enquired if it was part of the business and from our point of view, as insurers, was it part of the risk? He told me there was just one employer's liability policy so he concluded that it was and asked if I would need to look at it. Not needing a second invitation, and now back on the ground floor, we walked through a connecting door into an alleyway between the buildings and through another door into a press shop that was twice the size of the premises I had already visited. Within the building, there were approximately thirty machines including power presses, power guillotines, box formers and drilling machines. Every machine had an operator and all but the foreman were women from the Indian subcontinent. The foreman was an aged Londoner, which given the other workers smacked of a typical sweatshop using cheap labour.

Walking through the factory with the foreman, as the manager had left us, I was forced to ask the foreman, having noted so many unsafe situations, when they last saw a factory inspector. I had to explain to him who I was talking about as clearly this didn't register with him. Clearly the facility was operating to some degree unregistered and therefore undercover. Now we had a serious problem, given that there were some real hazardous situations and one where an accident of serious consequences was just waiting to happen. The foreman asked me what the problem was as they had never had an accident or the like. In reply, I asked to see the press register but this too drew a blank. Who, I then asked, inspected the presses? It was as if the enquiry fell on deaf ears. I asked if we could sit in his office, where I could run some things by him. There, I told him that what the actions of the HSE would likely be given there were so many breaches of statute. I ran many failings by him for good measure and all the time he was shaking his head.

The foreman grew even more pensive and suggested in his defence that he did as his manager dictated and that he was there to see that the production targets were met. I asked about the ladies' attire, being totally unsuitable for press steel working, which comprised silk saris, open sandals, no gloves and no ear defenders, with the noise level clearly exceeding 85 decibels. The foreman called the office and following him briefing the person on the other end of the phone suggested I walk back over to the other building and discuss matters with them. Back in the main office, I began enquiring about their trade description, headcount and wage roll. The representative gave me a headcount close to my original estimate so now confused I enquired about the employees in the press shop. This, I could see, was not registering as they openly suggested there were, in fact, more employees than the number I counted. So now I explained that the employer's liability premium was based on the wage roll and the rating for the trade. I also suggested that the headcount on the completed proposal only showed warehouse and administration staff, which was all very contradictory.

It was now becoming embarrassing, particularly since I had to inform the insured that I would have to make recommendations regarding the press shop activities and staff headcount. As there was clearly an attempt to play down the wage roll and the trade that would result in a considerable increase in the premium once the underwriter revisited the true wage returns. In addition, the insured would need to obtain certification for the power presses, proof of training and the provision of statutory documentation, all of which were missing. I also reiterated what I had said to the foreman that if they were visited by the HSE they would for certain prosecute with serious ramifications. Sensing that the insured was holding back other details I asked about the accident record in the press shop. Suspecting that I must have learnt something while over in the press shop the manager said that they had not completed the accident book for an employee who suffered a cut hand because she hadn't returned to work yet.

Now I had realised I was not dealing with one of the sharpest minds ever encountered I commented on the lack of safety apparel and unsatisfactory levels of guarding. I commented that the reason the employee hadn't returned was that she was probably seeking legal aid and if it reached the ears of the HSE there could be serious repercussions. Upon taking my leave from a somewhat bemused manager I reported my findings to underwriter who informed the broker that same week of the policy being cancelled.

Where an employer's liability is concerned, just occasionally, it is difficult to find grounds to repudiate a claim. On the other hand, where public or third-party liability is concerned, refusing to entertain a claim is not so problematical. The first example of this was an employer's liability claim, albeit due to contributory negligence on the part of the operator, which meant that the settlement was much reduced. Being reasonably experienced in the workplace, one never forgets certain dealings or ever loses sight of the extraordinary lengths that co-workers will go to beat the system. That includes management, when it comes to gaining compensation. I know this because of having spent the earlier part of my life in this kind of work, from an apprentice through to a safety engineer.

It is also relevant that, where the trades unions are concerned, a benefit of the membership is to be granted free legal consultations in the event of an injury, so it is worthwhile for a member to *test the water* without fear of expense. It also has to be appreciated that an injured employee could attract the wrath of his employer, regardless of a prosecution or a claim paid, if the injury resulted in a fine or an increase in premium, so with union membership it is akin to the employee being almost fireproof. One millwright at Ford openly boasted that the claims manager of Ford's insurers had the employee listed as 'claims mad' and needed watching whenever he reported being involved in an accident. Moving from the naive to the *professional*, I learned that what you hear and see is only part of the picture. So it turned out when I was called upon to conduct a post-loss survey at a general engineers and fabricators, where it was submitted by our claim inspector that a machinist had all but lost his right hand on a guillotine, I was on alert.

Sitting in on a prearranged meeting at the factory with the management and, surprisingly, the injured employee the first thing that struck me as at odds with the report was the injured employee's physical condition. A badly damaged hand inflicted by a guillotine to my mind means amputation to one extent or another yet there was the employee with his hand in plaster and his arm in a sling. Consequently, the employee's fingers were clearly visible so I simply assumed that our claims inspector had been provided with a prepared written statement in the employee's absence and taken the circumstances as reported by the management as factual. Addressing the employee, I enquired how he was now feeling as he sat there amongst the factory manager, his foreman and the company's accountant plus of course the broker. His reply was very predictable, stating that his sleep was badly interrupted and he was itching to getting the plaster off. Following some physiotherapy, he would hopefully be getting back to work. Showing some level of sympathy, I learnt does tend to lead to those involved dropping their guards somewhat.

At this juncture all present, save me, were *very* sympathetic. My reason for not being was that there was absolutely no evidence, even at this early stage of the proceedings, that the guillotine blade had directly inflicted the injury on the claimant. Resisting the temptation to make a sceptical quip about the blade of the guillotine being blunt, I asked if we could visit the scene so I could view the operation in the interests of preventing recurrence. All agreed and, save the accountant, we marched to the *guillotine*. Arriving at the machine I stated, "That is a PELS Metalworker and not a guillotine." I think everyone was surprised and the foreman pointed to the crocodile shear section, saying that the machine did indeed have a guillotine. "My point is that this machine has a number of functions but it is not a guillotine." I could see by the reaction of those present that they were just waking up to the fact that I was not going to accept all their observations.

The crux of the matter, I took time to explain, was the difference between a shear and a guillotine as the cutting or shearing actions are dissimilar. I thought it best to talk in technical terms to save any attempts by the insured's staff to hoodwink me with local technical terminologies. It has to be borne in mind that I had already shown some degree of knowledge by disputing the use of the word 'guillotine' so I felt the advantage was with me. I added that, unlike some cutting equipment, the energy source of the machine, as in the case of a PELS, is stored in the flywheel so that when the clutch is engaged the ram on the machine will continue until the resistance on the blade, as in this case, is greater than the energy stored in the flywheel. That is why it is a prescribed dangerous machine and should only be operated by a trained person or a skilled worker.

"In your case," I said, and turned to the injured employee, "you are *skilled* in the legal sense, thereby only requiring minimum supervision. As such, you are responsible for setting the machine up safely, including the immediate working area. By that I mean the floor surface being kept clear of anything that could lead to a slip or trip. As you can see right now the floor littered with the material, and therefore unsafe." The floor condition was a serious consideration so underhandedly I suggested to the employee that he would not have worked in such conditions as were presently underfoot. The supervisor, however, probably without thinking, intervened to inform me that the machine and the workplace had remained undisturbed since the accident. It seemed that the line of my enquiry was having a positive effect as was my status and therefore the resistance to my opinions was lessening.

"How have you managed to get by without this machine?" I enquired. Very quickly, the supervisor stated that they had two PELS machines and another skilled operative, identifying the other employee so that when one or other was off work for any reason they could use the other machine. Therefore, since the accident, this PELS had not been used. Some of the off-cuts and the remaining section of the uncut flat bar was still on the floor or in a metal rack nearby. "So it is as you left it?" I asked the employee. The employee looked the machine over and confirmed that it looked to be in the same state. "You were cutting flat bar?" It was all too obvious as cut sections were on the floor but I wanted conformation, which he affirmed was the case. I went on to explain as if those present knew little about the equipment that the PELS has some unique features and that when using one during my apprenticeship I was berated by the instructor for not adjusting the clamp fully.

The purpose of the clamp I stated is to ensure the work piece does not move through the scissor movement of the shear. A guillotine shears or cuts the material along its length at the same time, so there is no clamp at all, while it is an essential feature on the PELS. I quickly went on to explain that the weight at the blade on the down stroke of the shear causes the bar being cut to rise up against the underside of the clamp. I could see that the clamp was ill-adjusted and turned to the employee, stating quite clearly that I knew it meant he was using his own leverage on the bar, a common malpractice, in which people would put pressure on the bar to act as the clamp. There was one main difference: as the bar got shorter the leverage became more difficult and the cut initially, although not too obvious, was more at an angle.

At this juncture, all resistance had faded from those assembled so I continued with I what believed had actually occurred. "Look, I am sorry. But you were not using the clamp at all as by your own admission you said it was in the same position." I ignored the assertion by the employee that now it might have been adjusted by someone. The supervisor now clearly on side countered that it had not been used. "We can soon establish what position the clamp was in by the cuts," I said. Picking up a cut section I pointed out that the shear angle was not straight, and became more acute the more cuts were made, just as I had described. The foreman picked up a few pieces and sure enough, as was predicted, the shear was increasingly angled on each one. I requested to start the machine and make a sample cut with the clamp now adjusted as opposed to being in the same position as we found it, stressing that we didn't want to contribute to another unnecessary loss. We made the cut and I suggested that they look at the shear, which was clean as opposed to angled as was on the other off-cuts which I could see by the reactions of those present proved a point.

Now having everyone's undivided attention I suggested that we put the clamp back to where we found it and place the bar stock in the jaws of the shear. The supervisor foreman, now an active participant, depressed the foot pedal and the shear cut but the bar stock hit the underside of the clamp violently. All were somewhat taken aback, but not the injured worker. 'So you see,' I said, 'the blade didn't inflict the injury to your hand but the bar stock and the clamp. You accidentally hit the foot pedal while your hand was still holding the uncut bar, didn't you?' I didn't give him a chance to reply. 'One thing for certain, your x-rays will support my theory. You have a crush injury as you still have all your digits and therefore the shear was not directly involved as we can see by the condition of the machine.'

Regarding HSE involvement, they had been notified as the employee was off work more than three days, but as yet they had not visited. The machine's guarding appeared adequate so I asked them to counsel both machine operators regarding correct working practices as they were prescribed as dangerous machines under current legislation. The employee was sheepishly quiet all the time this was going on so, feeling a little for him, I wished him a speedy recovery. The rest of the survey was routine and at the debrief in the manager's office, with just the manager, broker and accountant present, I opined that there would likely be a settlement but much reduced as the employee was classed as 'skilled' and as such the claim reserve would be less. There certainly was a considerable degree of contributory negligence and there was no amputation, both of which would reduce the settlement. There was a downside to this, though, because I was requested by claims to accompany their inspectors on other losses regarding machinery and present at a number of their training seminars.

Another public liability claim arose in Australia, involving a plumbing contractor, during the insured's first year with us. They were currently engaged in upgrading the sanitary fixtures and fittings in a maximum-security wing of an Australian Department of Correction prison. We were notified of a theft while I was in Australia undertaking surveys, where the loss was over a six-figure sum involving sanitary materials that had allegedly been stolen from the insured's steel storage container on the site. The prison sited in South Australia was visited by a loss adjuster acting for us, and I viewed the loss report they prepared. The site was immediately adjacent to the visitors' car parking area and some hundred or so metres from the nearest external wall of the institution. Security was tight, as was to be expected but didn't stretch as far as the external areas of the car park, although floodlighting and some CCTV cameras were seen mounted on some lighting towers that would have covered the car parking area, service road and beyond. An area of the car park had been cordoned off with contractors' cabins and containers seen in that designated area. The location as such was in a semi-rural area that had a busy road on one of the four sides while on two of the other sides were arable farmland and a type of recreation ground. These external areas were segregated from the prison by fencing and a restricted zone.

The claimant alleged that they had taken delivery of the materials and secured them in the container on a Friday. On the Monday, when coming back to work, they discovered the lock was broken off and missing and the contents of the container gone. As I was a guest in the country and all the while not being suspicious, I obtained permission to look about the surrounding areas so as to get a feel for the route which the perpetrators took intending to prevent repetition. There being just one access route from the nearest accessible public road meant that there was possibly only one of two ways that a vehicle could gain access to the site, as a vehicle would have been essential to convey that amount of materials away. My obvious thought was of the farmland, which was flat and, for the most part, even. The only other possible access route passed by the prison staff housing, which was illuminated like most external areas of the prison at night. It should be understood that this insured was new to us and therefore, as usual, I was looking at the risk purely from a loss of property viewpoint.

The container in which the materials were stored was made of steel and the clasp and the lock cover were to the recommended antitheft standard. Obviously, the lock was unavailable but I was assured it was a five-lever lock to the required standard so my suspicions were never aroused. The one other notion that entered my head involved the materials being re-sited in another contractor's containers but the insured quickly assured me that the police had already searched those and found nothing. I visited the farm, where I enquired of the owner as to any unusual activities and given the land was arable had there been any unexplained vehicular movement? The farmer told me that, except for an agricultural vehicle, a car or lightweight truck would find it difficult to cross his land and that the farm was gated, having livestock and domesticated animals about. This gate was locked, especially at night. Drawing a blank I became suspicious as to how a laden vehicle could gain entry and leave undetected.

I later spoke with an off-duty member of the correctional staff in an external lodge, who got into a conversation as he asked me what I was doing near the staff quarters. Hearing my English accent, he asked where I was from and jokingly suggesting that they didn't have all their undesirables locked up! Giving him an account of the circumstances led him to helpfully suggest that there was no way a vehicle could enter and leave the site unnoticed and with the CCTV and lighting; something visible must be in their system. The officer couldn't have been more helpful and spoke over the phone to another correctional officer, again asking about the external CCTV footage. We sat and chatted for a while, and the officer was puzzled as to why I had come all the way from London to investigate a theft, given the travel expenses. Before I could enlighten him regarding other business dealings I had planned, the phone rang. According to the officer at the other end of the line, the log for the period was reviewed and it did not reveal the presence of any unregistered contractor vehicle. Not wishing to see the footage I asked if they would review what they had as there had been a crime. I was asked to leave my contact details and they would take another look at the footage but it was highly unlikely they would have missed a commercial vehicle registered to that or any other contractor.

Into the next day, the correctional services informed me that there simply was no evidence to support the loss taking place on site; therefore, it was treated as just another spurious claim. The insured, for some unknown reason, never believed that the loss would entail a post-loss survey, conducted by a surveyor all the way from the UK and that the claim would be repudiated as the materials were never on site. Of course, the insured complained bitterly, but our claims department simply told the insured to produce invoices, delivery details and the security padlock invoice as their policy required a specific quality. This was the last the company heard from the insured and their broker.

A post-loss survey that proved a real poser for me was due to me being advised and informed with only half the loss detail and further instructed only to deal with the public liability. The risk was a medium-sized general builder situated in South London where there had been a partial collapse when they were in the throes of removing part of a ground floor spine wall, making the ground floor into a through room in a semi-detached house, I was left to make the arrangements with the insured and was requested to give it priority. My workload at the time permitted me to be available the next morning with the insured's representative being very eager to get the survey out of the way. Unbeknown to me at the time they had suspended all their contracts until after the survey was completed.

I arrived at a private address some time before we had agreed to meet and sat waiting in my car until that prearranged start time. A little while later, another car drew up and, like me, the driver remained in his vehicle. I assumed it was probably the broker, although I had not been in contact with them. Within a minute or so of this unidentified person, two other cars arrived simultaneously so now, there were four cars all sitting there obviously waiting for the 8 am start time.

Being a prompt starter, I got out of my car at about 0755 which seemed to be a cue for all the others who had arrived and there was a procession walking down this path the front door of this private dwelling house. Before I could reach for the door knocker, the door was opened and the insured introduced himself and addressed me by name, at the same time acknowledging those walking in my wake. He apologised that his office, a bedroom on the first floor, was too small and that we would all be more comfortable in the lounge where there was more seating. We all moved in without so much as a word, in fact, it was eerie, and we all sat, with the insured perched on a stool in front of an electric organ. I still reflect on that which all added to the drama. The introductions followed including an exchange of business cards, where I learned that I had been joined by the two partners of the business, their surveyor and of course the broker.

Introducing myself, I explained the purpose of the visit was post-loss, never imagining why, in the eyes of those present, the public liability claim was taking precedence. However, the survey proceeded as per my underwriter's instruction where it transpired before the incident that they had engaged the services of a building surveyor where any future structural working was involved. This, to a degree, took the initiative away from me, as this clearly was the root cause of the loss. Apparently, two of their full-time workers were dispatched to the site where they were, to reiterate, proposing to convert the ground floor into a through lounge from two rooms, by way of by removing the spine wall. The work party included an experienced builder and a seventeen-year-old apprentice, who the partners considered to be adequate to complete the job in terms of both experience and manpower.

The work process was very simple: some of the bricks were to be removed at pre-set intervals from the underside of the ceiling and steel needles inserted so that these would protrude from either side of the load-bearing wall. Dead shores would then be introduced off sole plates on the floor and to the under face of the needle, thus taking the weight of the wall and all above. The work then involved a reinforced steel joist being inserted on the top of concrete pads sited on the top of the two adjacent columns in the existing brickwork spanning the opening. Once the RSJ was in place, now taking the whole load of the building above, the needles and dead shores would be removed, along with the remainder of the brickwork. This is a standard procedure that is adopted successfully daily in numerous home conversions.

However, on this occasion, the builder decided that if they removed sufficient load-bearing brickwork from just below ceiling level and insert the RSJ immediately, they would do away with the need for needles and dead shores, hence going against good, recognised working practices. The entire wall, ground and first floor, and parts of the ceiling however collapsed before the RSJ was in place resulting in the public liability claim all the while me being completely unaware of any employer's liability loss. While I was questioning the insured about the activities at the time I just knew something was amiss and that, as strange as it appeared, the survey was not going well. This was made even clearer when I asked about the other sites, only to be informed that the insured's entire operations had been suspended pending the survey. Now I was certain I had been on the wrong track, and I said I now wanted to talk about employer's liability when the insured remarked, 'I wondered when you would be getting around to that.'

Totally perplexed but choosing my words very carefully, I invited the insured to enlighten me on the way they viewed their management responsibilities given the collapse. The response astounded me when I was informed that this small contract had resulted in a fatality and the young apprentice was so critically injured that at this point in time the insured were unsure as to his ability to perform manual working in the trade in the future. Inwardly I thought that when I got back to the office the underwriter would be on the receiving end of heavy criticism from me as it smacked of a lack of trust in my capabilities. How stupid can a person be I concluded given the surveyor's task is to assess and report on the quality of the insured following the loss which was in this case by withholding pertinent information. The lame excuse the underwriter offered was that he didn't want the EL implications discussed, even though as I stated at a departmental enquiry it was unavoidable and as far as the survey was concerned absolutely relevant.

Whilst being critical of my underwriting colleagues on the very rare occasion for failing to share or divulge all the information they possessed about an insured, prior to them generating a post-loss survey request, I took great pleasure in surprising them just occasionally on my discoveries. I can recall in one instance where I purposely resisted verbally revealing what I had unearthed by nonchalantly confining my findings to the survey report. On the occasion, the loss history involved the theft of a forklift truck, possible loss of a hired-in replacement truck and an employer's liability claim, the latter two connected. Such post-loss requests were always treated as a priority and usually, through the broker the insured was forewarned of a surveyor making contact to arrange the visit to discuss the loss or in this case the losses. The insured was a well-established stevedore business based in the Falmouth area where the business primarily used mechanical handling plant and equipment to load and unload cargo ships. The main means of handling was a fleet of eight diesel powered forklift trucks and two quay cranes that the insured operated twenty-four hours according to the tides. When I spoke with the insured's representative, he proposed a time and date a few days hence as the recovery of the hired forklift truck was then planned and I would be there to witness it.

The reason for the loss was put down to unexpected brake failure on the forklift truck while operating on the quayside and with the truck suddenly out of control and heading towards the water the operator opted to jump clear. At the dockside, the truck toppled and plunged into the water several metres below followed closely by the rolling operator whose momentum also took him over the edge of the quay thereby following the truck into the water. The operator suffered a fractured wrist, abrasions, bruising, shock, cold and wet and was rescued by way of a lifebuoy and hauled out of the water by workmates. The forklift truck now sitting on the seabed within the dock was to be recovered with the aid of local rescue services who I was led to understand use such work as a training exercise.

Arriving as arranged at the docks the rescue services were yet to appear so it gave me the opportunity to talk through with the insured's representative the latest physical condition of their employee, the theft and their security arrangements plus the lease terms of the hired plant, testing, maintenance of the same and operator licensing. Having obtained all the details and moved onto the quayside it coincided with the timely arrival of the rescue services. As if there was an emergency, the selected diver was quickly attired in his diving apparel and breathing apparatus and lowered into the water by the insured's assigned waiting crane, disappearing from view in an instance. The diver remained from view below the surface for about ten to fifteen minutes, I assumed searching for the truck or assessing how best to recover it. When the diver re-emerged, he was now some distance further along the quayside so with the crane in tow we all moved towards his location from where he first entered the water. As we approached the diver having already removed his face mask looked up and asked 'Which truck do you want first?' There was a pause and the manager requested that the officer repeated his question albeit we all heard clearly what the diver had said. 'There are two forklift trucks down there, so which one do you want to haul up first?' 'Anyone' the baffled manager replied.

The diver then went on to direct the manager to reposition his crane and to nominate one of his staff to stand at the quayside to convey his lifting instructions to the crane driver. The recovery operations went smoothly eventually resulting in both forklift trucks being back on dry land albeit one truck was minus its engine cowling with the mast and both forks badly buckled while the other, the latest, was largely unscathed. Needless to say, the manager was now completely at a loss having been convinced that one of their forklift trucks had been stolen and subsequently a police report completed. There was even a suspicion at the time that one of the vessels bound for an African port may have been the means of conveying the truck out of the port. We later learned however that on the latest loss the linkage to the brake pedal had a weld failure while the reason for the other truck finding its way into the water was that it was probably struck by one of the gantry cranes. It was alleged that the insured's drivers habitually parked up alongside vessels occasionally leaving them unattended at the cessation of their shift ready for the next shift. Irrespective, I submitted to our underwriters that it was probably the first ever post-loss survey undertaken where any underwriter looking for a report concerning the loss of a forklift truck and its hopeful recovery actually ended up with two.

With the exception of the last post-loss survey, all of the aforementioned cases required a great deal of investigatory skills, that were very much order of the day during my time as a safety engineer at Ford Motor Company. Being thorough was crucial while following up on accidents and incidents, consequently, it all became second nature during post-loss surveys.

Surveying for Non-Negligence

Throughout the first twenty or so years in the insurance industry, I conducted approximately one hundred and fifty non-negligence surveys, and in many cases, they proved to be far more interesting than surveying for negligence. Briefly, this non-negligence insurance cover, which is usually recommended by the architects, is purchased by a contractor on behalf of an employer and is in addition to the existing PL (Public Liability) policy. Reflecting on surveying and loss control progression there arrives a time when your investigatory versatility comes to the fore; that essential skill that permits you to envisage the future whenever a hypothetical risk presents itself. When conducting a property survey, or examining a trade process and activities of the employees the deficiencies are in the main all too plain to see consequently easy to assess. Where non-negligence is concerned those luxuries do not exist as all you hear and see are to all intents and purposes the insured's imaginative take on the project in hand.

Civil and building operations can be hazardous if not properly managed by all parties involved and not solely by the contractor. This makes the survey all the more interesting and complex because, if there is professional input, and on the larger projects inevitably there are other active participants, then the extent of their input also requires examination. These professionals are the likes of architects, building surveyors, civil engineers and consulting engineers and, should there be a failure resulting in a loss, other than the contract works, which are excluded, they could be held accountable for perhaps overlooking something they were commissioned to provide guidance on. Recalling professional negligence, there were three cases where I identified shortcomings resulting in the successful repudiation of the claims by entering in the policy conditions supervisory responsibilities during certain operations.

Where non-negligence is concerned it is more a case of the unforeseeable arising consequently anything remotely predictable could trigger counterclaims, therefore, the insurance surveyor should be able to interpret building drawings and specifications, identify schemes and schedules of work, be aware of geological conditions, and it goes without saying site operations and plant required to be involved.

When assigning one such survey to a qualified building surveyor, with little to no experience in that line of loss control, he expressed doubt about his ability even though the procedure was set out in the provided aide-memoire that I had gone through with him, step by step. His parting comment was more a question asking exactly why as yet he had not been issued with his crystal ball. Just like that engineer, in my early days after a comparatively brief introduction to non-negligence surveying, I too was handed the underwriting guide for this category of risks and was required to not only conduct the surveys but underwrite them even down to setting the premiums.

I cannot honestly say that the added responsibility caused me further or indeed any anxiety because my survey findings were about three things: establishing the risk exposure, the ability of the contractor and the premium. Consequently, I set about the task always bearing in mind my job was to protect the business's interest above all else. I think on reflection that those added responsibilities made me even more aware of my role in the grand scheme of things. For the most part, these surveys were not as complicated as many believed they were and, while the contractor was effectively the insured, those parties on the periphery, if the terms and conditions were appropriately applied, were just as vulnerable, as some found out to their cost.

During the construction of the Metropolitan Rapid Transit, which is principally an underground railway network serving the Bangkok Metropolitan Region, a claim was submitted by a prestigious hotel for damage, allegedly caused by the tunnelling works hundreds of feet underground. The reason for me being there in Bangkok was that the six tunnel boring machines (TBM) were insured with us and their value was put at six-million dollars each. However, it was reported to me that the damage to the hotel involved the facade of a building insofar as it had suffered cracks in several places allegedly caused by the tunnelling below. The reason it was mentioned to me was due to us being the co-insurers for public liability and that the insured would be passing on the details of the claim.

As this damage was allegedly along the route, I requested to see the schedule of conditions of those buildings on the surface along all the proposed routes. We were dealing with two major insurers, one of whom I had been employed by some years before, plus my current employer. To my surprise, no schedule of dilapidation had been even discussed, let alone carried out, which resulted in some embarrassed planners and the international contractors, involved in this major joint venture between two of the respective country's major civil engineering consultancies and their Thai employers.

My opinions were two-fold: that the insurers had acted too hastily and the contractors not at all until it was too late. Nonetheless, a schedule was put in place from that point in time but I informed those that this was non-negligence consequently we heard no more about the claims. With hindsight the employer should have been properly advised; they should have identified those vulnerable structures and schedules of dilapidation introduced where any signs of defects were noted. This to my way of thinking would have involved the fixing of tell-tales to suspect elevations and their condition being monitored regularly while the tunnelling was in the vicinity underground. My report, following my examination of the alleged damage, suggested that the hotel had suffered from subsidence in the past, as had other buildings along the main thoroughfares, under which the tunnel was following, with some of these structures having previously been subject to remedial works before the tunnelling works had even begun.

The provisions of the non-negligence policy, primarily under the Joint Contracts Tribunal (JCT), involve the contractor taking out a policy that protects the developer in respect of any expense, liability loss, claim or proceedings incurred resulting in damage to property from the works due to: vibrations, collapse, subsidence, removal of vegetation, heave, removal of support and disturbance of the water table. Given that the list is not exhaustive there are occasions where even the most qualified can overlook the level and extent of the exposure, and it has been known for more than one of the aforementioned situations to impact on another making for an interesting challenge. Certain ill-informed parties having never encountered such problems and not appreciating that heavy losses do occur from time to time there is often opposition to a request to survey.

Opposition to surveys, therefore, can come in all manner of shapes and sizes; the most unlikely of contacts came in the form of a recently qualified architect, a very studious looking lady, and a throwback to a 'child of the sixties' with her doc martins boots, bobble hat and matching scarf, over length cardigan, long skirt and her spectacles hanging from a ribbon about her neck. I know about not judging a book by its cover but in this case, it was difficult as she was a carbon copy of my daughter whilst at university. Getting out of my car adjacent the scene of the contract, this lady skipped the niceties and asked, "Who are you?" I handed her my business card and hardly having the time I thought to have studied the details on the card she ticked me off a list attached to her clipboard, handed me a pack of drawings and a specification adding, "It's all in there so help yourself." I never once considered her to be rude or uncivil as I had dealings with many people like that over the years so I just put it down to her manner. After all, a lady dealing in the construction industry would have had to suffer much and probably this attitude helped her overcome some of those difficulties involved with male chauvinistic contractors. She was very business-like and I felt positive about handling this non-negligence contract risk, that was if the appropriate responses to my questions were forthcoming.

The site itself comprised a terrace of Victorian townhouses in North London where the foundations beneath the rear elevations had sunk leaving the whole of the rear wall in urgent need of remedial work in the form of underpinning to save it from collapse. Once underpinned, the contractor could then set about rebuilding the affected parts of the rear elevation, which had become badly bowed. At the very best, it would be difficult to know exactly where to start with the work; it would involve the erection of temporary support, identifying the most unstable sections of brickwork on these buildings and so on. As expected, the building had been served with a 'dangerous structures' notice, issued by the Architects Department of Islington Borough Council. I glanced at the drawings, which only told me what I could already see, along with the specifications regarding the underpinning and brickwork. I asked where the scheme and schedule of works were, as well as the temporary support detail. This drew no response at all save the lady commenting that such details would be up to the contractor. I told her that our insured was a builder, not a structural engineer or surveyor and he would need guidance regarding everything except laying bricks.

"Look," she said, "I have several other insurance people to see, so if you are not interested in quoting then goodbye." She turned away leaving me totally bemused, so I walked back to my car and drove off.

I knew that, as was common practice at the time I would probably be made responsible for underwriting the business, so in my head, I began putting my report together culminating in reporting an unacceptable risk, and therefore no quotation. Having previous dealings with the contractor, our insured, I found him to be quite competent and diligent at roofing, groundworks, bricklaying and other associated building works at the lower end of the trade. This, however, was altogether different so I called the director from my car informing him that it was highly unlikely we would provide cover as the job was to say the very least hazardous and would, therefore, require structural expertise including the design of temporary support. The insured in response to learning of my decision told me that he anticipated this and that he suspected something was amiss when, on inviting him to tender for the contract, the architect demanded to be made aware of his bank credit rating.

Believing that this was the end of the matter I had no sooner walked back into our offices, coming directly from the site, when one of the underwriters sarcastically suggested I had made a big impression with the architect as she wanted to meet up with me again to discuss what I wanted. It was clear she really didn't understand either the capabilities of the contractors who were vying for the work or the needs of the insurance companies. Apparently, we were the only insurer, out of the five the architect spoke of, who waited around long enough to ask any questions. At the underwriter's and architect's request I set out the most obvious requirements including the absolute need for someone with expertise in structural work, professionally qualified and carrying professional indemnity cover to submit a planned written sequence of work; they would also need to provide onsite supervision during the underpinning, approve the sequence and ensure that the temporary support involved was appropriate, as well as assessing the details concerning foreseeable removal of support. The policy conditions were accepted and, while the premium was high, I thought it fitting. Four months later we learned that the work had been successfully completed without a loss.

While the aforementioned risk ended satisfactorily some surveys did have their moments. In one such case, we declined cover and learned at a later date that there had been a large or significant loss. While hearing about these cases is rare, as brokers tend not to spread bad news, they do occur and another that came to mind involved non-negligence cover on a significant civil engineering contract where the client, the contractor or the consultant engineers all overlooked the geographical hazards of the area, we concluded each trusting the other to investigate such an issue. Working on extending a warehouse alongside an inland waterway, and with made up ground across the site, the contractor proposed constructing a warehouse building on piles and a ring beam, with the piles being percussion driven, as the subsoils were unsuited to bore piling. The site was extensive, as was the planned number of piles, which involved significant displacement and compaction of soil, a common hazard in driven piles. I ignored the vibration risk, as the adjacent building was excluded from the cover, due to this being the property of the developer, that would ultimately connect with the proposed warehouse. As for other structures, I measured the nearest as being another large warehouse over seventy metres away and of little consequence.

My major concern was the river, as the bed was very silty and the banks loose, plus the river was running very high at the time. I suggested that the client needed to be wary of these issues and that they monitor closely the river level and ensure the river banks did not start to erode through the vibrations set up by the piling. However, my opinions and misgivings were to no avail as the contractor had placed his faith in his consultants and the subcontracted piling company, who had conducted a site survey, allegedly taking into account such possibilities. On returning to my desk I researched the area and the river's flood history and learned that a holiday park and a public car park had been swamped previously so now I considered that we had not only rain to consider but vibrations, displacement and compaction. Explaining this to our head of underwriting I recommended decline, which he agreed with, much to my relief.

All was forgotten as far as I was concerned until three weeks later a claims inspector showed me a copy of a local newspaper. The banner headlines involved the flooding of a local supermarket and a few other retail stores due to the river rising to an unusually high level during heavy rain on the site subject to survey a short while ago. Upon further investigation, it was learned that the riverbed had in fact risen somewhere in the region of one metre, which was caused, according to appointed loss adjusters and their consultants, by the adjacent piling. These seventy driven piles and subsequent vibrations and displacement had a significant impact on the subsoil across the site that extended to the bed and banks of the river as these theoretically offered the least area of resistance. The claim never quite reached the seven figures spoken off but the brokers were quick off the mark in informing us that we were extremely fortunate not to have been on cover. On the contrary, our representatives claimed, it was because of the company's policy not to provide non-negligence cover without a survey, and not as alleged down to good fortune.

We were probably a little fortunate with another proposed non-negligent risk though, where again the policy conditions were ignored by the insured, who without professional civil engineering input went ahead on a somewhat high-risk building contract. The contract involved underpinning a party wall necessary to extent a large hotel. These surveys always involved ascertaining the condition of the properties in the neighbourhood, particularly where older properties were concerned. In the region of Carmarthen Castle, there were many, many historically listed buildings that had been subject to conservation works over the years. Taking this as a warning as we could never be sure of the unknown, we considered it essential that these underpinning works required the close attention of a consultant and a schedule of conditions undertaken before any work commenced. These aforementioned precautions were discussed with the contractor's principals while on site and they were informed that these would be the conditions imposed.

The contractor's appointed consultant engineer's practice was based over 100 miles away in Birmingham though, and apparently took little to no interest regarding our stance, so the underwriter imposed, in keeping with the survey recommendation, that there had to be a 'constant supervision' condition while underpinning was taking place. For whatever reason, this condition was ignored on the insistence of the insured's engineer, at least until such time as the wall of the hotel and the rear of the third-party structure collapsed. Too late, the engineer was summoned by which time we had paid the princely sum of one hundred and twenty pounds in legal fees for advice. Subsequently, the contractor having gone ahead without non-negligence cover was left facing rebuild and hotel loss of profits costs plus their consultants facing a significant professional indemnity claim that in total we later learned a total claim amounting to a little over four hundred thousand pounds.

There were cases when I was confronted with a non-negligence survey where the engineering representative of the insured had limited ideas regarding precisely what the work would entail, only being aware of what they hoped to accomplish at its conclusion? In these cases, I felt that the representative should be congratulated on their honesty although, as I remarked at the time, where insurance is concerned the underwriter respects the honesty but that is just about as far as it goes. These people deal in tangibles; they want details from the likes of me the surveyor naming probable and possible loss situations. Inevitably they would look to me to back up my opinion with the likes the schemes of work, operations involving risks and controls. In short, if the surveyor is comfortable, then the subsequent report will provide the underwriter with a feel-good factor. That was the problem in the Ludlow survey where the works engineer couldn't state with any certainty what they would need to do until they began conducting exploratory works.

The ultimate intentions were to arrest the movement in both a party wall, ground floor spine wall and the building's external wall by way of underpinning the corbeled footings and make good any work defects that the work processes may have caused; the standard RIBA wording was *making good all works disturbed*. The building was a Grade I listed, semi-detached, two-storey house that made up Castle Square, situated in the centre of Ludlow. It was fifty or so metres from historic Ludlow Castle, a medieval castle dating back to 1066-85. The buildings that formed the square were also extremely old, possibly with the original foundations in the contract site dating back three or even four hundred years. Consequently, the Works Department had no records detailing their age, construction and the like.

The ground floor was currently being used for retail purposes. As the elevations were suspect, the contract required the underpinning of the affected elevations and making good all works disturbed, the latter important because the

Works Department had little to no idea what that might entail. There were no party wall agreements in place clearly because they did not know where these started and where they finished as there were now no clearly established building lines. This is quite normal in very old buildings as it is possible that these may have shifted over time, or been part of one structure. In this case, the walls within the building were denser in one part than in another and the same was reported in the case of the neighbouring property where again over hundreds of years the elevation had been repaired and probably rebuilt; consequently, it was safe to assume the building lines had moved.

The task the Works Department faced was firstly to dig trial pits exposing the foundations on all the suspect elevations and then to assess exactly if they were the same through to the neighbouring property where party walls existed. Regarding the other elevations, the matter was less complex, as they could offer support ad infinitum and underpin all these if necessary. The works engineer reported that they were uncertain of two things: the condition of the party wall where it abutted their spine wall and its extent. After several hours of questions and answers it was clear we had no clear understanding of the full scope of the works, and therefore no idea as to the scheme of works, or the design of temporary supports necessary to both the insured's structure and that of their neighbour.

I had to cut to the chase in the end and express my concerns, predicting what the underwriters would say. Consequently, I informed the representative that I could not recommend cover because of the lack of information. For example, while conducting the proposed exploratory works a loss could occur as the position of the selected trial pits that purely by chance happened to be at a weak spot, leading to an unexpected collapse. Based on that, I had to inform the underwriter I would not be recommending cover. To my great surprise, the Works Department engineer said, "I told the committee so; that no insurer was going to provide non-negligence cover for the project."

There has always been a shortage of low-cost housing in London; consequently, a number of housing trusts exist, taking old and almost derelict central London properties, refurbishing them and letting them to social services for the homeless and lower paid families. In the Hammersmith area in particular at the time, many of the old Victorian terraced properties were being repaired, extended, upgraded and made fit for occupation once again. The works, therefore, involved all areas of the terraced properties, from the sub-ground floor to the roof and where the sub-ground floor didn't extend the whole length of the house then parts of the rear garden areas were being excavated to provide additional living space. The developer involved required non-negligence cover to engage many trades on a subcontract basis, working under their contracts manager, and therefore making the best use of the labour to keep redevelopment costs down. As a result, this would entail many of these trades people working on the developer's properties in a terrace on or about the same time. There were clearly two areas of concern: one being the normal policy conditions where the cover did not extend to the existing property; and, probably, more importantly, the removal of support, vibrations, excavations and underpinning that would be inevitable. Added to this and not to complicate matters further there could be more than one of those operations underway in any one single property at any one time.

Needless to say, the underwriters would have their work cut out to ensure the policy wording was suitable, if the risk appeared acceptable, on completion of the survey. This insofar as the survey had taken into account of all the suspect conditions of those involved buildings and the sequences of those proposed hazardous operations. Upon the survey findings reaching our underwriters, where no representative from the developer seemed certain of the planned system and contract issues, such as the sequence of work there was an air of mystery about the contracts. Putting aside the underwriter's misgivings, I called the appointed contract manager, who was the insured's contact, learning that one or two of the other properties in the terrace were privately owned all of which further complicated matters due to similar private works either proposed or underway in those properties.

Making our position clear I informed the manager that this would seriously complicate my proposed survey as it appeared that access into those third-party properties was nigh on impossible. The dilemma was one of exactly how would you set about controlling those third-party independent contractors' and subcontractors' operations where perhaps, as an example, both were involved in underpinning operations or were creating vibrations either side of a party wall? The analysis was unreal, with me never before having experienced such a tangle where building works were concerned; it took some careful thinking. With no understanding of what is happening on the other side of a fourteen-inch party wall then it is impossible to assess the risks.

The upshot of all this was that the contracts manager following deliberations and expressing my concerns felt that maybe my thinking was exaggerated. He said he would ensure, where a party wall was concerned, that he would restrict the work operations to one side only. Unfortunately, what was missing in all of this was a Party Wall Agreement under the Party Wall, etc. Act 1996. Thus, it was not as simple as the contracts manager made it sound when proposing his work activities would be restricted to the developers' property only. My thinking for this obvious oversight was that in some of the properties the developer either owned the party walls by virtue of being the owner of both neighbouring properties and that to undertake the underpinning, where there existed a party wall that required such work they never reached an agreement with the owners when looking for some financial contribution.

With so many potential loss-making circumstances and conditions it was going to be difficult to even start to think about the terms and conditions to be applied, even if the underwriters were brave enough to offer terms. The contractor would be hard pressed to guarantee the levels of control we should rightly expect, because of what others might be doing in the neighbouring properties. It, therefore, followed that the contractor would need to be totally in control of every single one of their activities, which, given the site manager's objectives and financial constraints just would not be practicable. In one instance, when fortuitously I actually visited the site due to broker pressure, I observed a percussion-piling rig where, within the schedule of works, it cited bore piling. Apparently, during a previous contract along the terrace, the contractor hit a snag during piling for the foundations in the property: insufficient headroom for the bore piling rig. Without informing us, they resorted to percussion pile driving, which entailed a whole new set of problems involving vibrations, soil rotation and compaction. However, there was worse to come; when viewing other operations, the piling problem became inconsequential.

The works were more complex and extensive than we were led to believe, not least that there were five properties to be refurbished, not two or three. Further, there were underpinning works being undertaken beneath the party wall, which were incomplete while at the same time floor joist hangers were being replaced in some already suspect brickwork in that same party wall. Added to this, all of the windows were being replaced with new UPVC units. This amounted to building works being underway in every area from the roof to the excavations at the rear of the property. The trades there were bricklayers, plasterers, carpenters, plumbers plus those workers involved in window and door replacement. In fact, it was difficult to absorb all that was going on through the verbal account delivered by the contracts manager.

Nonetheless showing willing I continued with a tour of the properties to obtain a clear picture of what was going on which while continuing through the first building I climbed a timber stair, without a handrail; all the while from the ground floor I could see daylight coming through sections of the roof, such was the condition of the building. On the first floor, the contractor had set aside the largest room for meetings and maintaining the documentation, drawings and specifications. While perusing the available contract, though, I noted there was no mention of the underpinning that was going on in the basement and the replacement of wall hangers.

Apparently when a subcontractor stripped off some plasterwork, to establish the extent of the vertical cracks in the party wall the exposed timber had wood rot and the floors were unstable so as a result, they decided to lift the floorboards only to find further decay thus the need for further work. Obviously the excavations going on at the rear of the property to extend the lower ground floor plus the underpinning under a section of the party wall to the front meant that there was every chance that the building could suffer further, with two large areas of support being removed. The reason I mentioned this to the contractor was that the sequence being adopted, to underpin, was incorrect and not in keeping with current building techniques. He countered this by suggesting that the work had been subcontracted to a specialist subcontractor and he had left them to get on with it.

Needing to make some sense of things I asked permission to speak with the underpinning subcontractor. The manager agreed but made sure I understood he did not want to be involved. Speaking to the foreman of the gang on the underpinning I asked what sequence they were adopting as I had never seen the like before. They admitted that the one-in-three sequence was not possible as the brickwork above was unstable; therefore, they were completing the work ad hoc. I asked why there were no needles and dead shores, which was met with a blank, sheepish look, because clearly, they were just hoping they would complete the work without a problem. Scratching around for an excuse, they told me that, to needle, they would require going through the party wall and as they were aware there was no Party Wall Agreement so they decided to adopt a different scheme in this instance. It was a lame excuse but I elected to hold one's peace as things were already going from bad to worse.

Thus far, I wasn't enamoured to witness so much risk taking. It was highlighted on the first floor near a chimney breast, where I noticed tell-tales fixed along the length of a major crack. Alas, all had broken due to what I assumed to be movement in the brickwork. As the property was being extensively worked on, I wondered how many other areas had been fitted with these tell-tales because it seemed clear that these monitoring devices had been ignored. I just had to ask the contract manager about the tell-tales: who fitted them, who was monitoring them and were the ones on the first floor the only ones? The manager said that the tell-tales were in place long before they arrived on site and he assumed the developers were monitoring them.

This assertion seemed yet another a lame excuse as the developers were not on site but the contractor and this manager knew that tell-tales needed to be surveyed almost daily. It was a sad state of affairs but the survey had served its purpose because there was nothing that made me optimistic that the work could possibly be complete without something untoward arising, whether that was negligence or non-negligence.

Being always forthright with our insured I expressed my concerns and said, "Look, I have to tell you that with so many unknowns we could never consider providing cover for this contract; it would be like providing you with a blank cheque, all the while praying that the phone will not ring informing us of a loss." I left the site and informed the underwriter that the odds of a loss were extremely high and should be avoided. No terms or conditions, therefore, were ever provided; contractors all risk or non-negligence.

When calculating the odds of something untoward occurring during a survey, having completed so many, those odds obviously get shorter. I witnessed one accident on an employer's liability survey, another during a public liability visit, but managing it during a non-negligence survey, where I was on site merely to assess, takes some doing. It still happened, involving by far and away, the worst non-negligence risk ever surveyed, in Plumstead, London SE18. I received a call on the mobile from our underwriter requesting a non-negligence survey for an insured builder who was refurbishing a terraced house in SE London and they were on site every day so I could call in anytime. Living close by, in Bexleyheath, I thought I could fit it in on a Saturday morning and have the report on the underwriter's desk early Monday morning. Little did I know that the property would not exist by then.

The terraced property was on a hill almost adjacent Woolwich Common and was midway along a terrace of about 25 similar properties, with party walls throughout. I was virtually kerb crawling, seeking the address and a suitable parking spot when I observed a dumper truck emerging through what was formerly a sub-ground floor bay window, up a crudely constructed timber ramp to empty its load into a large skip at the kerbside. I stopped my car and waited as I was at the only available parking spot save one or two next to the skip, which seemed too risky. Some minutes later the small dump truck came up the ramp again and this time the driver parked up, leaving with the engine still running and disappeared back into the property. I concluded that fortunately, this wasn't our site as my instructions simply read *refurbishment* when clearly this was no small contract. I decided to walk down the hill and find my address, leaving my car some distance away. As I got closer, it was clear that the dump truck was parked at what was left of the shallow front garden of the survey address. I crossed over to the other side of the road to get a better look and the first thing that drew my attention was what looked like a pagoda style roof. However, this was not Beijing, Bangkok or Hanoi but Plumstead, SE London! Why, because the roof was dished in the centre, almost a half metre lower in the middle than at either end, where the roof ridges of the neighbouring properties met, save now there were gaps at either end of the ridge and the ridge tiles almost on end.

Taking my eyes from the roof I noticed a portly man sitting on the running board of the dump truck smoking so I approached him and was taken aback when he asked me was I from the insurance. I handed him my business card and he gave me his name, telling me he was, in fact, the insured, and it was his business. I asked, "How is the work going?"

"Good, no problems, piece of cake and the weather so far has helped," he replied. "Come and take a look." He gestured me in explaining that they were excavating to extend the basement area and because of the amount of soil they needed to run a truck up to the dig as using a wheelbarrow was out of the question. To use wheelbarrow and more labour would take up too much time, therefore, he calculated it would be cheaper and quicker to take out part of the spine wall and the front of the bay and use the dump truck and the mini excavator that was there grubbing up the soil.

Once inside the property, I began taking notes. The bay had not been supported and therefore there had been some movement as the base of the bay at ground floor level had lost some of the brickwork and some tiles had also been dislodged at some time. One of the most obvious signs of movement was that the lower ground floor and the first-floor picture windows in the bays had cracked glass, a common indicator, plus according to the insured those areas had not been worked on up until the day of the survey. During this time, whilst in the sub-ground floor, I had to move away from the bay as dust was continually falling onto my clipboard, so I assumed that workers were active on the floors above. When I mentioned this, I was informed that no work was taking place elsewhere save on the lower ground floor. So, why the falling debris I asked. "It's an old house and things move, but nothing to get concerned about," was the insured's offhand reply. Almost ignoring the insured's response, I noticed that half the spine wall had been removed, minus any support, and there was evidence that the remaining section had been 'bumped' a little, as the insured put it. I was now more anxious than ever about the stability of the structure. I obtained permission to have a look around and getting the OK I ventured up the staircase and saw the effects of the loss of support as the floors above were also sloping. There were large gaps between the flooring and the timber skirting boards, which suggested there was movement throughout. Every now and then, plaster was falling away from the wall directly above where the spine wall was and I got an uneasy feeling that most of what appeared to be happening was literally going on over the head of the insured, due to him concentrating so much on the excavation. This was not the first case where the builder was taking a chance of undermining the structure. In some cases, they would get away without collapse; however, I also experienced cases where the builder didn't beat the odds with dire consequences, as previously reported on.

I tried a different tack with my questions by enquiring about at the sequence and scheme of work as it seemed like another disastrous risk I had surveyed. There were three problem areas of the building that could lead to collapse unless the insured took the opportunity to introduce shoring as a matter of urgency. When I expressed my reservations about the lack of support, the insured simply looked nonplus leaving me with nothing positive to report to the underwriter. The moral of the story is never take a risk and tamper with structural arrangements without first introducing temporary support. During the night, two days after we declined cover, the remaining part of the spine wall collapsed, leading to the total collapse of the roof which caused damage to both neighbouring properties. It was concluded by a consulting structural engineer, acting for us, that the building structurally was probably just about giving up the ghost during my survey with the dust and plaster falling being evidence of this and then, with the windy conditions experienced later, mother nature inevitably completed the job.

Purely out of morbid curiosity I visited the site several weeks later and found that the building had been demolished back to the party walls with raking shores having been introduced to those party walls and weatherproofing put in place, while the excavation, to the rear, was maintained by sheet pile and horizontal props. There was no sign of the road skip, dumper truck or mini excavator.

Surveying Services

The one issue I used to look at when assessing the contribution of a surveyor, regardless of their status, was their broker relationships. If they were considered good by the broker across the board, it got me thinking that they were being no better than those brokerages with their own surveyor teams. In short, they were not one for making waves and in the main keeping their recommendations down to a broker acceptable level involving limited costs. Just every now and again I would have welcomed a broker complaint and would bat away the wrath of our management where I considered that the surveyor was acting in the insurer's best interest, not the insured's and certainly not the broker's. While justifiably criticising some for taking steps to preserve their image it needed to be understood by those being judgemental that the situation, that led to a loss, may well not have existed at the time of the survey.

This happened in one of my own cases where the process was new and involved a selection of different materials. While both the insured and needless to say the broker claimed that the changes were insignificant, they proved to be quite the opposite. The insured and broker were correct up to a point, until the materials proved instrumental in a number of employees suffering health problems. Perhaps I am being unfair by criticising surveyors overlooking some issues but the problem was that so many did not prepare, which is why we were forced to produce our very own trade hazard guidance notes, detailing the most common hazards, that give rise to fire and other perils, liabilities, environmental damage and the likes of product failures. These guidance notes included underwriting considerations the like of which was prepared by a top underwriter with a deal of surveying experience.

Between survey work and broking, I am unsure after forty years in the industry who has the most difficult task. I was a servant of the underwriter when surveying, and therefore I only have one master, whereas the broker has to balance the client and the insurance market, both of which to a degree can be unpredictable. In this chapter, I am bound to mention the problems that surveyors have even though their focus should never stray from the underwriter's needs. Consequently, it just wouldn't be complete if I failed to mention the surveyors I worked alongside, both those who were a credit to their profession and those whose approach to their occupation left a great deal to be desired. Some were technically blessed but just couldn't accept the fact that their interpersonal skills left them sadly wanting. To this end, we embarked on a series of soft and negotiating prowess courses because so many surveyors were lacking where such important skills were concerned.

During the run up to putting on such training events, audits were conducted by senior surveyors to ascertain the levels possessed by their subordinates by way of them reviewing surveyor's reports. We found, to our cost, that it was some of those conducting the audits who lacked soft skills. Thereby, nothing was really achieved and the audit reports were largely based on technical content, making them of little value to the underwriter. What this tended to do was to drive the underwriter straight to the report's grading or the underwriting notes, both of which simply summarised the risk, minus the thoughts, behind those conclusions. On occasions I was requested to explain why some surveyors made numerous recommendations and requirements then confounded their findings by assessing the risk as one above average or better; this complete contradiction took some explaining with fear factors possibly suggesting a lack of conviction on the surveyor's part.

The survey teams were divided into property, liability, high net worth and engineering. The latter, closely followed by liability surveyors, were the most inept, more often than not led by people of a similar type and category. Being a liability surveyor myself I can recall, with embarrassment, that early on I too was guilty of surveying both the totally legal and technical perspectives with legal compliance taking priority. The reason for this was that, should an accident occur resulting in the employer being prosecuted for breach of statutory duty, the employer's defence would be extremely weak. Consequently, I began following the directives of my manager regarding the subjects to be covered, all clearly set out in the liability report format. Looking back, my reports were without substance unless my customer, the underwriter, was as technically informed as the author of the piece and therefore, in reality, they were of little to no value.

The best example I can recall regarding this question of surveyors feeling duty bound to include a recommendation or requirement in their reports, that had many of their customers, the underwriter, accepting it was to an accepted standard was on the occasion I received a call from a junior underwriter informing me that my recently completed report was incomplete. In response, I asked the underwriter if he had read the report through from first to the last page. I anticipated by his response that he hadn't, and based on that I suggested that he revisits the report and then call me again. After about an hour the underwriter called me back and told me he had never seen a survey report before that didn't have risk improvements and that he didn't initially see my overall opinion of the risk which was one of 'excellent'. That underwriter at least then appreciated that the risk didn't merit any risk recommendations. To sum up, many surveyors I had dealings with over the years were guilty of making needless recommendations so as to present a defence in the event of an unforeseen loss at a later date. It is a little wondrous that such a practice was pursued as some senior account managers and directors were equally guilty of making an issue of a survey report that lacked a specifically related recommendation especially in the event of the insured experiencing a large loss.

I should stress that I do not just have negative memories of my surveyor colleagues. Many were as good a salesperson as one could wish to meet and blessed with sound technical knowledge. In fact, it is true to say that, of the more than 250 surveyors I worked alongside, the top twenty were predominantly property surveyors at Independent Insurance and high net worth at AIG. Realistically those liability surveyors, like their engineering colleagues, would never have needed to develop other skill sets so when moving into the insurance industry their interviews would have been based on their expertise, qualifications and work experiences as opposed to the likes of interpersonal skills. Some engineer surveyors found it difficult to adapt, which meant they were themselves a liability and there were many accounts lost because of their inability to accept that the insured have many, many alternatives where the purchase of suitable insurance was concerned. Also, not resolving identified weaknesses or failures in a risk while on site, due to poor communications, meant that the survey was an utter waste of precious resources.

There were, however, occasions where the surveyor's personality and communication skill came through resulting in additional quality business being acquired or the risk transformed into a much sought-after piece of business. To reiterate the surveyor to all intents and purposes was the insurer so it was vital they created a favourable image and left a lasting good impression.

"Pop in for a coffee anytime you guys are passing," a managing director said after my property colleague and I had completed the survey of his business.

Responding to this invitation my colleague replied, "If the opportunity does arrive, we will. However, there are not that many quality risks like yours that permit us too much time for pleasantries."

Compliments right up to the end meant a piece of business highly unlikely to change insurers. On the other hand, one particular Australian risk surveyed resulted in the exact opposite being achieved where both insured and the broker informed me that should I attempt to send that same surveyor again they would change their insurer followed by the broker sending a letter of complaint to our CEO. The surveyor in question was a PhD, as highly technically qualified as one could wish for, with exactly the opposite to offer where soft and negotiating skills were concerned.

One case of soft skills that stays in my memory, was unrelated to surveying, and involved a misdirected phone call from a personal line insured, who was calling on behalf of her husband. His mother had recently passed away. They were requesting claims forms for the deceased's funeral expenses and the other claims related to property damage that had been passed onto their broker but thus far their request had gone unanswered or even an acknowledgement received. I explained that my department was commercial; however, I consoled her and requested her contact details, saying I would follow it up this as opposed to putting her call back to the switchboard. It goes without saying I gave her my details as a form of courtesy and assurance, promising to take the case up for her family. I didn't consider it anything other than the right thing to do since it involved a family tragedy of a policyholder.

As a result, I walked to the life division and spoke with one of the managers there who in turn took the details and moved amongst his team, seeking out the policy and the related broker. Within thirty minutes the claims forms were dispatched. I called the lady back and informed her of the progress made, adding that if she didn't receive the claims form within two days, she should call me back. Before the following weekend, the life manager informed me that regardless of the fact they were still waiting on communications from the brokers a cheque had been issued and sent out to the insured within five working days hopefully leaving the insured with a lasting good impression.

During the following week, I received another call from the bereaved insured on this occasion enquiring about our customer service relations and requesting to speak with someone of importance. Not understanding what the problem was I put him through to the life manager, wondering what had suddenly gone wrong. The life manager called me up when I returned to the office following some survey work two days later and requested that I get myself to the general manager's office at a certain time. Now totally at a loss as the life manager would not discuss the matter further even though, as far as I was concerned, I felt I had acted in the best interest of the policyholder. At the GM's office, I found obviously the GM, my manager, the claims manager, life manager and head of personnel, who were all smiles. Apparently the insured was a well-known public figure and author had taken the time to write to the company singing our praises regarding our customer services and public relations and in particular my involvement even though it simply started with a misplaced phone call. The life manager refused to accept any credit, which had resulted in the insured cancelling their brokerage, dealing direct and transferring all his insurance to us. The account was published in an insurance monthly news magazine as to how all should respond to an insured regardless of the line of business. I suggested it was just the way any of our surveyors would have acted.

Returning to the matter of survey working, I cannot recall a time when I conducted a joint survey where it didn't turn out well. This is opposed to conducting audits where I made it a point, no matter how difficult it became, not to get involved. Normally I would introduce myself but explain that I was present simply as an observer. In one case I received a complaint about a liability surveyor who was taking excessive time, way over what the insured's representative had prepared for. This I took as an urgent need to conduct the audit personally and to provide guidance, if required, as opposed to reporting negatively, as the surveyor did have a very pleasant manner plus possessing credible technical qualifications. We arrived on site and as was the norm I would introduce myself purely as an onlooker. The surveyor went through the report form headings albeit some were excessive as during the tour of the works the answers to many of those points would have been all to plain to see. After a while the insured became restive and the body language was lost on our surveyor as the individual's concentration was centred on the report document. With the surveyor's nose deep in the report, there was no eye-to-eye contact, no explanation as to why certain questions were being asked or an opinion sought, so everything was wrong and the survey laboured on. It literally became a question and answer session.

At long last, I had seen the insured suffer enough and was about to intervene when the insured's patience ran out first and he said that he could no longer spend time on this visit. I suggested we called it a day and I thanked the insured for his time and left his office. Well, you can't prepare for what happened next when we returned to the surveyor's car. The surveyor, in silence, started the engine and promptly reversed into the decorative dwarf brick wall at the front of the premises with the concrete plinth being dislodged and some brickwork hitting the MD's Bentley! The problems were twofold: we were the property's insurers and the MD's motor policy was with us. We had to have the claims inspector visit the insured and take him a gift as a sign of goodwill. I was required to revisit the insured a little later, where I had to admire his attitude and humour when he informed me that he took the whole visit as a form of penitence for missing his daughter's school carol concert the night before! As for the surveyor, we had a long discussion and irrespective of the size of the risk it was a requirement to manage time better in the future. I was happy that no further complaints were received regarding time and property damage!

On the subject of time management, I was personally embarrassed at a company sales and development conference, attended by over one thousand attendees made up of brokers, insured, sales staff, claims, underwriting and executives. During the presentations, the CEO presented a supporting broker with a significant cash sum, an annual award for the best business provider in terms of quality and quantity. In response to the CEO's address, the broker was asked for his views on the service he received and was unsurprisingly extremely complimentary. Pushing the broker further the CEO requested of the broker if there was anything that we could improve upon? The broker thought for a moment and said that one complaint he received was from an HNW client where the surveyor had been on site in his home for three hours on a re-survey; an excessive amount of time by any stretch of the imagination.

Now more than a little enraged, the CEO said, "Stuart, where are you? Stand up, what have you got to say on the matter?" I was totally at a loss as this was the first I had heard of it.

All the while my underwriting colleagues sitting around me in subdued tones were singing, "Goodbye, goodbye we wish you all the luck goodbye."

"I cannot comment without knowing all the facts and as this is the first I have heard of it and that it is rightly unacceptable, I will get to the bottom of it. In the meantime, Barry," I said to the broker, "please accept my apologies and I will respond to you and the insured as soon as possible." The CEO always wanting the last word told me he wanted my response in writing yesterday!

I investigated the complaint, establishing that it was an HNW assessor who had re-visited the home of an insured and, in line with sales directives, had got chatting to the insured on extending his insurance coverage. He didn't understand that HNW clients always have their commercial, motor and personal lines policies with us. I read the assessor's report and instantly established that he must have been on site as long as the broker had claimed as the insured's two dogs, Harry and Cissy, were named in the report. I made a case for the assessor and attended the next HNW's monthly workshop, instructing them to curtail their enthusiasm on the sales not overlooking the fact that almost all HNW clients are already totally covered. My report to the CEO went unanswered, probably because I purposely overlooked mentioning the dogs by name.

Continuing on the matter of time you occasionally come across some people who have little to no perception of time, yet at Independent, there was a punctuality code with a vengeance. It just didn't seem to concern one of our most technically gifted liability surveyors. We were invited to quote for a very large case that entailed six factories at different locations across the UK. My reason for being there was to conduct the introduction as the insured required an insurer who could provide loss control. I was to be accompanied by a liability surveyor who was dubbed by colleagues Sir Les Patterson, the fictional Australian character played by comedian Barrie Humphries, because of his scruffy appearance and smoking habit. Sitting in the boardroom we were all patiently waiting for the surveyor's arrival but after 15-minutes I got to my feet and suggested that I would venture out to the carpark to find him as he was not answering his phone. As I passed by the big window of the boardroom that looked down over the yard area towards the gate, I saw our surveyor leaning casually against the gatepost, smoking. Livid would not adequately describe my feelings as I simply said he was at the gate and I would fetch him.

As good fortune would have it, neither the broker nor the proposers had witnessed what I was seeing. Striding across the yard the surveyor recognised me and said, "Hi Stuart, I didn't know you were already here." I asked him what he thought he was doing when he casually pointed to a large sign that read *No Smoking Beyond This Point*. Furious, I repeated the meeting time to which he casually replied that he had hit a traffic jam, a bad accident. Not believing my ears I stormed back to the meeting followed closely by the surveyor; all the while those present fortunately had still not witnessed what I had. Upon entering the room, the surveyor apologised and spoke of the accident that had delayed him, making a few witty remarks on the way, and those present took to him like a long-lost friend. In all fairness due to his interpersonal skills and technical expertise we acquired the business and the surveyor established an excellent relationship with all concerned, save me, who let him know just how lucky he was.

The two worst incidents that damaged insured relationships and our reputation involved two extremely well-qualified surveyors. Both ironically were previously employed in a professional role as enforcing authorities. One incident involved a total lack of integrity plus an act of crass stupidity and the other a simple act of stupidity. The one surveyor visited a risk where he thought that the existing extraction system was inadequate and required upgrading, with additional expenditure on the part of the business. The insured was at odds with the surveyor's opinion, advocating that the visiting enforcing authority inspectors had not seen fit to criticise the exhaust arrangements. The dispute carried over to the underwriters who valued the broker and insured's business, that had been claims free since inception. Now between the proverbial rock and a hard place the underwriter decided that he would not pursue the exhaust system recommendation further, in the business interest, much to the dismay of the overzealous surveyor.

Unbeknown to the company underwriters and the survey management the surveyor subsequently contacted a former colleague, who was still employed as an environmental health officer in that area. The surveyor reportedly informed him of the situation obviously encouraging the EHO (Environmental Health Officer) to do his bidding regarding the exhaust ventilation arrangements. The EHO arrived on site unannounced, as was their policy and right, and went immediately to the operation where the exhaust system was installed. Looking over the arrangements, the EHO issued an improvement notice on the business, to complete an upgrade within a set time frame. Exasperated, the insured contacted the broker as he felt certain our surveyor was behind this, suggesting that the terms of the liability survey should be undertaken privately and in strict confidence. Now our survey management team were drawn into the matter and as the insured had intimated the surveyor was behind the visit, although the EHO was not available for comment, his business dealings with us were now at an end. My take was that it merited dismissal on grounds of gross misconduct while both senior management and personnel opted for a written warning. The insured carried out their threat, cancelling their policies, and the broker stated that in future where his businesses were concerned our rogue surveyor would not be permitted to survey.

Other surveyors who brought the integrity of the insurer into question did cause our company problems from time to time and when they did, to reiterate, it resulted in a loss of business. In particular, on one such occasion, the surveyor attempted to play the enforcing authority to the insured, which came across clearly as a threat resulting in the surveyor being ejected and the cancellation of all existing policies held by us. The owner took umbrage at both the tone and the attitude of the surveyor which resulted in considerable bad publicity through the broker network and a loss of more than a single piece of business. In the surveyor's defence, he clearly didn't understand that we were the insurers and the insured was a valued customer, so that he had no right to begin questioning the insured's morality by suggesting the business was ignoring situations that pose a threat to his workers. Notwithstanding the surveyor then suggested that as a law-abiding citizen he could feel morally justified in bringing such situations to the notice of the enforcing authority. He felt vindicated in acting according to his conscience and that he had in the past followed a similar line when he was employed as a health inspector with a local authority.

It was a difficult situation but one that I felt should have been dealt with using more diplomacy and tact, as opposed to threatening. As a guest, he should have treated the host with far more courtesy and respect. I later visited the same risk and it was true that there were faults that could have resulted in injury but then probably ninety percent of surveyed risks have a degree of shortcomings but without any intention of the insured's part and just maybe, as with the majority of cases, the proprietor was unaware. The crime, in my mind, would be the insured ignoring the problem irrespective of an injury being sustained or not. This would be left with the enforcing authority to decide on the course of action and the courts to decide on the sentence. Unfortunately, the damage had already been done as the insured was quick to put it out that we were not the best insurer to deal with. The proprietor also believed that the surveyor was going immediately to report his findings to the enforcing authority and therefore felt betrayed. The fact that the surveyor didn't go to the authorities changed little as the business was lost.

Just occasionally there were embarrassing times even for a surveyor of good standing. The most amusing one involved one of our property surveyors who, like me, suffered the indignity of a loss occurring in and about the time of the survey. Sometimes, reputation can be adversely affected by events out of your control and in that regard, two occasions had my direct involvement and the other one of our fire surveyors. Because of my appointment, I was the first to experience the board's wrath. Upon reflection, both cases were amusing as I could see the point of view of my managing director, made all the more laughable because they were totally outside of both mine and the surveyor's hands.

In Mitcham, a surveyor was conducting a routine visit to a long-time insured's business premises and following the normal question and answer session accompanied the factory manager on a tour of the factory. Having completed the internal inspection, as was routine, the surveyor toured the external areas including the outbuildings, which took in the plastic store, compressor house, electrical substation and security lodge. Having seen nothing untoward, the surveyor wrapped up the meeting with the usual courtesies and left. As the industrial estate service route was a dead end, his journey off the estate took him out the same way.

At the end of this road, the surveyor pulled into a lay-by and, as customary, made notes concerning the survey. During this time a fire truck came roaring onto the estate, lights and sirens active. The surveyor was surprised, as it seemed only minutes before he was at the far end of the estate and saw no evidence of a fire. He concluded it was a rescue call or drill and proceeded back to the office. I received a call, not later than two hours, from my managing director asking me what sort of surveyor I engaged.

"Are they of reputable quality?" he asked. "Do they wear glasses?" and so on. Interrupting his tirade, I asked what this was all about. Almost spitting down the phone he said that he could forgive most survey incompetence but that it stopped short of a fire surveyor failing to notice whether or not the factory was on fire! Unbeknown to the surveyor, just as he left, one of the workers of the insured reported smoke coming from the compressor house, which resulted in the fire services being summoned. The loss, fortunately, was small but it didn't help the surveyor who suffered many comments regarding his alleged incompetency.

My situation was no different. While in Sri Lanka I was there to survey Colombo Shipyard at the time of the Tamil unrest. The survey was set for the following morning; therefore, after arriving at the hotel, I took dinner in the top floor restaurant overlooking the city and the shipyard. I was being entertained as there was a firework display taking place that was quite spectacular, with the sky lit up and as good as display as I had witnessed, although the noise was not quite as loud as normal which I put that down to distance and me being behind double-glazing. I asked the waitress about the obvious celebrations to which she said she didn't know, however, less than five minutes later, the waitress came to me and reported that the Tamils had attacked a Sri Lankan naval gunboat!

Ironically I was in Colombo to check on both fire and security of the shipyard and another of other sensitive locations following similar attacks on a naval cum commercial shipyard that we insured in Galle, on the South coast of Sri Lanka. Unexpectedly in the middle of the night, my managing director was on the phone making similar sarcastic comments and questioning my ability. My survey the next day was a disaster, as security in the yard was substandard and fire precaution were some of the worst I had ever come across. Fortunately, however, the shipbuilders who built the gunboat had handed over the vessel that very day and it was therefore no longer the responsibility of the dockyard, our insured. Once in the hands of the Sri Lankan navy they crewed and armed the gunboat and it remained manned. The 'fireworks' seen were, in fact, the small arms ammunition and star shells exploding, which also damaged another armed naval vessel moored up alongside, with disastrous results. Investigating the incident, the next morning I learned that the crew assigned to guard the new craft had wandered onto the other naval boat tied up alongside during which time Tamil sympathisers had thrown a timed incendiary device into the craft and made off. Needless to say that upon returning to London I found some related items suggesting my eyesight was impaired.

One of the most hilarious occurrences involved junior underwriters, male and female who unwittingly prior to the survey dressed to 'kill' as far as the lady was concerned and the male looking like he had just returned from a day on a building site. It began with a senior underwriter calling me up and requesting that the I take one of his underwriters out on my next survey in the southern area, for the purpose of understanding what a site survey was all about. Obviously, there was no problem as my duties extended to underwriter training which where possible did entail at least one accompanied site visit per annum. I informed the underwriter about my schedule for the next week and as luck would have it one of the engineering risks was written out of his office. The trade did entail metalworking and in the main, a highly skilled workforce utilising a range of machinery.

I had been given the underwriter's name and address, which was close to my home, and as it was on route to the survey, I agreed to collect the underwriter at 9 am the next day. Being in the insurance world the superintendent underwriter simply asked me to go to an address and collect Sam Wilson who had been with the company just six months. I arrived as usual at the given address early, as was my policy, and was pleasantly surprised to see the front door open as I drew up so I guessed Sam was watching out for me. My first impressions were incorrect because I was expecting a male colleague, not a pretty, twenty-three-year-old female, dressed as if about to have a night out on the town. I continued looking at the front door to the house half hoping to see a man emerge, but no, this was the Samantha Wilson, junior underwriter.

My mind raced regarding what to say as this attractive lady, who was without doubt inappropriately dressed for the survey of an engineering works, or any risk save an office or hotel. Full of confidence she slid into the passenger's seat with a friendly, confident, "Hi Stuart, nice to see you again!" With that, the situation became even more tricky as Sam clearly knew me but she was lost on me.

"Hi, Sam," I replied. "Have we met before?"

"Obviously, I impressed you," she remarked, "I attended one of your liability presentations about four months ago."

"Oh, of course," I lied, but this allowed me to comment on her appearance. I complimented her on the way she looked and suggested that if she entered a place where had I been working a machine then I could be forgiven for being distracted.

Jokingly I added that as insurers we could be facing claims for industrial injuries for the next decade if she entered a risk looking the way she did. Any distraction is ill-advised as the workers would not expect to see such a sight from one year to the next. I explained that at Ford we had a large number of visitors and the appearances of some were not wasted on the workers. Sam blushed and apologised for not thinking and asked permission to quickly go back into her house to change. In less than five minutes Sam came back out with a tastefully fitted trouser suit and flat shoes totally suited to visit a risk without the employees having their attention taken from what they were doing. It is worth mentioning that Samantha transferred to surveying later in her career and with her knowledge of underwriting and subsequent claims experience she turned out to be one of the best surveyors I had ever had the privilege to work with. As for the incident, even though there were no losses reported during the survey, it became a topic of conversation whenever we met up.

Returning to the other occurrence with a junior male underwriter, he decided that, to create a good impression, when accompanying me surveying an extremely large international civil engineering business, he should arrive at their offices wearing jeans and rubber boots! Unfortunately, no site visits had been arranged at this juncture, as the purpose of the survey was to introduce ourselves as potential insurers. I have to admit the directors had a sense of humour, particularly the chairman who asked when introduced to the embarrassed underwriter if his attire was our company's usual dress code or perhaps it was a dress down day? For the rest of the meeting and the subsequent site surveys, the incident was forgotten and considered acting with 'initiative'.

Certainly, one of the toughest tasks I faced internally, by way of an external incident, was keeping one of our senior liability surveyors employed, with the board and senior management calling for his employment to be terminated.

Looking at the facts in the cold light of day you could have been forgiven if you took the board's side in this matter. However, on the other hand, I was finding it exceedingly difficult to recruit the quality of the surveyors the company desired. Dealing with heavy risks you need top surveyors and they do not just appear as at that time there was a big market demand for quality surveyors. We had already taken on the loss control engineer with a doctorate only for this individual being found seriously lacking in the demands of the work plus there were others that were causing us problems when facing our insured and brokers. While I am not suggesting we were being swamped with complaints but serious questions were being asked regarding some surveyors level off competency to identify a loss-making circumstance from trivia.

The problem was quite simply that the senior surveyor in question caused an injury to an employee of our insured during the survey. On the face of it, that was just about the worst scenario you could imagine when we were claiming to be the best in the market where risk management was concerned. I suppose the most daunting part was me having to visit the business where the incident occurred and coming face to face with both the management of the insured and the injured employee. The insured at the centre of it was a commercial printer who was being subject to a routine employer's liability survey; a simple, almost courtesy, visit. The surveyor given the assignment was one of the best, having exemplary soft and negotiating skills, and was as well informed of the statutes governing people at work as any I ever came into contact with. You can imagine my surprise when one of our directors informed me that this same surveyor had injured an employee while he was conducting the survey.

Initially lost for comment the director went on to explain that the surveyor had operated a multi-colour printing machine being worked on by a maintenance engineer, trapping the individual in the moving parts. The size of the machine has to be appreciated, measuring some fifteen metres long, three metres wide and two metres high. Below floor level, there was another metre of machinery. Consequently; from the aisle way the maintenance engineer was not visible as he was working below the bed of the machine and to the rear. Our surveyor was being accompanied by the insured's financial director, who was in truth unfamiliar with the machine's characteristics and much that went on in the works. Consequently, when asked by the surveyor if he could turn on the power to view the guarding, he got the approval all the while being unaware that this six colour printer had two speeds: 'run' and 'crawl', fortunately for all concerned our surveyor selected the latter. A GM's complaint was raised as the insured's technical director had sent a letter to the company with a comment that they now had an entry in their accident book which, up until the survey, had been clear! I was directed to do whatever I could to resolve the matter and ensure that at the very least we were not going to receive notice of an injury claim. This seemed a bit ambitious knowing that there had been amputations and crush injuries on similar machines.

Upon visiting the risk, I met firstly the three directors, including the financial person who had accompanied our surveyor. Needless to say, I apologised unreservedly and enquired about the employee's wellbeing. He apparently was a long serving member of the staff and while at the time was badly shaken up he had since returned to his normal duties with no ill effects. The employee engineer did admit that he never isolated the machine or posted his 'danger' tag on the machine's controls to warn others against starting it. Nonetheless, this was not the appropriate time to be contentious so I asked permission to speak with the engineer, as we would like to offer our apologies in person and perhaps offer him out for a meal as I was staying in a local hotel? The insured's management was delighted and left me in a side office with the elderly engineer who was extremely amicable about the whole episode.

Staying overnight at a local hotel I was able to take both the maintenance engineer and his wife out to one of the more expensive restaurants in the town and ran up a bill with the assurances that the matter was closed. About three weeks later I was called up by one of our general managers who wanted to discuss the incident, which had me believing that perhaps the employee now had second thoughts and was pursuing a claim. I was greeted with "Have you seen the restaurant bill? I know you told me over the phone it was on the high side, but how many attended?" I told him just the employee and his wife as my meal was within my hotel bill.

"What do you think, should we deduct if from the surveyor's salary?" was the general manager's final words.

Yet another unsavoury incident involved another liability surveyor, where again, I was required to investigate the reported incident and take appropriate action. Making the most of a bad job came during a products liability survey where a casualty surveyor, with limited products liability experience, was sent out to conduct the survey of an electrical component manufacturer. There was nothing revolutionary about the switches, adapters, sockets and associated extras, as all were to British Standards and the risk ISO accredited. In fact, the business probably did not require special attention at all, given that it had no loss history after almost two decades which is possibly why the survey was given to an inexperienced surveyor, at least in products as the engineer had considerable experience where health and safety were concerned.

Following the headings in the products aide memoir, the insured obviously became impatient as the surveyor was detailing every heading: another case of the surveyor failing to notice the insured's frustration. Finally, the MD snapped and asked why the surveyor wanted to be made aware of the production statistics for a certain item. The surveyor admitted he didn't know, and simply said it was a question in the report. This further infuriated the insured, who suggested that the survey was at an end and that our company should send along someone who knew why these questions were included and the thinking behind them. A complaint was immediately dispatched by the insured to their broker who in turn contacted our directors, as it was a director's complaint from a very important broker connection.

Needless to say, the complaint landed on my desk to investigate and to quell the storm where both the insured and broker were concerned. Being only partially briefed I was unable to confirm if the complaint was the result of anything other than technical issues; there was no discourtesy, tardiness, confrontation and so on. Consequently, I visited the insured the very next day unaware of where and exactly why the problem arose as the surveyor involved was an extremely courteous individual, a graduate engineer. In fact, the complaint came as quite a shock.

I entered the offices somewhat at a loss but prepared for the worst, as both the broker and insured seemed hell-bent on attack. The insured took my business card and studied it for an age, asking me what some of the abbreviated qualifications stood for and just why I was involved, given my status? I immediately detected some reticence so I explained that we took complaints seriously and that I was personally very surprised given I knew the surveyor very well and I had always been impressed by his professionalism. The insured assured me that he liked the surveyor who was polite and honest and it was his honesty that made him somewhat regret his fit of pique. I enquired if we could start again and get to the bottom of the complaint, which he remarked was already a marked improvement as his time was important.

Here I was at least knowing what the complaint was about so, to avoid a lengthy dialogue, I asked whether or not the insured was informed of the likely duration, which apparently he was not. I apologised and explained that where products were concerned, we were like glorified bookmakers, working with the odds of a loss. He then interrupted and said now he half realised why some questions were included, and asked about the one concerning numbers. I went on to explain that these numbers were not so important should the company's defective products tally remain in the house, which apparently the rejects were. With this, the problem became clear; the insured had taken umbrage because the surveyor didn't know why he was asking the question! I suggested that I should go through the bullet points in the aide memoir, explaining the pertinence of each which I concluded within 30 minutes, much to the satisfaction of broker and insured. The insured asked that I convey his apologies to the surveyor and that when the surveyor was next passing would he please call in for a chat.

The most difficult decisions surveyors are faced with are moral issues. The ordinary person in the street, should they witness a crime in progress, would likely pass that information onto the authorities. If someone was being hurt or were simply being threatened, driving under the influence of alcohol etc. it could involve a responsible citizen passing that knowledge on to the police, thus leading to arrest, prosecution and maybe a custodial sentence. For surveyors, the issue can come up far too frequently. Often, when entering a place of work, if I saw that clearly the law was being broken or at least the statutes were being ignored, resulting in lives being put at risk. Understandably most serious-minded proprietors acted immediately, but there were a number of those who never reacted even though they were clearly aware of the law. I recall the managing director of a group of companies, who I met during a post-loss survey, and who I believed didn't care about his employees. All this leaves the surveyor is in a quandary: do they simply report the hazardous situation to the underwriter and let the power of the underwriter, in terms of policy conditions, impose sanctions, or the cancellation of the policy? Do they ignore it? Either way the same dangerous situation would still exist leaving people's lives at risk.

Putting the human interest above the insured's activities and experiences, as a whole, proves to be far more informative and interesting. The reality is that as a surveyor we meet every type of person in all manner of industries with duties ranging from the janitor to the chairman of the board. However, it is the latter we usually see because these are the policymakers, but they can often be accused of giving a slanted view of the general business dealings. If you wish to know what the janitor's duties are you do not ask the managing director because he will tell you what he believes you want to hear and not the reality. Ask the janitor though and they will tell you what the duties entail in detail. Speak to a middle manager and again while providing an opinion you know the response will certainly be guarded which means that the surveyor will have to use their eyes and ears to better effect to obtain a clear picture.

While sitting in a meeting with the board of a multinational business, where both the chairman and managing director were in attendance, it was usually easy to see who was the boss because when answering a simple question, the board member would look towards the chairman or MD for a sign of approval. The one individual who usually seemed to be above that was the financial director because rarely if ever did they have much to offer where loss control was concerned. On the other hand, I recall that, at one meeting, I asked about their stress management policy, with only the FD responding by asking me why that was important to us as insurers. *What a great question*, I thought, since, even though the individual clearly didn't think things through before speaking such was my immediate response it clearly went some way to eliminate any further questions from this financial director. For the record I informed him of a senior executive, emphasising the 'senior director' having an alleged work-related nervous breakdown and we the insurers having to put a six-figure reserve against the claim. The chairman responded by suggesting the FD keep his questions to himself as clearly, he was not on the same page. This risk was one of the very best and I had to meet up in the Far East and Pakistan with the MD and chairman at the insured's location, such was their commitment to loss control.

Whilst dwelling on the subject of stress I couldn't help casting my mind back to those really interesting moments while in insurance because I cannot ever recall preparing to go to my work with daunting thoughts or trepidations. That didn't mean that others were without stress when it came to my work though. In one case, it seemed that me undertaking a long drive from my Surrey home to Inverness, starting out at 0345 gave my senior management serious concerns and got one or two apparently hopping mad. I was in Aberdeen just before noon when my GM called me asking my whereabouts as he thought I had a survey to complete at a diving school on Loch Ness but up until then, he hadn't seen my flight request for sign off. I informed him I was just about an hour's drive away and in plenty of time to keep the 2 p.m. appointment resulting in him wanting to know what possessed me to make the journey by car. I explained that I needed to carry all my survey equipment such as high-visibility clothing, foul weather gear, hardhat, safety boots, torch, noise meter, camera, tape measure, first aid kit, briefcase, notes and policy documents plus overnight personal effects.

Considering I had two other surveys to complete in the vicinity of both Glasgow and Edinburgh the flight costs and car hire would be three times more than my fuel plus additional accommodation as I would now only be out two nights, rather than four. Still not being completely sold he made arrangements to have me take the car sleeper train back to London from Waverley Edinburgh with an instruction not to repeat this type of driving excursion again. The point was that travel was an essential part of the job and working to my own demands I was really relishing meeting this challenge. I simply detested routine, which was totally incompatible, I felt, with the demands of corporate and international insured. Working in tandem with underwriters and corporate insured, the latter paying millions in premiums, the role demanded flexibility and as far as I was concerned, they merited my time and best endeavours.

It was true it did take a great deal out of me at one time but surveying in Bahrain, Chennai, Singapore, Hong Kong, Taiwan, Manilla, Sydney and New Zealand, on a round trip of seven weeks, would have taken up to almost six months to complete had I made individual trips. The times that galled me most were when I found myself flying over countries knowing I had work to do there. On reflection, I think I simply got into a way of working where I just wasn't happy unless I was busy surveying, which always requires considerable travel. Where Independent was concerned, CEO Michael Bright's comment about me being in the office as opposed to surveying was unwittingly retracted some years later when he called me up in Sydney, telling me I spent too much time out surveying, particularly overseas. He like many other directors and executives spent countless hours pursuing their objectives and while a percentage of my time was overseas it was probably more noticeable but nonetheless extremely productive.

Before concluding this chapter, providing an overview of survey work, there is one remaining issue that you will rarely hear surveyors speak of, the like of which happened to me on no less than four occasions: requests to report favourably for inducements. Where an insured feared to expose all of their underhand dealings, where their insurance was concerned, they might choose to incentivise the surveyor to overlook certain matters. On one such occasion an insured, whose liability policy was up for renewal, asked me details concerning my children: their ages and schools. As a major school outfitter, they would welcome me bringing my children to their factory, at the weekend, to enable them to be fitted out with their appropriate school's summer and winter uniforms. All I was required to do was report positively on their business, based on just their main factory and showrooms, ignoring their other establishments scattered around the London area.

Without out so much as a second thought I declined and insisted on seeing their other manufacturing facilities which turned out to be establishments using many young persons, mainly from minority ethnic groups, and immigrants. The director, sensing my displeasure, added of course that it would probably mean some payment but far less than the sums I currently paid for school uniforms. All those people labouring in three other out of the way premises laboured in what could only be described as Victorian conditions; so bad were these working conditions my thoughts turned to wondering what the education authorities and the schools would have made of it all. Following a consultation with the underwriting managers the insurers suggested that the insured seek out another insurer for renewal of their liability cover. The word inducement was never used either orally or in writing as it was solely my word against a reputable insured.

The second instance involved a double-glazing and conservatory manufacturer who I established were engaging teams of uninsured fixers to install their glazed units. The exposure came about, not from the insured but when speaking to a team of fixers installing double-glazing in a semi-detached house in Surrey. The head of the gang did possess insurance for both his team for personal injuries and for accidents to the public and any property, for which he paid the premium to the insured on an annual basis. All of this was contrary to the information provided by the insured's representative, who informed me each subcontractor made their own insurance arrangements. Without discussing and disputing this with the insured I informed them I would need to see other sites currently underway, where I established the same situation of each paying the insured a premium. Armed with this knowledge I went back to the insured, realising that I had completed my survey and established the facts, suggested that he could arrange for my property to be fully double glazed for a pittance, as he put it, for me to forget the subcontractors. My response was that it was best that he found another insurer because I couldn't ignore subcontractors working without public liability insurance on the insured's contracts. Once again, the matter was discussed behind closed doors and renewal was not invited.

The other cases were to a degree minor but due to being offered incentives I had to report the circumstances regarding those insured's undisclosed business dealings, hiding these undertaking under the cover provided by us the insurer but not the offer of goods and payment in kind.

Brokerages

A major part of the insurance surveyor's time involved, to one degree or another, insurance brokers. Essentially the broker being the intermediary between insured and insurer. Some books of business I found were split between 'direct' insured and those policyholders whose business was acquired via a brokerage where in those cases the business dealings went only through that source. At another insurer the entire book of business was obtained via brokers of which there were several classes such as 'club' and 'select' where in those instances our company was the preferred insurer. These dealing were principally through the provincial brokerages with the insured based primarily in the UK and the Irish Republic. However, based at one head office the underwriters worked in the *London Market*, as it was known, dealing in the main with the large international brokerages who boasted of branches worldwide.

The quality of the insurance broker is like any profession dependent on the experience and levels of knowledge within that organisation. These brokerages profess to be professional advisers who understandably work solely on behalf of their clients as it is through these businesses that their commission is forthcoming. Was one to read a typical broker sales presentation they inevitably claim to help would be clients by identifying their exposures and risks by way of awareness of the client's business, thus being able to determine their required cover. It goes without saying that as with any profession some brokers have specially qualified personnel capable of dealing with specific types of industries plus, in some of the larger organisations, field staff able to provide on-site guidance to reduce any exposure.

Based on my experiences with brokers, there are two distinctly different animals; the office-based account handlers and those that venture out into the field. Dealing first with the account handlers I found them generally proficient possessing a deal of soft skills plus their knowledge of the insurance market insofar as those insurers best placed to provide the appropriate level of cover and in some cases practical loss control guidance. Occasionally, when the actual account handler accompanied me on surveys, they were an asset and handled some difficult instances with tact and diplomacy. Some of the very best account handlers I had the good fortune to meet up with were in the Far East, Australia and Caribbean and this was where the surveys were being undertaken following claims. Regarding dedicated field staff or those attending the survey as if duty bound principally due to the size of the business, such as in the case of the actual account handlers, they for the most part proved a hindrance due to their pompous and dogmatic approach usually adopted to disguise their lack of technical knowledge and understanding of their client's undertakings.

Overall, I found dealing with brokers to be generally positive. However, where would we be if that was to apply to all brokerages? Competition is harsh in this field and therefore, brokers will do all they can to maintain positive relationships where their clients are concerned. So, while not always seeing eye to eye with broker representatives, I did respect the broker's situation as they were more often than not placed between the proverbial 'rock and a hard place'. On many occasions however, I found the broker would provide me with the insured's contact details, based on previous positive experiences and dealings, knowing that my adopted approach and manner would hardly ever cause them heartache.

Under normal circumstances, in respect to surveys, the broker would firstly contact their client and explain the policy conditions. The insured would designate a member of their staff most suitably equipped to deal with the surveyor, usually a technical person or perhaps even a consultant engaged by the insured. For the most part, the insured's contact was the manager or director who oversaw the day to day running of the business, whether that involved a building site, factory, office, shopping mall or any other insured business. With the likes of an SME (small or medium enterprise), the director or owner would likely be the person to be seen, which was all the better, because that individual would know the business inside out. It therefore follows that being the top person you could very much gauge the quality of the risk, particularly where risk recommendations are concerned, by simply measuring both the person's attitude and their commitment when such matters were discussed.

Undoubtedly, the worst situation the broker faces is where they are trying to place a business with an insurer where poor claims experience exists. This would often entail the broker finding it difficult to obtain cover at the best possible terms and conditions at an acceptable premium. Added to this, there are mandatory insurance requirements for the like of employer's liability or workers' compensation and third-party motor insurance. Consequently, cover has to be in place at all costs. At the very least, placing substandard business would require substantial effort on the broker's part. In a more drastic scenario, the would-be insurer might demand additional draconian conditions such as a survey, where the findings of the appraisal would become conditional including within a fixed time frame. In an attempt to avoid the imposition of these tough measures, and fearing the worst, businesses have sometimes decided to dispense with the services of one brokerage and resorted to finding another, less informed broker, applying direct to an insurer with the business name now having been changed. As such I gained knowledge during the survey of companies falsifying both their claims and decline history.

One such broker took on an allegedly established business, going under a trade description of steel erectors, having no claims history and an acceptable credit rating, resulting in the business obtaining employer's and public liability under a commercial combined policy from my employer through a preferred brokerage. As was the norm due to the trade of steel erection the insured was to be subject to a liability survey within thirty days of inception, save that we would select the site, as the insured had informed the broker of having at least two site contracts ongoing at that time. Being assigned the survey, I made the necessary arrangements through the broker for several days hence. The underwriter also requested I enquire of the broker why, following the issuance of their policy documents, they had not transferred the premium. During the setting up of the survey, I asked exactly that only to be informed by the broker that they were still waiting on the insured. I had never encountered this before but didn't consider it too much of a problem as I was sure some accountant somewhere had overlooked the payment. During this telephone conversation, the broker provided me with the insured's largest current site address, which I learned was a school being extended by way of a new gymnasium in Richmond, Surrey, just a stone's throw from my home location. The broker also asked me if I would ask the director about the unpaid premium.

Arriving on the site, I did not meet with the principle of the insured as he was allegedly on the other site so I had to make do with the senior rigger and site agent of the main contractor. The work process was on an unoccupied school as at that time it was half-term. That meant that no school activities which from a risk perspective was healthy. The site was being managed well by a known, reputable main contractor but the insured's crane and steel erection operations seemed on first impressions to be haphazard, to say the least. I considered the insured's site activities very poorly managed and therefore, not free of hazard; the steel waiting for erection was poorly placed and almost all the riggers were without all the necessary safety equipment such as appropriate footwear, hard hats and fall restraints. As the riggers were working at height without any safety harnesses, I asked the senior rigger why not. His response was one of indifference and he continued to work. Consequently, realising I was going to obtain little by way of policies, safety arrangements, training and so on, I returned to the site agent's office for a sighting of the subcontractor's insurance details.

Following a formal request for our documents, the agent retrieved them from a drawer and handed them over. Whilst handing them over the agent informed me that the contracts department, from head office, had perused the same and made no comment during their site visit. Looking at the EL certificate, however, I immediately recognised that it was not genuine; in fact, it was out of date and not ours, therefore bogus. This led me to speak over the phone, direct from the site office, informing the main contractor's contracts department of the situation. The person at the other end of the line expressed serious concerns and said that they would contact their contracts director. The director called the site agent requesting that he speak directly with me. He requested that I get confirmation of the situation as, being a contractor of repute, he rightly didn't want their reputation tarnished. Being reasonably well informed about the circumstances now, I, in turn, called the underwriter, informing him of the type of risk the insured represented and the puzzle concerning the EL certificate of an unknown insurance company. His response was predictable, informing me that as the broker had not received payment therefore as the policy effectively did not exist, there was no cover. He informed me that he would contact the broker himself. Returning to the site agent, I found that he had spoken with his director, who had, on learning of there being no insurance in place, instructed him to suspend the steel erection immediately. The contracts department had been ordered to cancel the contract until they could produce a genuine policy document.

Regardless of my underwriter's intention, I made the broker aware of the underwriter's intent to state that the cover as such was cancelled. Within a few moments of leaving the site office, the steel erector's main person called me, threatening all manner of reprisals against both me and the company. In return, I informed him that he had firstly furnished the main contractor with a falsified document, and could face prosecution by the enforcing authority. I also told him that the reason this all came about was because of the unpaid premium as neither the broker nor our accounts had received it. The director of the steel erectors hung up. A short while later, we learned from the efforts of the diligent broker that together we had apparently uncovered a trail of corruption and deception involving three insurers, with us being the only one to have escaped without a claim being submitted for damage, loss of equipment and minor injury claim. In two cases two claims were paid, one involving theft and the other material damage, which I suggested probably covered their insurance premiums.

I faced only a few difficult cases led by brokers within my fourteen or so years at Cornhill, all thankfully having satisfactory conclusions, which at the time did seem only a remote possibility. The first involved a case of alleged racial discrimination which was at that a time a very sensitive issue, with race relations offices reportedly bursting at the seams with complaints. The insured was situated in south London, with the business producing plastic bubble wrapping for pharmaceutical products. Visiting the risk, I met up with the directors who on completion of the usual introductory meeting left me in the capable hands of their factory manager. The manager, a first-generation British Pakistani, was both well-educated and knew the work processes and equipment extremely well. He had apparently commenced employment with the insured on the shop floor as a packer, was promoted to supervisor, then, following continual excellent service, was promoted to manager. Given my background, I naturally had some empathy for him.

I completed the survey with a few recommendations involving the like of blocked firefighting equipment and fire routes that were congested in one or two areas. In fact, these issues were immediately rectified by the manager the moment they were identified. The recommendations were simply recorded for future reference and did not, due to the swift resolution of the problems, influence my overall impression of the business, which I rated as an *above average* risk. Some four weeks following on from the survey I was summoned to head office, where I learned through the broker that I was being accused of racism by staff at the bubble wrap risk recently surveyed. Obviously, Cornhill was concerned and while they were clearly defending me, they wanted my version of the alleged incident or incidents as no one seemed fully informed apart from the broker. I was sure it was nothing I had said as if I were a racist or accidentally prone to the odd racist remark how, given Ford's workforce dealings in far more hostile and confrontational environment, did I avoid such an incident there for all those years? Realising management was in a difficult position, I was permitted to speak with the broker to learn a bit more. The broker clearly was on the side of his client and was to a degree quite uncommunicative at the outset; in fact, I felt he was enjoying the situation.

Having experienced so many difficult industrial relations situations in the past and knowing that the accusations being levelled had no basis I was adamant that the broker should not be so vague but to get to the crux of the matter and inform me of the situation or situations. At length, he read from the communications section of my report which stated, "Even though the manager was from an ethnic background, and given his perfect command of the English language, there lies the conclusion regarding communication problems."

My first question to the broker was about my report as it was headed and footed, *For internal use only*. So how, I enquired, did he obtain a copy of it given its confidentiality? There was a silence and he informed me it was sent to him by an underwriter from our company and because it involved recommendations, he dispatched a copy to the insured and it was the insured's board that allegedly raised the issue. In reality, he added, how they got the report and who received was of little consequence as it concerned a matter of race discrimination and client prejudice and in that regard someone needed to be taken to task, even stating that it was against the law.

I double-checked it was as the broker had reported, and the Private and Confidential notes had been inadvertently sent out by an underwriting clerk at the branch. Taking my findings to senior management I requested that I be given permission to speak on site with the insured, certainly with the broker present, thus avoiding any further future misunderstandings. My manager was an extremely astute individual and he made the call, setting up a meeting the following morning. Making my way to the factory I was greeted by the MD's PA who informed me they were waiting for me in the boardroom and that I should go right in. To say the atmosphere was icy would be an understatement but I weighed right in requesting they should listen first then comment; after all, we were we speaking of a confidential document and if racism were proved I and my employer could be charged under the Race Relations Act 1976.

I believed that by me citing the law and therefore the possibility of fines, or dramatically at worst, custodial sentences rather took those present a little by surprise. They in all probability being fed by the broker never took all the possible implications into account. I explained that if such a case were proven it could involve legal action and on the other hand to be unjustly accused it could involve civil proceedings with the plaintiff or plaintiffs seeking damages against those who were alleging racial discrimination.

The room fell silent as I felt my words began to sink in, which had obviously come as a shock to some of those present, as they clearly saw this beforehand as a cut and dried case. I took their silence as a good sign because at least those present would think twice before uttering something that could be used against them. Finally following this pause, gesturing with his hand, the director granted me the floor. Taking up my report I suggested those present should take note of the front page of the report where it itemises *Number Employed* with subheadings that include *skilled, unskilled, female, young persons, supervisors, disabled* and finally, I emphasised *ethnic* numbers. I added that the underwriters required this information, as did the law under the Health & Safety at Work etc. Act 1974, where, for example, if the workforce is made up of a large number of non-English speakers, there is a question of how the company discharges their statutory duties regarding safety induction, safety policy statement, terms and conditions of employment, safety warning notices and so on. I never imagined that the meeting could have turned so favourably in such a short space of time, but it did.

Continuing with something now becoming a presentation I mentioned several cases including a Turkish bakery here in London where their company's safety policy statement, a statutory requirement, was in Turkish following a visit from the HSE as before their statement and health and safety documents were all in English. For another of our insured, a Lebanese business, their documentation was found to be in both Arabic and English. Still, silence reigned, so I now requested that they turn to the part of the report headed up, *Private and Confidential notes to the underwriter*. Here I quoted, "There were no communication issues albeit the workforce was virtually made up from ethnic groups. The works manager, while being from an ethnic background himself, was fluent in both English and Urdu, there were, therefore, no language or communication difficulties."

Without waiting for a response, I asked where racism was either during my time conducting the survey or in the contents of the report. The MD, now getting gingerly to his feet said, "Whoops! How embarrassing, I would like to offer both you and Cornhill my sincere apologies." In turn, in a conciliatory tone, I suggested that we should drop the matter as there was a clear misunderstanding regarding the reasons for those thoughts, led by a person or persons who were not present during the survey. The broker knew who I was referring to and as was wise remained deathly silent and was clearly put out by the final outcome. I did follow up by informing those present that because this was an internal document Cornhill were changing their policy regarding liability survey reports whereupon my suggestion the *Private and Confidential* notes in the future had to be typed on pink paper and the risk recommendations section would be replaced with a completely new form that should never to be attached to the main report going forward. That policy was still being rigidly applied some 14 years later.

The second most affected unsuspecting insured through an unprofessional brokerage involved a relatively new established house painting and decorating company where regardless of the insured being involved in a non-hazardous trade the underwriters thought that perhaps it was one that required a routine survey. My feelings upon receiving the survey instruction and seeing a copy of the underscored policy conditions concerning 'work at height' were that perhaps, the underwriters had suspicions regarding the extent of the insured's site activities.

I made contact directly with the insured making the usual appointment to attend an active site. I was informed that in fact they only had one contract at that point in time and it was taking place next to their new offices and their warehouse, adjacent 'F' Wharf, Chatham Royal Naval Dockyard. This address did not concern me as I assumed that the insured probably stored their paint and equipment there in one of the sheds, although as I mentioned previously, assumptions can be dangerous. For the record, the weather at the time was foul, with heavy snowfall overnight so that the roads and walking underfoot were treacherous. At the gate of the dockyard, I was directed by dockyard police to the wharf address which was a warehouse adjacent a dry dock in which a 26,000-ton ferry boat was berthed. I went into the warehouse and found it was almost stacked to the roof with large tins of paint, all lead-based, decidedly toxic and flammable. I found the insured and another worker in a small office, huddled around a small electric fire.

At the door to the office I gestured to the paint, asking was it a job lot or had he obtained a major contract? He confirmed that it was for a large contract that was in fact already underway in spite of the inclement weather.

"Where?" I asked because I estimated he would need a fleet of vehicles to cart that amount of material about.

"Here, outside," was his response, which completely threw me. I was surprised as firstly it was snowing with below freezing temperatures, and surely painting buildings in this weather was unwise?

"So you are doing some internal painting then?" I enquired.

"Yes, I will show you around but lucky for us the contract does involve as much internal work as external, it's just that the outside where the hull and superstructure will have to wait for the spring."

"The hull and superstructure?" I repeated.

"First take a look and I will explain things as we go," the insured said getting to his feet and putting on an anorak. We stepped out into the weather and taking a few steps towards the vessel towering above he gestured with his hand.

"That's a boat," I said.

Sarcastically with a grin, the insured quipped, "Now I see that you surveyors don't miss much."

Ignoring that, which in other circumstances I would have found amusing, I told him we needed to talk. We trudged back to the office where I drew out the policy schedule and missing out some of the print I informed him that there were policy restrictions and conditions such as no work above 30 feet, no work on tunnels, bridges, docks, wharves, railways, airports, adjacent tidal water, 'vessels' I emphasised, and so on. I added that those employees, if they were his, seen grit blasting the superstructure were approximately 40 to 50 feet above the deck while the worker on the radio mast, assuming he was again a member of his team, was way, way over the height working restriction.

Surprisingly unperturbed, the insured casually informed me that his broker was fully conversant with the project and had already received the go-ahead from the insurers. Just for good measures, he informed me that they also painted, in the recent past, the M2 motorway bridge over the River Medway that was way higher; in fact, the clearance alone was 116 feet and spanned over 500 feet. He said that he would need to speak with his broker as he thought everything was OK. In response, I said that I was going back to head office now and I would talk it through with the underwriter who would undoubtedly speak with the branch underwriter and his broker, as I was sure there had been some misunderstanding. Having got a full account of what the painting contract entailed I left the insured and drove back to the office informing the underwriter of what I had found.

The underwriter seemed unmoved, simply took up my scribbled note and a copy of the policy and went straight to the head of underwriting. I guessed there probably was a history here so I knuckled down to report my findings when the phone rang. An extremely irate broker was screaming at me down the line, threatening me because I had allegedly told his client not to speak with him. Of course, I assured the broker that was not the case but I told his client that I would have to report back to the underwriter who would talk over matters with those involved, namely the local underwriter and his broker. I added that I never told the insured not to speak with his broker at any time, as it was an underwriting matter.

Now, with the broker continuing to shout and curse, I put the call on speaker, which stopped production in the underwriting room, and so I said that if he continued as he was I would hang up and as his mood and tone never changed, I did hang up. Needless to say, I didn't have to report the incident to the head of underwriting, who had upon hearing the broker emerged from his office. Having ignored the threats, as it had gone way beyond that and as the head had been briefed by the account underwriter, he told me to forget it as the situation was no longer a survey matter. It transpired that the broker and the local underwriter colluded with one another, the latter having exceeded his underwriting authority on this and a number of other policies, surprisingly enough involving the same broker. The result was that the local underwriter was dismissed for gross misconduct and the brokerage was cancelled. I never heard from the broker again.

Independent Insurance after two years as the liability insurers of an extremely large poultry processing business we established total cooperation regarding risk management that resulted in a much-improved loss ratio where employer's liability was concerned. Following yet another successful year the underwriters decided that they should make a financial award to the insured, preferably to be used for risk management initiatives. Much to the delight of the insured's CEO, the business was contemplating where to make the best use of the five-figure sum when they received an unannounced visit from the broker's head of risk management, who had flown in specially from London to their client the insured's head office.

With the brokerage believing that the substantial sum was 'burning a hole' in their client's pockets, so to speak, the broker's risk manager appeared, unannounced, on the scene. As reported to me, the CEO was surprised and wanted to be briefed regarding the reason for the impromptu visit. Clearly not understanding the relationship that the insurers had now established with the insured after several years where great headway had been made regarding losses and absenteeism, the broker had presumptuously brought with him his ideas on how to spend the cash award. The CEO was an extremely astute businessman and one not to be duped into thinking that the brokers were not looking to benefit from some or perhaps a heavy part of this windfall. The type of individual the CEO of the insured was can best be described by his character which came very much to the fore in my very first survey of the business that we had just underwritten. Following a very brief introduction on a Monday morning, the CEO told me to help myself regarding what I wanted to see and his safety manager would be there to ensure there would be no obstacles. During the following four days having surveyed all five of their plants, I was back in the CEO's office for the debriefing.

Being as diplomatic as possible, I reported positively to him on the matters that would make him comfortable, or so I thought. To my amazement, he told me in no uncertain terms that he didn't want to know what they were doing right but wanted to know want they were doing wrong.

Taken aback by his frankness I listed them, to which he replied on the conclusion of my report, "Thank you, now let us get to work on putting those matters right."

The CEO informed me that he considered the broker's risk survey team inadequate, making the point that, during all their previous years as business partners, they never mentioned any of the issues that we were now identifying, such as kinetics and noise. This was an excellent example of why some broker survey teams do their clients a disservice more often than not.

Returning to the broker's risk manager unannounced attendance, the meeting was apparently short lived with the CEO informing the risk manager that in the future the risk arm of the brokerage should be accompanied by the insurer's risk manager. A call from the insured followed to our underwriters suggesting that I should return to their head office meeting yet again with the CEO, with some ideas on how best to invest the monies. Apparently, those broker risk management initiatives, now in the possession of the CEO, left very little funding for any ideas the insured's safety people had, which more than angered the board of directors and in particular the CEO. Arriving at the insured's plant the next week, the CEO, a fairly intolerant person at best, was almost inconsolable, such was the audacity, he felt, of the broker's risk manager. What had been proposed amounted to one of the broker's risk team personally conducting kinetic assessment and training, which accounted for approximately 85% of the award, with a further 10% for the production of a training manual, leaving a measly four-figure sum for the insured to use, which would just about upgrade the guarding on two of their eviscerating machines, when in fact there were many other worthy causes and issues to improve the risk.

The insured presented me with the broker's recommendations and asked for my comments, which to my surprise given the history in the industry and the plant, apart from the odd repetitive strain injury, were predominately mechanical related; hence the noise. As another mark of goodwill, at little to no cost to the insured, we used our own audiometric qualified risk surveyor to undertake audiometric screening and audits, as well as upgrading some mechanical handling equipment, and almost as importantly we upgraded the temperature controls at the cold store doors. Here, icing up was a serious problem in these very large cold stores as the doors were constantly jamming up, which led to yet more icing on the floor surfaces and in turn resulted in some slips and falls of staff and impact damage through skidding transport. That excludes the constant additional electrical power that was required to energise the blowers necessary to control the temperature. Going forward, approximately 50% of the award was spent sensibly in the following two years, to the complete satisfaction of the insured and the underwriters. The broker's head of risk management never once accompanied me again, although he once did send a broker surveyor who was just a passenger during the survey programme over the following six years.

Of course, there were other broker related cases that gave rise to poor relationships where surveying was concerned and, in my opinion, where some of their surveyors were doing their clients an injustice by treading softly around them as opposed being frank with them. Take, for example, arguably the world's largest container terminal: Container Terminals in Hong Kong. We were facing a claim for a badly damaged formula one racing car on route to a Grand Prix in the Far East, allegedly damaged at the port. I met up with the port manager and the broker's surveyor, who I thought to be a bit on the inexperienced side, and possibly lacking the necessary skills and knowledge for such a large and potentially hazardous facility. Risks in ports and terminals are considerable, with natural perils ranging from storm, fog and sea mist that can give rise to poor visibility; specialist mechanical handling plant, handling of dangerous goods and substances, road transport both port and visitors, deep tidal water and the vessels themselves.

The broker's surveyor, in this case, was a graduate engineer with less than one year of experience and without any meaningful loss control experience. My first concerns were to listen to his findings, but there were none, as it turned out he had never conducted an audit or proper survey but had on a few occasions been shown how the terminal operated. The surveyor, in response to my question of familiarity with the terminal, showed me the insurance proposal document completed by the insured, with no input regarding risk quality or opinions from the brokers. Regarding the claim, this had not been investigated by the broker with the insured's opinion only being available. As I turned my attention to the manager I was rightly quizzed about my own experience regarding terminals and ports. In response, I informed him that I had undertaken work in the Far East in Chonburi and Singapore while in Europe, I had surveyed in Felixstowe, Rotterdam, Dover Harbour Board, Southampton and Hull plus Dubai, Bahrain, Aden in the Middle East and almost all Cypriot ports.

Somewhat taken aback, the manager's mood changed, and he asked me if I had seen anything untoward concerning the single wharf I was able to see while standing on the top of the insured's multi-storey office block or on my way through the port from the main gate? I informed him that I had, to which he replied, "I might have guessed as much by your remarks concerning the broker's report."

I informed the manager that four issues entailed precautions against collisions:

"Firstly, why are your Rubber Tyre Gantry's (RTG) warning lights at high level only?" I asked. "I realise the numbers and locations of the warning lights are generally the purchaser's decision and while I can see your operators in their cabs have the benefit of cameras for a lofty 20-metre high piece of equipment intermediate lights would certainly have been included in my purchase order. Being that the RTG is a very substantial mobile item of plant, other RTG operators and those travelling at road level need be made aware of the plant's presence, don't you think? Secondly, why do you not operate a one-way traffic system, given you have regular visitor transport who are not familiar with the layout? Third, why are some of your shunters operating without hazard warning lights? Last, but not least, where is your hazardous cargo isolation facility?"

Surprisingly, the manager thanked me for my observations and informed me he had made similar comments at the business's quarterly reviews, but now having a third-party passing comment along those lines, he felt that would help his cause. The one outstanding point the manager confessed that took him a bit by surprise was my suggestion regarding the directional signs to the isolation facility. I explained a situation where a high hazard toxic load was leaking consequently the vehicle needed to be dispatched at speed to Dover port's isolation point via an emergency route. The port's security staff were instrumental in getting the vehicle to the area without incident, and with the emergency services on station a major incident was averted. However, I suggested that being that Container Terminals' facility was probably six times larger, appropriate road signage should be in place. All the while the broker's risk manager stood by silently, which gave me no satisfaction because simply it was not this individual's fault but the brokerage's. Regarding those recommendations, the insured were as good as their word, completing them in a very short space of time. We still never got to the bottom of how the racing car was damaged but just maybe a collision or a dropped load were my guesses.

The least impressive broker surveyor I met was in the UK, where, upon arriving at the risk, he told me that he would show me around and if I had any points to make I should tell him first and he would speak with the insured, who was, he emphasised, their client. We appeared to be getting off on the wrong foot so I requested he took a good long look at the business card that I had provided him with asking that he note my title and the qualifications behind my name. I also informed him that if he wished to conduct the survey then he should go ahead and I would return at some other time once we got the rules straight. I then requested where his loss control qualifications were, as he was clearly an authority, but was he too modest to have them printed on his business card. In my case with my company, it is a requirement.

"I cannot see any insurance qualifications, so I can only assume you are perhaps a graduate with an engineering degree or perhaps Masters?" It turned out that the surveyor possessed a degree in Business Studies, which was not at all helpful when attempting to assess a risk, but I let sleeping dogs lie. What I did pursue was his findings during his previous visit and recommendations presented to the insured. As expected, this was his first visit and he admitted he had never seen a survey report on this client.

In response to the surveyor's desired strategy, I informed him that while I was quite happy to follow and had no wish to either make him look or sound inferior in the presence of his client, I would be asking questions and making observations if merited. The surveyor understood and then, with the manager of this main commercial vehicle dealership, we started the walkabout. As the survey progressed, the surveyor upped the pace considerably, until we came to the compressor and generator cell in which two large items of plant were located. The 3.3KVA generator had a vertical exhaust that vented through the roof, with the exhaust pipe bound with some loose fibrous material that was designed to prevent accidental contact when extremely hot. Having dealt with licensed asbestos companies, the lagging looked like Chrysotile, which at the time was in common use. It was very restricted inside the cell so that it was not even possible for two people, to pass each other without a squeeze due to the position of the exhaust pipe. However, such was the surveyor's rush he brushed against the lagging, leaving the right sleeve of his suit covered in the dust.

I spoke loudly, telling the surveyor to stop as he still hadn't noticed his sleeve and surprisingly neither had the manager. He stopped and asked what was the problem to which I replied, "You are, if you go out into the service bay like that."

I suggested that he should look at his jacket sleeve before taking another step. Turning to look, he did what I imagined he would attempt to do and I said, "Don't even think about brushing that off inside here. Given the estimated age of the generator and the lagging, I would hazard a guess at Chrysotile. If you want to contaminate the area then go right ahead, but let us all get out first."

With him now frozen, I suggested that he make his way to the washroom and wash the material off. The manager gestured the way and about five minutes later they returned with the surveyor having a wet sleeve.

Not wishing to make matters worse I simply recommended that, given my guess that the material was Chrysotile, the insured should get licensed contractors in to either reseal the material on the exhaust or have it stripped off and replaced with a suitable substitute, of with there were now a number available. Either way, the manager would need to contact the HSE with their suspicions, but what I strongly advised them against was attempting to seal the material themselves or remove it, as the HSE were vigorously clamping down on breaches of the regulations. In the final analysis, I found it difficult to believe that neither the insured nor the surveyor realised what was around the exhaust and its condition.

Yet another unsavoury brokering incident started very simply, with one of our top underwriters asking a favour of me: that I should support one of his London Market brokers on a quest to win, against the opposition, one of the top financial houses in the UK. This potential client, having worldwide connections and business interests in all manner of industries, was looking for a brokerage that could provide risk management on a global scale and, where and when required, provide guidance on the ground. It sounded like some risks we already catered for, so I thought little of the request not knowing the upheaval it would lead to. The problem arose due to bad timing with the underwriter never for one moment imagining the implications of batting for a very supportive brokerage against another or others.

Not bothering to prepare as I had worked with the brokerage on previous occasions, I imagined it would be very much a run of the mill presentation if my input was required. Following on from making myself available the broker suggested that I would only be in attendance if he needed additional support when and if the meeting involved issues concerning risk management, as he had previously informed them of our company's levels of expertise. Entering the prestigious premises of the targeted business, situated off the Strand in London, we were shown to an outer office, adjacent a lavishly furnished foyer, where we were each provided with a brochure about the business and the extent of their undertakings. They truly were involved with everything from mining, to forestry, to armed services support throughout the UK and overseas postings. It was an expansive task but like any of our insured, they could be risk managed so it was not as daunting a task as it first appeared.

We were summoned, exactly to the minute, to the main conference room where following introductions the business was clearly set on searching for a broker or insurer who could help them with risk management for any of their undertakings wherever they were. I suspected they were like some US-based organisations who specialised in providing risk management guidance, which we had already had dealings with. With the client almost ignoring the broker I was requested to briefly summarise how we were organised, our international capabilities and availability, our experience and not least of all how confident were we to deliver a creditable service. It was all very straightforward and, following a short, off the cuff account of the loss control people we had in our team, who included those with experience with armed services, some with security clearance, it was clear we were what they were seeking, particularly given that I was spending at least a third of my time overseas.

We left the offices, with the broker suggesting that they were very sure that they would be getting the business and that in turn, we would be providing the risk management. As we emerged from the lift into the foyer there was a small assembly of people sitting there who I immediately recognised as another leading London Market brokerage, including their CEO. Members of the team obviously recognised the competition but when the CEO identified me his rage became apparent. Needless to say, a serious complaint reached our chairman about

Independent apparently giving the opposition favourable treatment by using me in their business presentation.

It was never a case of being innocent until proven guilty, more a case if you upset a broker you were guilty, end of discussion. Consequently, I was subjected to some serious abuses from the very top of our company, at least until I pointed out that it was one our own directors, in collusion with the brokerage, who had decided that I attend the business meeting. Had I refused, I asked, what would have been the ramifications? Further, feeling unjustly criticised I tried to cite the number of times I had been used in such a way but, as usual, with the CEO wasn't listening. I eventually explained that the very broker who had filed the complaint had asked that I was in their general manager's office to support them when they themselves were in competition with other brokers just four weeks before, again at our underwriter's request. Not leaving it there, I suggested that the complainant should be reminded of those times, naming two of those companies. Fortunately, I never heard any more about the incident, as the first broker acquired the business, as did we, resulting in continual support to both brokerages. So there were both negatives and positives to broker relationships and the difficult world these businesses operate in.

Undoubtedly, every now and again, I encountered a broker's representative who liked to pontificate on matters that to a layperson sounded credible but to an informed individual were inconceivable. The information provided was delivered with such authority it sounded unquestionable, which was as far away from being accurate as possible. For the record, it was the same international brokerage whose surveyor was present at Container Terminals in Hong Kong. Perhaps the individual wished to be seen as an authority, but he was obviously unaware that anyone amongst the gathering who was informed would speak up. The broker's representative had been holding the floor and finally arrived at a question and answer session, before my own presentation, which up to that point in time had not covered loss control or risk management issues. The venue was in Iraq, where those present were safety representatives of a Defence Base Act insured, who were there to hear something on loss control. A simple question was put to the broker by a safety officer, requesting guidance on improvisation, employing unsuitable equipment in an effort to get the job done, citing lifting equipment as an example.

The broker, in response, had the temerity in front of me, to suggest that if having to lift a three-ton weight it was acceptable to employ a two-ton hoist if that was all they had available, adding occasionally. Initially, I was stuck for words as I couldn't believe what I was hearing. This individual was an account handler, clearly not an engineer, therefore, had no concept of what he was advocating, and consequentially all I could think of was that he was trying to impress those safety representatives present. Given that the range of workplace equipment that I imagined that could be misused was extensive, and that only slips, trips and falls have worse accident returns, being about thirty per cent compared to the one in five accidents related to lifting and handling.

Now uninvited I got to my feet, interrupting, and said that what the gathering had just heard was against the law, leading me to citing US law, followed by the UK and European Health and Safety statutes governing lifting and handling, which the US adopted. Being more precise in so far as all lifting equipment must be visibly marked with any appropriate information, to be taken into account for its safe use, such as the safe working load. In addition, I stressed, it must be accompanied by the appropriate test certificate for the lifting equipment, which states the weight limit. It was, I insisted a statutory requirement one designed and introduced to guide workers from using the wrong equipment 'occasionally'. Needless to say, there was a momentary hush and, to save losing face the broker suggested once would surely be acceptable? With all credit to the broker for not completely backing down, I then challenged him to know just how many times before had the safe working load been exceeded adding once, twice or perhaps five? The broker had now lost all credibility as there was no answer; he was incorrect for even thinking such a thing. I hadn't finished, so I added how would it be if I had sat there and said nothing and something went awry and a load did collapse, perhaps killing or maiming a worker?

There was now complete and utter silence so as this was a serious matter I put the question again, adding this time, what if the situation were to become a working practice, how many other times would it be OK to exceed the load? What about keeping a log or perhaps then taking the equipment out of service until it was tested by a competent person once again, not overlooking the need for that competent person to be a qualified lift engineer? Not waiting for a response, I asked those present to dwell on the following scenario: imagine attempting to lift the turret off the hull of an M1 Abrams, after the ordnance has been removed, and the turret ring snags on perhaps the ring gear. This, I added, was not fantasy and indeed not uncommon resulting in two of those present adding their support saying once some mechanics forgot to remove one of the gear covers. Continuing, I said the strain on this already overloaded equipment and lifting gear would then not just be twenty-two tons but given the weight of the forty-tons hull who could even begin to guess what the strain would be or for that matter the effects. What is sure is that it could result possibly in the load collapsing and even worse an employee suffering severe crushing injuries, as well as damaged equipment and a vital armoured vehicle being further delayed in returning to the field.

Would you, I asked them, feel secure facing an enquiry with the defence being that the broker said it was OK? How about overloading an electrical circuit, just the once, by replacing 12-amperage fuses with 20-amperage fuse because the system kept blowing? At that point, I had made a statement that left all those present in no doubt that misuse of equipment is unsafe. Nothing more was said, even following my presentation. The account handlers and the other broker's presentation party, out of New York, moved onto Qatar, where I refused to attend. It still remains the worst piece of advice I have ever heard where safety is concerned involving an insured and the assigned broker representative.

Just maybe I am being a little severe where some brokerage participation is concerned, but by and large, I found that most of the failings were down to the incompetence of some of their field staff, who were simply not up to the task. If their client was a corporate business paying a hefty premium, and therefore commission, a more senior broker was assigned regardless of whether or not that person had the necessary levels of field experience, or more importantly the knowledge of the trade or occupancy of their client. On occasions, in discussions with one of a number of insured one was hypercritical of the brokerage claiming that the only time he ever got to see his broker was when he arrived at his office smiling, once a year, to collect his premium.

At least one client suggested that the insured should deal with us directly as they had no faith in the broker acting in their best interest. This changed as a result of their accounts department complaining that their broker was difficult to deal with: not returning calls, requests going unanswered and the phone lines answered with a recorded message, and we all know just how frustrating that can be. However, ultimately matters came to a head when, during a board meeting concerning finances, the managing director suggested that the renewal premium was very high given the market. Returning to us, the insurer's accountant was directed by the managing director that we deal with them directly, which of course was against company policy. Consequently, the managing director pursued the matter, asking one of our principals for a fresh quotation, given their no claims record. It has to be mentioned that the MD in question was a high net worth client, having all his personal insurances with us. A new quote was submitted, through the broker, that was almost half of the renewal sum previously quoted. Consequently, the insured, now exasperated, changed brokers but we retained the business. Speaking with the insured during a subsequent HNW survey he remarked that it wasn't his job to obtain favourable quotes, but that of his broker, and he concluded that they, were only interested in the size of their commission.

Misinformation is a bugbear, but there have to be acceptable limitations and on one occasion, receiving incomplete and unconfirmed accounts meant that I entered a war zone for only the second time when visiting Iraq during the hostilities there. Initially, the survey was going to be limited to Kuwait, however, when surveying, the limits can be exceeded in the interests of the work requirements. In this case, the broker simply quoted from some accident returns from the insured, which made horrific reading, just like Swan Hunter, where we discovered incidents were either blown out of all proportion or simply we learned nothing and achieved even less. A transportation contractor insured by us under the DBA (Defence Base Act) submitted reports listing five incidents: three fatalities and two serious accidents involving the contractor's drivers. To cut to the chase, I ended up on the Kuwait/Iraq border, surveying what appeared to be reports of a substandard risk. The inference was that local civilian drivers, under warlike conditions, being untrained to deal with military requirements, plus not being able to cope with extreme working conditions.

The contractor's base in Kuwait operated out of two large vehicle compounds and a major warehouse that contained military provisions that were being transported daily up to Basra in military controlled convoys. I was to learn that the drivers of these transports were from the Middle East, the Indian subcontinent and Africa, so my initial feelings were that there might possibly be poor communications and this would be particularly pertinent when the officer in command expected immediate compliance with any instructions. In addition, driving standards in those regions are considered poor when compared to many parts of the world. Armed with the accident statistics and my own feelings I never expected to learn so much as there was firstly an obvious lack of guidance and preparations on the part of the hauliers' management. Firstly, I needed to understand the conditions and failings regarding each of the five accidents so I sat down with the management team to discuss each as they saw things. Clearly, there had been meetings regarding the three fatal incidents, as the manager's accounts and views were very much consistent with the information the underwriters provided me with.

The first involved the worker's bus, which was in a collision with a truck in Kuwait City, a common or garden motor accident where a truck ran into the bus and the driver of the truck was pronounced dead at the scene. The truck was adjudged to have been in the wrong, allegedly running a red light, so the insured's driver was exonerated by the police and for the record walked away unscathed; consequently, the first fatality didn't involve our insured and was not a loss situation. The second incident involved a transport driven by an African driver struck and killed a soldier in an Iraqi US army vehicular compound, resulting in the driver's arrest and charges being brought. The driver was alleged to have been reversing and was unaware there were pedestrians about him even though he should have been assisted by a marshal while manoeuvring. Exactly how we, as insurers, were involved was beyond me, save that it did suggest a level of incompetence and indiscipline existing amongst those employed, as my report suggested.

The next incident was far more interesting and again suggested more than a hint of indiscipline was the root cause when a convoy heading south back to Kuwait ran into a sandstorm. The sandstorm was such that the visibility was almost non-existent so the convoy was ordered off the highway, as the route was an extremely busy one for troop and armour movements. It was a standard military practice that certain routes used to be kept clear at all times and in fact there were occasions where the convoy commander received forewarning that a military convoy was on route and that the transports must remove themselves until they received the all-clear when the military had passed them by. Sandstorms are common in the desert and can turn up unexpectedly and I was somewhat surprised to hear that it was almost a case of reckless disregard of care when one truck driver decided not to tailgate the vehicle in front, as required, but take an independent route off the highway. At *panic speed*, as described to me, the truck, all forty-tons of it, ran into another vehicle that was already parked, with the impact being so severe the driver suffered fatal injuries. The review suggested that the driver was inexperienced and had possibly never experienced driving in a sandstorm before, which led me to question the level of training and competence involved. I reviewed the driver-training manual and found that it fell well short of that required. The driver's surviving family would have been compensated irrespective of the driver possibly being the victim of his own actions.

The last and most interesting incident involved a catastrophic set of circumstances when a convoy heading north towards Basra allegedly came under hostile fire from an unidentified enemy position, resulting in a truck, approximately positioned in the centre of the convoy, bursting into flames. The military could have been excused, as it is a customary military tactic to target the centre of the convoy so as to bring at the very least half the column to a halt. Consequently, the experienced military commander was convinced that they were under attack and required the vehicle next in the convoy to drive around the damaged vehicle in an attempt to keep the column moving. However, by the time the commander reached the stricken vehicle the driver of the following truck had stopped and jumped out of this cab with the good intention of rendering assistance. The military commander, believing the convoy was in a perilous situation and keeping with his orders, wanted the column to continue moving, ordering the driver at gunpoint to remount and keep his truck moving.

Moving back to his truck this driver was struck by another vehicle, sustaining serious injuries. Consequently, two trucks were now technically disabled but the convoy got underway without further hostilities. These accounts were presented to me in report form, the preparation overseen by the broker which were in my possession when viewing the two recovered vehicles. In addition, the insured's manager provided me with other pertinent details in response to my questions once I had viewed the stricken vehicles. What I was about to be made aware of was that following the incident, still remaining at the roadside they were inspected by the military police, whereupon they made a startling discovery. The vehicle that was thought to have been hit by a weapon system had in fact not come under fire at all because the explosion and fire started and finished in the cab of the vehicle. There was evidence to show that the driver had been cooking rice on a portable, petroleum fired cooker that had probably overturned and the fuel exploded, killing the driver and giving all the appearance of the truck being struck by a weapon system. The military reaction was severe, with each and every truck from then on being inspected by the column military commander before setting off, with contraband, such as cooking and food preparation items, confiscated. While the incident resulted in minimum settlements and serious lessons learnt there had been prior to and since no broker loss control involvement which was typical as the insured suggested. Just for the record, we made four risk recommendations involving tightening up on recruitment, driver assessment, compound speed limits and review of the driving manual being translated in different languages the latter two never considered previously.

While the work involving DBA overseas wasn't without difficulties, I walked into one unscrupulous UK broker who was willing to go to almost any length to get a recently acquired piece of business placed. During my short time as a consultant, I encountered two brokers who illustrated the very good and the excessively bad side of the brokerage business. I was called by a provincial brokerage, who specifically sought out my services as he flattered me by singing my praises and reputation in the industry. His approach was a little wasted on me for I suspected that it was more than likely they intended to use my reputation to promote a client of theirs to the market with a glowing report. I have to confess it never came into my thinking that, to date, their initial approaches to potential insurers had proved fruitless as after all, they were a reputable brokerage. The case in point was a large crankshaft, connecting rods and axle beams producer where these internal combustion engine components were for commercial use; probably marine engines and electrical generators. Briefly, this business had changed ownership during the 1980s, 1990s and again in 2001, and was now with foreign ownership, therefore, having bases in the UK and other European countries, with Italian directors.

The processes were considered 'heavy' and high risk due to drop forging, machining, heat treatment and mechanical handling of components weighing over 350kgs. All these undertakings were at premises that were well suited to the processes and had been in use a decade or more before WW2; in fact, the site activities dated back to the previous century. Reviewing such a risk for a brokerage didn't pose any problems; in fact, unlike surveying for an underwriter they could completely dispose of the report or release part or all of it within reason. One thing for sure was that the task in hand had to be conducted professionally, treating the broker as a would-be client in every respect. The broker made all the arrangement and as always I arrived slightly ahead of the scheduled time, at the security lodge. The security man directed me to the nearby parking lot and getting out of the car I couldn't help but notice the white, chalky substance on the surfaces about. I guessed that it came from the processes of the business so I thought no more of it. The security man informed me that the factory manager would collect me in a short while but right now he was tied up in an unscheduled meeting.

Now idly sitting in the security lodge, my curiosity got the better of me and I asked where the white powdery stuff had come from as I had never seen such material ever being used in a forging business before, certainly not during my Ford days. Security advised me that it wasn't chalk and it came from the old warehouse, which had very recently been demolished, making way for additional parking. Still way wide of the mark I pursued the matter further by asking if the dust had been redundant stock or what was stored within? The answer was a positive 'no' but the remains of the corrugated asbestos cement sheeting that clad the building; elevations and pitched roof. I said that the licensed demolition contractors should have watered down the residue and swept the site clean as in dry windy weather conditions this could end up everywhere inside and outside the factory.

"What contractors? I did it!" the security man said, who went on to explain that one morning one of the new Italian directors arrived on site but was unable to find a place to park his car as they were short on parking spaces and those available were allocated.

Later that same day the director apparently established that the old warehouse building had been empty for some time and as there were no plans to make use of it he suggested they demolish it. Seeing it as a priority the director asked the security man if he knew of a demolition contractor, with an available mobile plant, who could get the job done over the following weekend? A little while later the same director asked the security man, if he were to hire a JCB, could he operate it over the coming weekend, on overtime, and demolish the building? Claiming to be capable of driving the plant, a JCB was subsequently hired and on the following weekend, the portal frame building was demolished by the security man. Proudly, the director even claimed that the sale of the scrap metal paid for the plant hire and the employee's overtime. However, their biggest problem was yet to come and that was the disposal of the broken sheets of asbestos cement. There was a considerable heap that was unsightly and still taking up space as the scrap metal merchant who collected the steel had refused to get involved, I would guess wisely. They were obviously aware of the strict asbestos licensing regulations and the fact that it can only be disposed of in or at a registered tip after being appropriately bagged and transported.

When the manager arrived, I informed him what my task entailed and that I needed some background details concerning safety organisation, accident history, training, safety audits, numbers employed, skilled and other workers, supervisory levels, and so on. He suggested that I should venture out alone and tour the site and he would, in the meantime, have those figures and details ready for me when I got back. The first area was the forge where almost white-hot ingots were taken mechanically from the furnace and placed into the die in the drop-forge. The heat was obviously intense even at 15 to 20 metres which prompted me to ask the loader operating the mobile plant where his protective clothing was and particularly his lack of noise defenders. Also, where had the guarding about the forge got to? He looked puzzled, suggesting that this was the way it had been since he first came to the company years before and he had apparel but it was uncomfortable to use. Consequently, the negatives were already mounting up and I had barely arrived.

Entering the machine shop, you had to be impressed with the number of machines, ranging from milling machines to lathes, drills to grinders. The operators were all mature males but safety apparel was apparently not on the agenda. I approached the horizontal milling section as these were the most hazardous of the machines installed. Noticing again a lack of guarding I spoke with the nearest machinist, asking about the guards on the two machines he was operating that were either missing or inappropriately adjusted. Informing the operator of the dangers he laughed and raised his right hand and said, "You mean something like this may happen?" The three middle fingers were missing to the second knuckle on his left hand. Now lost for words with this worker who simply had not learned the lesson, I asked him where his supervisor could usually be found.

The operator pointed me towards some offices, deliberately using his almost fingerless hand, where I found the supervisor on the phone.

I introduced myself and he surprisingly said, "I know who you are and what you want." I told him what I had seen thus far and he said that he was not responsible for the drop-forge but the machine shop. "Without wishing to spoil your day, the guy with the missing fingers seems not to have learnt his lesson so why hasn't he been disciplined?"

"I don't wish to be presumptuous but have you ever worked in industry?"

"Look, I am not wishing to debate the issue but surely to date, your man has been lucky but what about the next time? It could be what is left of his hand," I added.

"You avoided my question," the supervisor replied.

"Well, I cannot see your reasoning but for the record, I served an indentured precision fitting apprenticeship. I spent a few years on the tools in Ford on toolmaking and as a supervisor."

"OK, so you know what it is like: if you don't get management backing it's impossible to instil any discipline." That was the end of the conversation.

Leaving the supervisor, I returned to the manager. Briefing him on what I had seen with his response being, "I thought as much but I do my best and that is all I can do given the lack of leadership from the top." I made my excuses and returned to London. Over the next two days, I compiled my report, which made for depressing reading, but I was paid to do a job of work and like it or not, unsavoury as it was, my account was a true reflection of the risk as I saw it. I emailed it off with my account. Almost by return, I had an irate broker on the phone questioning my judgement and the conclusion regarding the risk bordering on the unacceptable, as the existing management team had almost given up as a result of the director's cavalier approach. The broker threatened me with all types of retribution and even suggested that he would make the risk sound better with a few omissions and appropriate changes to my report.

Obviously, this was a case where the risk had either been one where, due to their loss history, renewal terms had not been forthcoming alternatively due to the claims history the market was simply shying away from it? Either way, the broker was attempting to have me make it into an acceptable, or at least an average, risk. I warned the broker that I had retained a computer copy of the report I emailed them, and if it came to a dispute involving my professional indemnity cover, I would release the whole report to my insurer. A stony silence followed and then the broker, in a more conciliatory manner, requested if I could remove certain parts as it was based on hearsay. I had to explain that the report, except for what I witnessed, was based on testimony, such as the supervisor's, manager's and security man's accounts and opinions.

Nonetheless how on earth are you ever going to get over the fact of a pending prosecution because an insurer would require the details of that and the loss history?

"You would leave yourself open to a claim of non-disclosure if any of these facts got out," I added.

"I have no wish to question your experience or integrity further but you do realise that the businesses manager is holding an HSE letter and that they are being prosecuted and if there is a warrant out for the fleeing director you would be best advised to step away from the risk as there could be other claims pending and that they did not reveal even to me?" That was the end of our discussion and I received my fee about one month later, a conclusion being that insurance broking is not for the faint-hearted.

A great success story where brokerages were involved was following Independent acquiring the insurances of BH&HPA (British Holiday & Home Parks Association), a national organisation for home parks where holidaymakers and tourist can either park up their mobile home, camp pitching a tent or simply hire a static caravan. There were additional facilities on some of the bigger sites that included swimming pools, boating on a river or lake, restaurants, bars and clubs plus children's entertainment. Most of the parks were located near water such as a river, lake or at the seaside. My involvement began after visiting a few parks and getting a feel for the activities and then being asked to look over the BHHPA's safety manual, which provided park owners with guidance on a whole range of issues including health and safety. This document was apparently drawn up by the brokers and listed needs such as fire extinguishers, first aid and keeping an incident cum accident book. Personally, where I found the manual informative it smacked of 'legalese' and needed to be more user-friendly. So I set about rewriting the multipage document, as if I was a park owner seeking practical guidance listing in order of priority what my business required to avoid losses, much to the delight of the brokers and the tourist boards of the UK and the Association.

Feeling very much at home, after surveying a large number of parks and meeting up with many park owners, I was invited to speak at their annual conference in Blackpool. Having spoken to groups on many occasions over the years, I have to confess I was a nervous wreck on this occasion as I was expecting the small usual gathering of 30 or 40, but instead, some 1,400 were present, with there being so many wishing to attend that there were insufficient seats available. To make matters worse, amongst those attending were both the parliamentary government minister and shadow minister for tourism. I was there to introduce the manual as the author and surprisingly my nervousness disappeared when the shadow minister questioned my opinion regarding liabilities where there were unsafe conditions due to frost, ice, snow and wet fallen leaves, as some parks were open all year round. The shadow minister had got to his feet and facing the audience, as if addressing the house, took issue, claiming that I had not covered the subject adequately at all.

Somewhat taken aback, what could I do but reply saying, "If I had overlooked the point then I do apologise."

Suddenly, a lady close to the front of the assembly got to her feet and said, "But you did cover the point very well under reasonable care." Then another also added that he understood and that he felt the matter had been adequately covered, followed by another and another until there seemed to be a host clapping. At that point, the shadow minister retook his seat. I never felt so pleased that I not only got the support of the floor but also they were I concluded dealing with a dedicated insurer. Later, at our stand in the adjacent hall, I was quizzed by a host of owners asking for Independent's intention to visit their parks, in answer to which I could only suggest that they speak with the chairman who would liaise through the brokers.

Following the work, we did after large flooding losses running into GBP millions, I visited the principal caravan manufacturers in the UK and learned that continental caravans are constructed with waterproofed chipboard whereas for the UK these are built with bulk standard chipboard. The latter absorbs water and swells, leaving no strength, while the continental specification resists water for several days before it breaks down the structure, with the difference in cost being a miserly additional GBP 400 for a GPB 30,000 caravan. This surprised many park owners, and further enhanced our standing as an insurer. With our rating being so high I was invited to the insured's head offices, where the broker was discussing renewal terms. It was during a quiet moment that the broker's representative approached me requesting that I put a good word in for them as the insured every year, as part of their internal policies, seek out alternatives regarding all their business partners. Fearing the brokerage would lose their biggest client I spoke in an off the cuff manner to the company secretary about how highly we thought of the brokers. The secretary, smiling, said, "They shouldn't worry, we do this every year and they will be with us for years to come as I hope you and Independent will be."

Very briefly my experiences with brokerages were mixed ranging from pleasure to disappointment not so much from the interpersonal viewpoint but largely due to some of their number failing to have the courage to inform their clients where they were found wanting. Almost akin to them doing all they can to avoid antagonising their clients regardless of the implications. That simple lesson I leant from an astute CEO of chicken processors previously mentioned, and I quote, "I don't want to know what we are doing right, I want to know what we are doing wrong." Priceless!

The Unexpected – Be Prepared

I never imagined what was in store for us as insurers once Independent began venturing overseas and yet in those ten years, while my role never changed, my attitude and approach had to. It is true that I continued conducting surveys and reported back to my customers, the underwriters, regarding what the insured did and from a loss control point of view how they managed their undertakings. Surveying a small-medium engineering risk in Derbyshire was one thing, whereas surveying an open cast mine in the Borneo jungle or an off-shore pipe-laying interest in the Indian Ocean was another matter. My surveys could cover everything from a bakery in Belfast to rock boring 100 metres below the ground in New Zealand, cutting a new tunnelling system for a passenger rail service in Bangkok, or a small cement quarry in Kent, a building site in London or gold mining in the USSR. That is not to overlook those non-UK active military bases in the likes of Iraq, or dam construction in central Africa, maybe oil fields in remote areas of the Argentinian pampas, that, while all being poles apart and out of the ordinary, nonetheless required surveying, constructive reporting and opinion.

The problem is where to start given the variety of those risks, yet still making allowances for culture, overcoming language and literacy obstacles and beginning to get some idea about putting the value of life in perspective, which were concerns that were particularly pertinent in some third world countries. There are allowances of course but where the problems increase is where these insured import cheap labour which in many instances went hand in glove with the levels of risk management. The building of a fossil fuel power station in Chennai was different to the one I surveyed in Rayong, Thailand, where employees and public safety standards were concerned; however, when a tower crane collapses it doesn't matter whether it is Sharjah or Singapore; the material loss results in terms of claims for a similar amount. These issues pose problems during the surveys when trying to persuade an insured to protect the workforce with the same level of care as his mobile plant. The employer has a queue of people outside the proverbial 'gate' just waiting for employment whereas the availability and value of the insured's dumper trucks or those tower cranes in Dubai come at a heavy premium.

In first world countries, we can bring pressure to bear on haphazard businesses by them being made aware of their statutory duties, enforcing authorities and exactly how much clout they have. I mention the enforcing authorities because when it comes to applying the country's statutory requirements, the level will be greatly dictated by who the employer is and their level of investment. Alternatively, in third world countries, your opinion could be met with a shrug or more often or not a plea of the insured simply not understanding. The best example that comes to mind was the building of BTS (Skytrain) in Bangkok where, along the entire unprotected edge of the elevated road, there were posted signs 'Safety First' while immediately next to the unguarded edge, some sixty feet above the road below, were several workers without fall arrestors even though there have already been three fatal falls. While being critical of lax safety, while the Burj Dubai was being constructed several workers fell over 100 feet to their deaths. Against this type of apathy, it was a tough ask to get the insured to respond positively and maintain their standards over a protracted period.

Of course, there is a saying that *risk is a risk*; however, just for a moment, throw into the mix additional factors such as climate, environment, location, other unusual hazards such as those that existed in the likes of Afghanistan, Chechnya, Iraq, Yemen, Libya, Bangladesh, Pakistan, Ethiopia and Somalia etc. In many cases, your presence as an insurance surveyor is unwelcome even though we are the business connection providing essential insurance coverage. The climate coupled with the environment can play a major part in a surveyor's thinking; for instance, while in Kuwait, I was conducting a survey with a temperature above 46°C. Here, the labour law was being broken, but the employers took no account of the unbearable temperature, save the wood mill operations where the insured simply sprayed water onto the cut timber and wood dust to prevent fire but offered the labour no such luxury. While on another Middle Eastern site, in Oman, some construction employees collapsed due to the heat. They were carted off to the sickbay, cooled off with a water spray, hydrated and then sent back out into the heat. In fact, it was so hot that on the same site where workers were drilling the rock to lay explosive charges, the laying of the charges was suspended for fear of a premature explosion.

On this occasion, I was accompanied by a broker's surveyor from India who, in his enthusiasm, wished to view the rock boring taking place on a hillside 20 metres away from the nearest access point from our vehicle on a track. I warned him about venturing out of the vehicle due to the heat but he clearly didn't appreciate my concern. Within ten minutes he staggered back to the vehicle, wet from head to toe, as if he had been in a shower. He was clearly distressed, so we had him remove his tie and loosen his collar before he collapsed back into his seat. When he recovered he stated the obvious concern by remarking that if he was affected just walking and watching, what about those workers involved in manual labour? He began to see the problems more clearly following that visit.

Another problem that I encountered involved civil unrest where high levels of security were being provided by the armed services of that country. At a location on the Indian subcontinent, the insured lived with it day in day out; however, my presence and my movements allegedly made the insured's task even more difficult simply because of the fear for my safety and his own by virtue of accompanying me. Security was provided at the location, which was a key point installation, being one of the country's main sources of income, where gas from off-shore wells was being piped in, refined, stored and distributed. Normal activities were being conducted acceptably; however, the armed militia was in the area with high-velocity firearms backed up with two armoured cars, mounted with 70mm main armament and secondary armament. I quickly established, even though the military commander was very guarded in his responses, that that there were no real terms of engagement, thus putting the gas tanks, premises and the surrounding areas at risk should there be either a stray high-velocity round or random small arms fire. Once again when the risk was written the underwriter had not been informed about the army providing the site security as the provided information only detailed the high-security fence, floodlighting and manned security.

Nonetheless, there was so much diversity to surveying that it followed there had to be some pleasant, albeit somewhat bizarre situations that I found myself in, such as the products liability survey undertaken in the People's Republic of China. The business was Taiwanese, engaged in the production of baby and junior products, which were therefore considered high risk, and insured through the London Market. These products ranged from strollers to carrycots to baby feeding bottles where all were for exports to the US, Europe and Japan, but designed and developed in Taiwan. They were at that time a brand leader producing, as far as baby strollers were concerned, over 55%, of the world's market. Following the survey of the research and development establishments in Taiwan, surveys were required of the manufacturing plants based in Shanghai, Guangzhou and Shenzhen. Due to perceived language difficulties, I was accompanied by two English speaking Taiwanese brokers for the entire survey, which took about five days to complete in the PRC. Once in Guangzhou, we met up with senior quality and production staff who were briefed on the intended programme to commence at 9 a.m. the next morning. Making a point of never being late, I suggested to the brokers that we should meet in the designated meeting room at 8:45 a.m. sharp so as to ensure we at least were setting off on the right foot. I had never worked in mainland China before but by and large, I had already learned that punctuality was not on most Asian countries' lists of priorities.

The next morning at 08:45 a.m. we found that the pre-arranged meeting room had been set up with fourteen nameplates, all in Chinese, that I was to learn held the person's name and designation. Obviously all this meant nothing to me so I never really got to understand who was responding to my questions. Regardless, the room quickly filled and all were seated by 08:55 save for an empty place at the head of the long table, adjacent me. As if designed to impress, the entire assembly were clad in very smart grey overalls and as I recall the same colour and type of male/female footwear. All of it was very impressive which made me change my opinion of Chinese punctuality at least.

Now the position at the head of the table remained vacant which was to me insignificant for two reasons: firstly, everyone was so prompt and secondly there was unlike every other position, no nameplate for that seat at the table. As I like to lead, I proposed, through the brokers, that we could proceed given that we had a long day ahead of us. My translator, Ms. Wo, put the proposal to those present and without having the necessary language skills the responses were unanimous and an unequivocal, *Bo*. I can safely say that was almost the first word I ever learned in Mandarin.

With that reaction, my first thought then took in the empty chair and I assumed that a very senior staff member was due, probably running a bit late and was going to make an 'entrance'. I was wrong on both counts as it turned out because precisely at 09:00 a.m. the door swung open and a young lady entered the room; medium height, and immaculately dressed in a dark green two-piece woollen suit; over knee-length skirt with the jacket buttoned up to a Mandarin collar. The arrival of this person prompted all present to stand, that is save the two brokers and me, as if caught a little by surprise, due to the reaction of the remainder present in that meeting room. Without the slightest hint of any acknowledgement or introduction the lady sat at the head of the table, stone-faced, simply bowed her head, so as giving her approval for the meeting to start.

As was usual, Ms. Wo would make the introduction: who I was, where I came from, the purpose of products insurance and what exactly we hoped would be achieved. During this five or so minutes I was looking for reactions which involved smiles, nodding heads and so on save the lady at the head of the table who sat stone-faced and silent without so much as a blink. Handing over to me, I explained what I needed in terms of information, knowledge of supervisory levels, quality accreditation and so on, all adequately I assumed translated by Sharon Wo. The problem faced was that even what I considered a simple question took an age when translated. In fact, some of the responses were so time-consuming I was continually making sure I remembered what I had asked in the first place and the reason why. Unsurprisingly, the meeting was taking much longer than I anticipated but nonetheless I was getting good feedback and felt that positive headway was being made.

After an hour or so, the lady at the head of the table had offered nothing but continued sitting motionless and impassive throughout the entire period. This lack of involvement had me wondering why at all she was present. Finally, when at long last I mentally noted that everyone present had offered something in response to my questions, I turned my attention to the lady seated at the head of the table. Speaking through Sharon, all the while observing the lady, I felt certain she knew exactly what I was saying. Over the years you soon learn when interviewing whether or not that person understands or is interested, so I decided to challenge her.

My question was more of a statement which was simply put, "Please excuse me but you are understanding every single word I say, do you not?" To which she responded in a superior manner and perfect English, "Mr McCreadie, every single word." Admittedly I was taken aback but not being one to come second in a debate and being as diplomatic as I could, I suggested to her that while everyone else present appeared to have contributed, why not her? Or did her role entail working on a different agenda? She then spoke directly to me, again in perfect English, explaining that just as I had a job to do so did she, adding that her role was in many respects similar to mine, insofar as she firstly had to ensure that both my questions and staff responses were being correctly translated by Sharon. Second, she had to make sure that the answers to those questions were correct, again insofar as they were a true reflection of the company's efforts and they would not in any way shape or form damage the reputation of the People's Republic of China. I had heard of the USSR's strict political approach but I was a little stunned experiencing the same thing first-hand in China involving strictly speaking Taiwanese products.

Her appearance and aloofness were clearly no act; in fact, during lunch, she sat next to me again whereupon I complimented her on her English. Her responses were again not so surprising with her actual reply going along the lines of, "I know, I have a Masters from Beijing University and attended language courses in the United Kingdom."

Purely out of curiosity I enquired exactly how long she had worked for the insured and true to form I got it all wrong yet again. "I do not work for your insured," she responded. "I am employed by the People's Republic of China, the lady mentioned the department or bureau but it slipped my memory. We have an unjust reputation regarding the quality of our manufactured goods; therefore, the PRC wants people such as you to see first-hand that we are a nation that promotes quality."

Taking a chance with this government employee I said, "I have never met a commissar before which I have to say has made this trip worthwhile." She laughed for the first time and asked me for my opinion which, for the record, read: *The insured rated extremely high as the workforce was totally dedicated to producing products to their ISO accreditation, and all in a positive spirit.* Understanding the way of the Chinese was difficult at the outset but I did learn that their manufacturing philosophy was one of identifying defective products as early as possible and the need to encourage as opposed adopting a culture of blame.

This quality control approach of identifying defective products very early on in the manufacturing process was identified in another manufacturer that regardless failed to avoid seven separate claims for injuries allegedly due to defective products. The Taiwanese insured at the outset I identified as an above average risk, this following my survey there some eighteen months before. The risk surprisingly during that period of insurance, based solely on claims experience, had rapidly deteriorated to one rating almost uninsurable, in fact, our underwriters were refusing to offer renewal terms. Apparently with all seven of the claims being so quickly settled in the US it initially left me doubting the integrity of those involved excluding the insured and the insurer. In fact, initially because I had conducted a products liability survey of the business, I began to question my own ability to differentiate between a substandard risk and one above average because I had placed the insured's products in one of the highest of categories. Now following my involvement where the precise circumstances and chain of events were established, I believe there was a conspiracy and not as it first appeared a catalogue of incompetence.

So now in Taipei yet again, undertaking some surveys of other major manufacturers the broker's representative was very persuasive requesting that I should revisit the insured, a garden furniture manufacturer, as they were beside themselves as they just couldn't understand where and why after years of successful trading the design and quality of their products were now failing. After explaining that I could and should not become involved, as it was an underwriting decision, the badgering continued until I submitted with the proviso that the visit had to be off the record. The reason for the change of heart was that we had an excellent broker relationship; the client just wanted my opinion on the quality of the furniture in the face of the claims given that my previous assessment was so positive.

These claims came about due to faulty plastic garden chairs and one faulty garden hammock collapsing, all of which resulted in the users suffering injuries. This left the manufacturer extremely vulnerable to increased premiums once they secured terms elsewhere and this to what allegedly was a highly reputable designer and manufacturer. The business was housed in a heavily industrialised area, yet the premises stood out from the other units by way of being particularly smart: organised car park, neat flower beds, etc. The broker and I were met in the main reception by the owner, a smart middle-aged Chinese lady, who, in very presentable English, thanked me for coming yet again and assured me the visit was unofficial. My first impression was again how well laid out the factory was: the workforce was smartly dressed and productive; nothing had changed! Given other conditions, I began wondering why and where things had gone so wrong. Upon viewing the insured's range of garden chairs, I was once more taken aback by the quality of not only the chairs but also the other plastic items being produced. What really perplexed me was, in particular, the garden hammocks that incorporated a safety feature to avoid collapse. This entailed two spiral anchors that had to be unwound naturally and would have had to defy the laws of physics to result in a collapse as was the claim.

Perusing the quality manual, as the business was ISO accredited, meeting the quality manager and so on, it was difficult not to be impressed by the whole organisation. All the while in the back of my mind were the seven claims. My initial thoughts were that there must have been a faulty batch or that the chairs at the centre of the claims had possibly been misused, abused or that there had been some other reason for the failures. Added to this, how could the insured's dynamic and static loading tests have failed to identify these alleged defective chairs; not one but at least six? My conclusions were that just maybe the goods had been damaged during the journey from Taiwan to the US as perhaps the packing arrangements were substandard. However, the owner informed me that they already had checked with the carriers and that they had their US counterparts checking the consignments on arrival, after which they were unsure because it was the wholesalers who delivered to retail outlets.

Having looked at all possible avenues where damage could have been inflicted, I wanted to look at the product manufacturing process again, just in the event, I had overlooked something. As these were plastic injected products and the supplied plastic granules came from an accredited source I was fast running out of possible causes regarding the strength of the chairs. It couldn't be the design, because this had not changed in a decade and had not been suspect before this latest batch. In the final analysis, I looked at the testing, quickly concluding that there had to have been a defective batch. We reviewed the load testing and I suggested that while they were weight tested, they should consider fixing a label to the chairs indicating the maximum loading and that the chairs should be used on a firm, level surface particularly, as all of their products were bound for the US markets. I was, of course, envisaging overweight users dumping themselves into the chairs, where the static weight for the average US male was about 88 kilograms while dynamically as much as ninety-five kilograms or more. I added that, as a form of defence if the user was found to be over the recommended loading, it could prove decisive in the events of a claim.

To my astonishment when I requested a sighting of the defective products, I was informed that they had not been recovered, which had me now questioning why we had sanctioned claims settlement? The insured informed me that we had, following notification from the retailer's legal team that the claims were settled following a loss adjuster's report, again with us approving the appointment. I had to confess to the insured that my previous rating remained but what they should demand that the defective products are recovered. Once back in their possession I suggested they examine these items without prejudice and make necessary design changes, if warranted, to prevent a recurrence. The insured assured me they would recover the chairs and hammock and keep the broker informed bearing in mind I was not officially involved.

On my way back from Australia and New Zealand to the UK some three weeks later, I received a phone call from the Taiwanese broker requesting I contact the owner again as there had been some interesting developments. Speaking over the phone the owner informed me that they had received back from the US their alleged faulty chairs and in an attempt at humour added that they were not in fact manufactured by her company, in fact, the products were bearing the trademark of another Taiwanese company! Following a moment of silence, she thanked me and informed me that while protecting my involvement they were seeking legal advice as she felt that the claims reflected badly on her business. Feeling both sympathy and justification, due to the poor claims handling of the case, I requested that I be given the opportunity to try and put matters right at our end before they did anything, to which the owner agreed.

Once back in London, I immediately made my way to the underwriting room and sought out the individual who handled that account. The underwriter was a close colleague and friend so I was about to enjoy his moment of predictable panic then have the satisfaction of providing him with the solution. I informed him that I had visited the insured to which he responded by chastising me about the visit and that I shouldn't have got involved as the case was soon to be off the books. I suggested that he closes his office door as I had something rather important to tell him.

Simply put I said, "How do you feel about paying seven claims for faulty products that were never produced or marketed by the insured?" Now startled, the underwriter leapt up from his desk and in one movement had closed the door and resumed his seat. As if he hadn't heard properly, he asked me to repeat what I had just said. I put it as succinctly as I could. I explained that upon receiving back their 'defective' chairs they discovered that they were not in fact the manufacturer at all and that by virtue of us paying the claims the insured had lost credibility, which was impacting on their sales, since we were suggesting their chairs were of inferior design and manufacture.

As the instructions came from our claims people to appoint legal representatives in the US to settle these claims both they and the retailers, who allegedly identified the supplier, had been anything other than diligent, which had resulted in both ourselves paying out vast sums, and our insured's reputation being in shreds. That is putting it dramatically but by some retailers, it could just prove to be the case. I had already come up with the solution which would ensure the underwriter appeared in a favourable light and we could invite renewal to the satisfaction of our insured. My suggestion was that the underwriter, due to previous good loss control reports, suggested that while in Taiwan I should conduct a post-loss visit in the interest of maintaining good broker relationships and to investigate whether or not the quality standard in Taiwan was acceptable.

The upshot was that the US attorneys were left to deal with the fiasco that included the return of the claims paid, legal costs incurred and the manufacturer's losses, which did, as I was led to understand, include the consultants and the retailer who falsely identified the chairs and whose subsequent report mentioned the insured and the substandard quality. The pleasing part was that the insured and the brokers, the latter due to their efforts in looking after their client's interest, made good use of the publicity. Contrary to poor publicity and the likes of the aforementioned case, Chinese manufacturers were generally found on a par with those in Europe and Australia. So there ended another positive input from brokers that made life so easy for us in the Far East and Australia.

Just to show how diverse the surveyor's role can get, I could be looking at a plastic goods manufacturer in Taiwan one moment and the next surveying the Circus Proprietors of Great Britain. This is the best example of where facing the unexpected can be stretched to the limit. Here I had my most frightening experiences, where the circus owner and ringmaster kept a Kodiak bear, that he personally rescued from a wild animal refuge when the bear was less than a few months old. The insured was a circus fanatic, educated but having run away to join the circus as a teenager, was brought back twice, but after the second time, his parents promised to give him their support if he knuckled down and finished his education, which he did.

The insured found the bear kept in what were described as appalling conditions by the owner of an animal refuge, who incidentally could not get near to this very young cub for fear of injury. The insured explained that when he was looking for an animal, he was not thinking about a specific breed but nonetheless something of interest when he arrived at the animal refuge. The owner described the bear as a 'pet', to raise the sales asking price, all the while keeping the animal at a safe distance. The insured suggested that the bear cub was simply reacting to the cruelty shown by the refuge's manager, being left cooped up in a dirty cage and fed only on scraps and water. When our insured saw the animal, he was moved and immediately bought it, in effect rescuing the bear from a refuge.

Consequently, over the next few years, the bear was cleaned, well-fed and obviously as the proprietor only tended the bear's needs, they became close. Kodiak bears when fully grown, stand three metres tall and weigh in excess 600kgs and so represent a very large carnivorous animal with a dangerous reputation in their natural habitat of Alaska. During the survey, the proprietor took time to explain that the bear did not perform but he kept the animal in an extended show road cage when the circus was open. Fixed to the road cage was an enclosure that came with a safety rail set up between the cage and those wishing to view this ferocious animal. There were also safety and warning notices fixed to the cage warning the public not to stray beyond the barrier, to avoid feeding, and taking precautions to be found at any zoological garden.

Imagine my surprise when the proprietor went into the cage and whistled to attract the bear's attention. The viewing cage was empty as the bear was nestled down in a mountain of straw at the back of the road cage. At the sound of the whistle, the heap of straw moved and the bear emerged down the ramp on all fours to stop at the insured's feet. At the time of the visit, the circus was not open to the public, and consequently, there were only circus staff about plus the proprietor and me at the cage. The bear stopped inches short of Jay and reared up to its full height of approximately 2.75 metres. Jay was tall but the bear overshadowed him by something close to a metre. What happened next took some believing when Jay put a polo mint in his mouth and motioned the bear to take it which the bear gently did. 'See,' Jay said, 'no problem'. He followed this with an invitation for me to enter the cage and have a photo taken which I replied in no uncertain and unprintable terms that he must think me mad?

'Seriously' Jay said that the bear was not a problem and was in effect a bit of a pussycat! My response was an unequivocal 'No'! Adding 'Suppose your little pet there takes a dislike to me, perhaps even mistaking me from that cruel animal refuge manager you spoke of. What would you do about it and given your performance thus far just how many packets of polo mints do you have handy?' Laughing loudly Jay stroked the bear, handed over some more mints and left the cage, locking it behind him. I wrote in my report that it was unnecessary to re-survey this risk!

The other circuses proved to be more hazardous than they first appeared, as they were, by and large, bigger; as well as performing animals there was the size of the 'big top' that traditionally involved members of the public offering their labour to help erect and then strike the tent for the reward of free tickets to matinee performances. Our concern was of course where wild animals are involved and the danger they posed to members of the public if they were to escape or were accessible while on the show, not overlooking at that time the potential of the animal right activists to add disruption. By and large, the circuses usually approached the local council to erect the tent on common land; however, the tent would involve spikes and poles being driven into the ground, which in two cases damaged an electrical power line and a foul sewer, both resulting in claims. The risk of injury to the members of the public was our priority as the activities can only be described as 'heavy' and labour intensive, plus of course the risk of causing damage to public facilities.

The second event that was slightly, but only slightly, less frightening involved a survey of a zoological garden in the Far East, where one of the residents was a Bengal tiger. Once again, the insured invited me to move towards the tiger, which was sprawled out on a very large rock within the confines of an open cage. The tiger was chained and was lying passively, indifferent to either myself or the owner standing a few metres away idly chatting. However, I had already taken note of the distances between me and this feline and the amount of slack in the restraining chain about the animal's neck. Besides that, I was strategically keeping the insured's manager between the tiger and me. It shouldn't be overlooked that I had previously been provided with a plain coloured jacket as it was explained to me that 'stripes' and 'spots' could catch the eye of the tiger. Relieved by this piece of assurance I have to admit I thought at first he was joking. But no! Later I learned that this was a normal precaution.

The underwriter would need to understand the activities and as I was not impressed, I would resort to using my camera, just to show evidence and the level of my misgivings. Requesting the use of the camera the manager said he could do better than that and I should take a seat on the same rock and he would photograph me with the tiger. I declined but I did take a shot or two until the tiger turned its head towards me, looking me straight in the eyes. At that point, my life flashed before me and I figured that if she had moved so much as a muscle, I would lose face and leap to safety, sudden movement or not. I learned that photographs with animals were common practice at the park and many, many visitors prized the possession of a snap showing them stroking a Bengal tiger. My report write-up was damning and as a result, the risk already on cover was not renewed. In a short time following my 'safari' there were two further fatalities by way of mauling; however, not being involved we never learned of the findings or the levels of the awards.

In keeping with wildlife and safaris, in the likes of Africa, these are particularly hazardous activities, largely down to the apathy of some of those who organise these adventure trips. To me these safari businesses appeared to be nonplussed about the risks and the loss statistics where fatalities were concerned, not overlooking those tourists who are so badly injured they are crippled for life, possibly mentally as well as physically. On one occasion I was requested to a survey a top safari business who had gained their reputation by operating in the heart of Africa as opposed to the likes of Kruger National Park, Kenya's Buffalo Springs or the Serengeti. Being a member of a party of eight tourists made up from the UK, Canada and Ireland I would be experiencing what these tourists had spent considerable sums on: to visit African wildlife and be able first hand to measure the extent of any exposure to hazard.

Believing that it was a pleasure for me would be completely wrong as, by keeping focussed on the reasons for being there, I got little out of it save the number and extent of the hazards. The tour took in Malawi, including the lake and the Nyika Plateau on horseback, which I will endeavour to explain later, and the Okavango Delta. It probably sounds all very exciting but once putting things into perspective it was anything other than that. One thing the organiser's brochure did not explain was the necessity of an armed guard who, along with the driver-cum-guide, was present throughout. Before getting too carried away with the level of security being offered, the armed person was there, along with his Lee Enfield rifle, in the event of poachers and not the wildlife. I felt so much better knowing the reason why!

Looking into those risk exposures, five events made me realise just how close a tourist is to real danger as, during my 21 days, there were two fatalities, one involving another tourist party, while the other involved a wildlife exchange employee. We were at Lake Malawi and some of the party decided to take a swim until a local came up to our guide and reported that hippos were seen in the vicinity that morning. The tourists were quickly ushered out of the water, all while both the guard and driver stood to watch. Later that day, we witnessed a kill by a pride of lions and were watching the carcass of a hippo disappearing when the driver spotted a lion sidling along the side of our vehicle towards a lady with her arm leaning out of the vehicle snapping away with her camera. Screaming the warning the lady drained of colour closed the window, dropping her camera outside.

That night at the camp where we stopped the staff reported the death of a Japanese tourist who was at the very same kill as our party. Apparently, he got out of the vehicle, unseen by either the guide or the man's wife, to get a close up of the feeding with his video camera when he was set upon by two lions. The tourist's remains were later retrieved by rangers who allegedly shot the animals. These rangers were in action again two days later when a visiting ranger from Florida's game reserve went for an early morning jog unbeknown to his assigned minder. After a search, they found the man's towels and trainers on the bank of the Shire River. The rangers somehow identified a crocodile and shot it and upon opening the animal up they found the man's arm while the rest of the body remained a mystery. During our stay near the Nyika, we were housed in two large bungalows and those of us in one were summoned to attend dinner at sunset in the other. As the five of us, with two houseboys, walked the 50 metres to the other bungalow, one from the party reported that there were dogs following us; the houseboys urged us to run as they were not dogs but hyenas.

Regarding the use of horses on the Nyika, this was explained as being to improve the chances of tourists getting closer to the likes of the Eland antelope and leopard, both inhabitants. They apparently can smell humans, particularly deodorants, but on horseback the scent is less so consequently people can get closer to both quarry and predator. The problem with these types of holidays is that they are an adventure but with real danger because no matter how well you prepare a momentary slip of your guard could prove to be fatal. My report was pretty damning as I saw that those who were there to ensure safety could, like any of us, become preoccupied or complacent, which ultimately leads to many deaths on these types of holidays. Needless to say, the business was never considered as the risks were far too great.

The most involved post-loss survey undertaken was one where the local police force could not have gotten matters more wrong, purely by making assumptions based on hearsay, a common practice, and as a result, two boat boys were unfairly castigated which was made all the worse as both were fatally injured. The insured also came in for some criticism and again without any justification. My instructions were to survey a holiday facility in the Caribbean that catered for couples, with two of the seven resorts catering for families. The holiday centres were located in St Lucia, Jamaica, the Bahamas, Antigua, Grenada and Barbados. These were upmarket resorts where the accommodation involved villas, hotels offering full board and a whole range of activities including water sports, golf, other organised sports and tours of the islands.

My instructions were to conduct a post-loss survey following one claim and another as yet reserved or received involving guests at one of the resorts. One suffered fatal injuries while the other had serious burns. My contact was the insurance manager of this risk, which had worldwide appeal and a good reputation. Through time constraints, my survey only took in resorts on Jamaica, St Lucia, Antigua and the Bahamas. Reading the police report, it was clear that the two boat boys who lost their lives, were identified as being wholly responsible for the tragedy by virtue of them 'hot-wiring' the outboard motor attached to one hull of a catamaran. It was clear in my conversation with the underwriters and with the insurance manager that there had been malpractice and that as the two guests suffered we were going to have made significant recompense. The reserve for the male who died was set at US $10 million. As for the female who suffered first degree burns and trauma, caused by the fireball and the force of the explosion hurling her a distance into the sea, no reserve had as yet been set as the extent of her injuries was at that point in time still unknown.

The guests had booked with the water sports centre to go scuba diving and they were, as was the norm, to be ferried out to the most favourable parts of a reef by the catamaran, crewed by two local boat boys employed by the insured. The boys started the first outboard on the boat and tried starting the other conventionally but without success. In an attempt to start the Yamaha motor, they decided to hot-wire it to the other engine, which was now energised. This is pure speculation, as there were no reliable witnesses, but the engine was thought to have overheated, resulting in it exploding and the force ripping through one hull, with the blast killing the guest sat on the hull and the two crew next to the outboard motor. Such was the force of the explosion the female on the other hull, some seven metres or so away was blown out to sea but was recovered.

To those at the insured and the police, it all seemed very plausible that the malpractice was the root cause. I wanted, out of curiosity, to see the catamaran, as I never witnessed either in the armed services or during my time at Ford an engine exploding, but then, I convinced myself, it was never too late to learn?

We obtained police permission, as we were the insurers, to see the boat in a secured boathouse. The boat comprised twin fibreglass hulls with top decking constructed in similar material, with hatches spaced along its length. My first observation was that one of the Yamaha engines was still secured to a hull while the other outboard was found under a tarpaulin nearby. Upon removing the tarpaulin, it was obvious to me that the submission that the engine had blown up was false and in fact, it had by force of the explosion been blown from its anchorage.

My first comment was, "The outboard didn't blow up; it is still intact." The engine had obviously been blackened and physically damaged by an explosion but it appeared not to have been an internal failure, as the cylinder head remained on the block, while the combustion chambers were by all accounts were also intact. I explained to those present that fuel is vaporised to cause internal explosions within the combustion chambers so there was no evidence to support that theory here. Now there was silence when I asked why the hull was split as there was no sign of external force or scorching. My suspicion grew when it was obvious the engine failure, while being considered the root cause of the explosion and ignition, was simply leading others to jump to conclusions due to a lack of credible witnesses.

When hot wiring there is every chance of an external spark, but how many millions of people from all corners of the globe hot-wire or jump-start an internal combustion engine in their vehicle or on their boats daily, yet the engine doesn't explode? I believe it was this very point that others had not considered in reaching a conclusion; consequently, I submitted, the fault had to lie elsewhere? There had been a massive explosion, but, with insufficient fuel within the confines of the engine, I thought that it was either the fuel line or fuel tank failure. The hull was split like a banana peeled from the centre leading aft towards the engines, so I requested to see the fuel tank in the other hull. The tank had been drained but along with the fuel line was still fixed in its mountings. The positioning of the tank was below one of the hatches, thus making refuelling easy. It was clear at this point, to me at least, that the failure was due fuel leakage, a build-up in the bottom of the hull by way of the boat boys continually 'turning over' the engine to obtain ignition. All the while, fuel was leaking from the fuel line, making for a highly explosive atmosphere in the confined space of the hull.

It was little wonder that the attempt at hot wiring was not working because quite simply the engine was starved of fuel. Every revolution of the engine pulled fuel from the tank and, because it is pressurised, to avoid air getting into the supply, it began escaping through the wall of the damaged fuel line. The situation, I submitted was akin to a large empty can being filled with petroleum spirit and then ignited. While my opinion was still theoretical, I inspected the rubber fuel line where suddenly my suspicions were justified. The rubber fuel line was showing signs of major deterioration, due, I suspected through being continually subjected to saltwater, which is known to harm such materials. However, given the serious nature of my findings, I enquired if the same equipment was available at all resorts or simply the one where the accident occurred.

It shouldn't be hard to imagine the looks on the faces of those present as clearly, this was a major equipment failure. Products liability within the automotive industry had become a specialist area for me, particularly recall, so the message was that all the fuel lines should be inspected, better still, immediately replaced with nylon or strong, resilient plastic tubes. They also needed to establish who initially supplied the tubes, if not Yamaha; better still they needed to work out who had installed the engines and the fuel lines as I felt there was potential to subrogate. If we could establish a defective or unsuitable product or simply that the installation and user instructions were inadequate, the Insured and ourselves would be in a strong position to look for compensation elsewhere.

I have to admit my first thoughts went out to the families of the boat boys, as I felt there was some considerable unfair criticism, which led me to suggest that the insured take a different view regarding the boat boys' alleged failings for two reasons: firstly, I am sure if management were aware of the practice of hot wiring the deceased could hardly be held responsible; thereby, if proven, it would help ease the families' suffering. Further, I asked about the guest who lost his life, asking whether or not he smoked, which was followed by stony silence. Adding weight to this I submitted that while we could never hide behind this as an excuse if it were found to be the case then the boat boys would be further exonerated. My submissions were taken very seriously and while the one case was being heard in New York the others were at that time unknown. I understand that, after we ceased to trade the matter was still being investigated.

From the tranquil Caribbean to the Indian subcontinent is half a world in distance and far further where culture is concerned; nonetheless surveying, to establish the quality of the insured, makes no allowance, and therefore underwriters adopt the same policies. The examples regarding both the holiday tourist and a telecommunications insured, which I was called on to survey next, are just about as stark as it is possible to get. The survey took in more countries and posed more personal risk to me than any other, including the likes of Yemen, Afghanistan, Iraq, Pakistan and Libya.

The insured was a telecommunications business who suffered an appalling loss by way of the kidnap and slaying of three of their field engineers while working on a project involving the installation of a telephone system throughout the Republic of Chechnya. It was understood that this was the type of project the insured undertook, often paid for by way of UK foreign aid, whereby the government hoped to improve the country's basic needs thus avoiding the provision of direct funds that could be used illicitly. There was a fourth engineer held and murdered who worked for another telecommunications business in the UK, who I was led to believe was involved on the same project. The insured, a major reputable telecommunications contractor, undertook this type of work, mainly in third world countries as a way of improving that country's infrastructure, so a creditable, well-established organisation who we were involved with by way of providing employer's liability, general liabilities and contractor all risk cover wherever their staff worked.

The survey was called for due to the claims repercussions, and serious underwriting concerns concerning the types and levels of exposure. I was assigned the survey, to take in at least one of the insured's current overseas contracts, strictly avoiding the contract works, currently suspended, in Chechnya where the atrocities were committed. Being left to select a country I was determined to visit one where I could establish the extent of their services, working conditions, the quality of their management in the field and, where necessary, their levels of security. However, my survey began at the insured's head office where, upon arrival, I saw the company pennant at half-mast in respect for the loss of their engineers. I met with the entire board, even their head of finance, who I would suspect had little to offer from a risk management perspective of staff operating in the field, so I looked on it as a good sign of unity.

During the long meeting, I was provided with a complete library of working procedures and policies that covered almost everything a risk manager could think of. The areas touched upon included welfare, health care, security, health and safety… in fact, everything that would come to mind from a loss control point of view and of course compliance with the UK statutes covering the workplace. Following a thorough grilling of those present, I gained the impression the board were at a loss to explain the events given their written and practical approaches and procedures. I even ventured to question those present on management selection which drew some sharp responses as the work required skill sets that were difficult to find; therefore, they tended to go for experience by promoting from within.

At the end of the meeting I obtained a list of their current contracts and being aware of the political climates in a number of those countries, their third world rating and being largely Islamic, much along the same lines as Chechnya, I selected Bangladesh. The contracts work, unlike Chechnya capital Grozny, extended from Chittagong in the south of the country through to the capital Dhaka and then on up to Sylhet in the Northeast. These were technically more complex as the contract was all about the electronic controls on the gas pipeline flow valves, this gas pipeline entering the country at Chittagong through to the northern city of Sylhet. Covering the whole country would have meant a constant change of accommodation, with extended travel, made all the more difficult at the time due to poor roads and mass flooding. Coupled with these issues, I considered the country wholly unstable politically, where only a few years before there had been mass uprisings that led to the fall of General Ershad. While it was unlike the war in Chechnya many people died and a state of emergency was declared. I arrived at Shah Jalal International Airport, which is the largest and main airport in Bangladesh, located about 10 miles from the city of Dhaka. I was collected at the airport by a taxi booked by the insured and ferried to their main location.

The turn of events that followed put into perspective the unnecessary levels of risk and the blasé manner and attitude of some of the insured's staff in the field. This adopted approach was adequately portrayed by their field manager located in Chittagong, who with the other managers was in attendance at the

Dhaka compound. Whether or not the individual was displaying bravado was to me immaterial as this person was responsible for ensuring the policies and the procedures of his employers were being adhered to. What had occurred in Chechnya seemed to have been wasted on this engineer and I believe as a form of defence he decided to enlighten me on working in foreign climes as opposed to being employed and working in the likes of Europe. The general manager was, I felt, slightly in awe of this individual but to his credit, in the end, instructed him not to make further comment unless directly asked something by me. In response, I thanked the general manager and said, "I am a big boy now and what I am hearing I have heard many times before." Speaking directly to the belligerent manager, I said, "I am pleased to hear your opinions and take on matters as, I have to admit, they do for the most part tend to fly in the face of your board of directors' take on things at the head office."

Not waiting for a response, I added, "Can you enlighten me on how many different countries you have worked in for your employers, as it would give me an idea of your experience, especially working overseas?" The manager cited about six contract countries in total, that included some in Africa, so I gained sufficient knowledge to learn that he spent most of his years overseas and was wholly experienced working abroad. "I am interested to establish your knowledge of your employer's policies regarding health and safety," I said, and ventured down the road of healthcare, asking him about his inoculations and again displaying his masculinity, he replied that if he took the number of inoculations required by management he would be like a pin cushion.

"But what about those staff who report to you? Do you take their healthcare as lightly as your own? Further, who completes and maintains their health records, you?" Now there was silence for I felt that the manager realised he had trapped himself, as the contracts director at head office had informed me that field contract managers outside of the home country were responsible for looking after their charges' health, safety and welfare.

I swiftly changed the subject to working practices on the communications lines and installations, covering security and emergency procedures. Clearly, the radio would be an asset, but the foreign aid that provided the telecommunications equipment and materials also included vehicles, among which there were several new Land Rovers. Unfortunately, the insured were forbidden to fit radio antenna boxes to the wings of the vehicles; therefore, they had to make do with cell phones and existing landline phones. The reason for this was that the Bangladeshis did not want the vehicles drilled or defaced in any way as they would be their property on completion of the contract. The existing Bangladeshi telecommunications systems were substandard though, and wholly unreliable; consequently, communications were not particularly good. I proposed a scenario of an employee falling from height and injuring himself, thereby requiring urgent medical assistance and enquiring as to whether or not the field supervision was constantly updated regarding the distance to the nearest appropriately equipped hospital and doctor. Always to be relied on, the field manager from Chittagong cut in, informing me that in Bangladesh travel is measured in time and not distance.

Now having gained the trust of most of those involved I turned again to the Chittagong field manager as he seemed to be the weak link where probing questions were involved. Looking directly at the Chittagong representative I asked how many of the staff employed were married. Somewhat surprised, he told me he was single as the job meant that home life was not conducive and at 28 he didn't need the burden of marriage. While many may consider my next question bordering on the unthinkable, I asked him what he did in his spare time, given that he was a healthy young man who spent so much of his time away from home. His response was what I anticipated as he was full of his own self assurances, "Go to any of the villages about and you can get what you want for the price of a Mars bar."

Partially ignoring his reply, which I anticipated, I asked about his knowledge of religion and if he was aware that Bangladesh was predominantly Islamic. Further was he aware how the local population would react to his self-confessed antics or for that matter those of their women? Before he could respond I turned to the general manager and suggested that to avoid the possible wrath of the locals he should even consider flying his men down to Thailand, one-hour flying time away, monthly if his staff were so desperate that they were tempted to venture out of their compounds unaware and unprotected. The final comments said it all for me as the theory at the insured's head office was clearly wasted on even the managers in some of their contract sites. As a parting shot, I told the Chittagong manager, in response to him questioning me on my experiences, that I had surveyed in over 70 countries, some far more hostile than Bangladesh, and I made it my priority to learn something first of the local culture and religion and that he would best be advised to do the same.

The role of the surveyor to some is pretty much cast in stone; however, the depth of the role doesn't really have any bounds. The extent of the investigations will vary from one piece of business to another; plus, the more experienced the surveyor the more they pick up on, where less experienced people tend to stick rigidly to the subjects listed in the aid memoir and report form. One of the first questions that were put to me by an engineer cum prospective insurance surveyor, following a brief description of the duties and requirements the position entailed, went something in the order of the length of time it would take to gain the necessary level of experience. To a layperson that I thought was a realistic response, as you can never with any certainty predict what the next appraisal will turn up and what lies in wait in the next few days or even years consequently I replied, "Never believe you know it all as there is always scope to learn. Nevertheless, ideally just keep in mind what the underwriters are seeking: first-class pieces of business over a protracted period that will bring handsome underwriting profitability."

To that end, an aide-memoire is a very useful guide for surveyors, although with experience it becomes less influential as top surveyors work with flair, imagination and lateral thinking. Their thought processes extend beyond the usual parameters that guide lists provide, regarding associated perils and other dominant factors. The permutations that an aide-memoire throws up usually go further yet bulk standard wordings were often encouraged as a means of churning out reports that did not in my mind aid the surveyors' development. To compound this, matters become even more problematic where more than one site or location is involved. True, there are issues that the underwriter wishes to be covered but these tend to involve updates on the likes of trade activities, wage rolls and future plans such as premises and products simply because these issues can have a significant impact on the likes of the premium.

To illustrate the influential standing and multiple locations problems, I was once assigned a survey of a family business involving three brothers, each running their own individual operations out of three separate factories, 50 to 60 miles apart yet all insured under a common policy bearing the group's name. The three premises were all very similar in age, construction and dimension, located on modern industrial estates. As far as the processes were concerned, here too they were similarities insofar as the insured were producing spark plugs, generators and electrical looms used in motor vehicle manufacturing. One of the establishments undertook generator repairs, although the amount of work was small. Two of the brothers were considered risk aware and clearly understood the clout that an insurer possesses; consequently, they were very cooperative and responsive to considered risk improvements. On the other hand, the third brother was nothing short of confrontational and adopted a cavalier approach to risk management and in particular health and safety. He took umbrage that an outside organisation, such as ourselves, regardless of effectively being a business partner, because that is what the insurer is, could have an opinion. This left the insurer with a serious dilemma: did they base their opinion of risk on the two good locations or the one very likely to experience claims?

This is one where the broker and two of the brothers played a significant part by persuading the influential individual running the non-compliant operation, explaining the scenarios and serious disadvantages of going it alone or alternatively making amends. My opinion was that in multiple locations the worst dictates the opinion. Common sense, however, prevailed and while clearly irked the business remained and my observations were adopted, certainly not in spirit but reportedly in practice. Just to put another slant on multiple sites insured a less experienced surveyor appeared not to have been influenced by peripheral perils where a neighbouring business was involved in highly hazardous activities. The oversight did give rise to internal problems where, following a third-party loss, the neighbour's failings resulted in property damage and business interruption claims. While the report was positive regarding our insured's undertakings, the surveyor failed to notify the underwriter about the negatives, which was a case of the surveyor becoming the inappropriate decision maker.

Some risks were discarded quickly. Amongst those discarded risks was another London business where it was hard to believe the lack of care regarding the wellbeing of the workforce. Initially I was at a loss; however, after travelling the world surveying, I put it down to the owner's country of origin where the workplace standards were not so rigid and enforced. The reason for me being on site was that we had received a claim under employer's liability where a female employee suffered a severe electrical shock and was now suffering an anxiety disorder or phobia for anything electrical and hadn't worked since. This may all sound very suspicious to the sceptic but then it does depend on the level of shock received and if a person has ever experienced an electrical shock before. I, for one, wasn't of that mind-set as I had literally been sent spinning on one such occasion by an electrical shortage on a piece of equipment, so I reserved my judgement. I arranged the survey myself and agreed to meet up with the factory manager, as he ran the business on a day-to-day basis. Arriving on site on a very cold, snowy January morning before the 8 a.m. appointment I observed an employee unlock the premises and enter; shortly after, the lights were turned on. Some five minutes before the allotted appointment time another person arrived, who looked more likely to be the manager so I got out of my car and introduced myself before we entered the factory together. The interior was cold and the manager's office dark and dank, just above freezing.

The manager, without taking off his topcoat and scarf, turned on a small electrical fire causing me to immediately think about Bob Cratchit in Charles Dickens' *A Christmas Carol*. I explained the reason for the survey again and requested more detail because the claims document simply mentioned electrocution of an employee. The manager briefed me firstly on the company, which he described as a medium-size business employing about 40 full-time employees: males and females of mixed races but predominantly from the Indian subcontinent, as was the owner, incidentally, he added. The incident entailed the electrostatic coating of a wire letter rack where the claimant, employed as a packer with extended duties, including inspections, simply observed an incomplete coated article on the continuous overhead conveyor after the spray station. As were her duties she removed the partially coated piece and was in the throes of replacing it once again on the moving conveyor in front of the electrostatic spraying station when the accident occurred.

The manager set about explaining the work processes from start to finish, which involved just six production stages with the first being the unpacking of their customers' products. In stage two, the articles were hung on the overhead conveyor, which dipped down below floor level, submerging the hung article in a subfloor bath of trichloroethylene, a strong defatting agent which is non-flammable with a sweet odour. Trichloroethylene is used principally as a solvent to remove contaminants such as grease from metal parts and when exposed to air evaporates quickly. As for the health risk, even short-term exposure to trichloroethylene can result in harmful effects on the nervous system, liver, respiratory system, etc. The product would remain submerged for three or four metres of travel before reappearing along the track, ready for electrostatic spray coating. Station four was the electrostatic spraying station, which entailed plastic powdered particles being sprayed by a powerful electrostatic charge onto the surface of a conductive article, such as, at the time of the accident, a letter rack. Once fully coated the conveyed articles entered a gas fire oven that cured the coating, thus completing stage five. Finally emerging from the oven, the articles were removed from the conveyor and packed ready for shipment.

To reiterate the accident occurred following the woman removing the letter rack from the conveyor with the intention to replace it on the conveyor. However, before she could do so, the sprayer, in sheer ignorance, on being informed it required reworking told the lady to wait. Without permitting this female operative to rehang the article the sprayer incredibly told her to identify the surface area missed and hold it while he sprayed the uncoated area. Clearly without being aware of the obvious hazard, and now acting as the earth, the lady suffered high voltage electrocution. The act was irresponsible and given the further unfavourable conditions it could have proven fatal; nonetheless, it was now subject to a claim for negligence on the part of the employer.

Following the briefing, by which time the factory was fully operational, we moved out of the office to the spraying station and we were standing alongside it, just off the aisle way when I was actually brushed by a passing forklift truck, travelling with a high load to the front; clearly, the driver had impaired vision. Just past me, the truck collided with a stack of metal pallets, scattering them and the workers employed in the area. It was a close call, so momentarily I felt constrained to enquire of the driver why he was firstly driving so fast and secondly why he did not have the load behind him. He was lost for a response and simply remarked that the work area was too congested. I then politely enquired whether or not he had an operator's certificate, to which he replied he didn't need one as he had a UK driver's license!

It was all too much. I concluded that I was indeed in a disaster zone and decided to cut short the survey. With experience in surveying there comes a point during a visit where you just know the quality before you, irrespective of any claims. Consequently, I was about to take my leave when out of nowhere a very well-spoken gentleman, expensively dressed, asked me who I was. I explained who I was and handed him my business card, informing him that I was just leaving. He walked off in the opposite direction while I made my way to the office area and the exit determined that this risk would be off our books before the week was out.

Now sensing my displeasure, not helped by the actions of the forklift truck, the attitude of the owner and the general state of the factory, the manager and as it turned out the company secretary, pleaded with me to stay promising that whatever I wanted he would see it carried out. He asked me to forget the owner as he only came into the factory once a week for less than a few minutes. Having marginally calmed myself I agreed and we walked to his office whereupon I requested their accident book, if indeed they had one. Much to my dismay and surprise their accident book was produced. Perusing two pages of details including the electrocution, I noted that one name kept cropping up involving a cut, fall, abrasion, dust in the eye so I mentioned it to the manager who informed me that the person was the labourer, a retired employee, who the owner had kept on after retirement age to help out, as he put it.

I read at the bottom of the page, of the accident book, that the man had amongst his accident history suffered burns to the hands and one side of his face. Consequently, I asked the manager for more details and was continuing to study the accident book entries when his office door opened and the owner came striding in. Sarcastically he said, "You are still here then?" I couldn't resist saying that it was just as well as I was now aware of two very 'near misses' so I was already dreading what the underwriter was going to say? The owner's response, given his attitude thus far, didn't at all surprise me when he remarked, "Don't concern yourself, there are plenty of insurers out there who would gladly take on my liability business. Next, you will be telling me the asphyxiation was our fault too!"

This latest remark was like a bolt out of the blue but from this insured; an almost throwaway comment. On occasions such as this, it is wise to keep your own counsel because the arrogance of the man clearly meant that he was master of all he surveyed and that others' opinions counted for little. I had already decided that the owner should live in his own dream world and almost ignoring him I continued to idly read, concentrating on the entries in the book. Turning over to the next page I did the proverbial double-take where two entries caught my attention that I just couldn't take my eyes off: one entered under 'oven' and the other 'asphyxiation'. Now I was understanding the owner's comment. Apparently, the incident took place within the trichloroethylene tank. Initially, I was beginning to believe I was part of a hoax save the severity of the three incidents made me dismiss the notion that it could be real almost as soon as they entered my head.

"Obviously, there is little that goes on in your business that you are not fully aware of?" I put to the owner, appealing to his obvious ego. He confirmed this, so I asked him, purely out of curiosity, could he enlighten me regarding the 'oven' incident? Without hesitation, the owner described how he employed a retired person, who was generously given overtime to commence work some 45 minutes before the normal start time. The duties assigned to him entailed firing up the gas-fired oven so that firstly, the works were reasonably warm when production started, as this was the only source of heating in the factory, and secondly, production could start on time, as the process required the application of heat.

Apparently, on the day of the accident, the worker arrived as planned on a frosty morning some time before shift start and, being cold, he sat inside the still relatively warm curing tunnelled oven with his flask of tea and a copy of a daily newspaper. The aged worker snuggled down and subsequently fell asleep! The manager arrived and, noting the oven was not fired up, with no sign of the labourer and with workers due to be arriving shortly, he purged the gas system and fired up the oven. This may well read like a comedy sketch but it was anything but. All this time the manager failed to notice the sleeping worker in a small alcove within the tunnel where it dog-legged. The gas flashed over, setting part of the man's clothing and hair alight so that he emerged screaming out of the oven, whereupon the stunned manager grabbed a fire extinguisher to douse the flames. Following hospital treatment, the labourer was given the rest of the day off! He was apparently grateful that the owner never took disciplinary action against him and the worker therefore never made a claim.

Putting my question directly to the owner I remarked, "So that was it then?"

His response was again priceless, "What? Do you expect me to pay for his damaged clothing, buy him a newspaper? He was sleeping on overtime, so he certainly won't be doing that again."

This was turning into a farce so now even more anxious yet intrigued I asked about the trichloroethylene tank, fast believing it cannot get any worse, it could and did. He explained that once every month, on a weekend when there were no planned production runs, the open top trichloroethylene tank was cleaned. The process involved firstly emptying the trichloroethylene and then removing the residue lying on the bottom and sides of this deep sub-floor tank. To complete the cleaning, the worker used a stiff broom, a shovel and a metal waste bin. I decided not to ask where it was emptied but I could imagine!

Following the removal of the highly toxic gunge the tank floor and walls were hand cleaned, followed by the tank being refilled with clean trichloroethylene. Not understanding that this liquid is a known asphyxiant, the worker presumably climbed into the now empty tank via a stepladder, just as he did every month, without any form of breathing apparatus on his person. As he worked, releasing the fumes from the residue, he began inhaling which was exacerbated on this occasion by him smoking! Needless to say, he passed out and it was only by chance that another worker, assigned to haul out the filled waste bin, noticed the labourer lying prostrate on the floor of the tank. He called for assistance and without waiting for help he unwittingly climbed into the tank and now with the aid of another two workers pulled the labourer out by way of a rope sling. Once lifted from the tank, the unconscious employee was finally conveyed by ambulance to the local hospital where he fortunately recovered and within the week was back working. As for the risks taken by the rescue team in getting the labourer out, I asked about breathing apparatus. 'The man was smoking and he couldn't have done that masked up now could he?' replied the owner.

The circumstances and consequences were obviously wasted on the owner but I felt constrained to submit, now in such a way that my contempt was obvious, "What about the others who probably saved the labourer's life? Didn't their health matter?" For the very first time, the owner was silent so I took my leave without looking back. I have to conclude it rated amongst the worst risks that I had ever surveyed in over four decades of loss control and survey work and it goes without saying the policy was immediately cancelled, with the business I assumed going elsewhere.

It shouldn't come as too much of a surprise when I say that some managers or at least supervisors should not be in the position of leading or managing a workforce as they are completely incompetent. In loss control, we are speaking of peoples' safety, but many seem not to understand that. I witnessed incompetence first hand, such as the plasterer supervisor whose fall from a height was caused by a manager advocating shortcuts, or the steeplejack manager who expected staff to experience a fall as part of their learning curve, or female machinists being expected to work without hand protection because the manager informed me that sticky plasters were a cheaper alternative to gloves.

With all this incompetence, there just had to be someone like those mentioned who got a taste of what it was like to experience a serious accident, and it happened when I was conducting a post-loss survey. I was really surprised by the hostility and mistrust shown by a plant manager towards an injured employee who had allegedly lost the tips of a number of his fingers while attempting to clear away a build-up of metal swarf from a chain conveyor, linked to a machine the employee was minding. The manager was a total sceptic, it takes one to know one, and was of the opinion that the employee had to have been engaged in something other than what he reported. Needless to say, as the accident was involving a claim, I thought it prudent to at least examine the views of the manager just on the chance of there being something where there was a degree of contributory negligence. Consequently, I informed the manager of me being open-minded and wished to see what exposures, if any, still existed. I was assured that the machine was safe and that the management had examined it and found no dangerous parts were exposed. Looking over the machine, it did, at a glance, appear as the management had suggested: it was securely fenced. However, the opportunity arose where I could speak with another machinist who said that he believed, after speaking with his colleague during a hospital visit, that it was the conveyor that caused the injury and not the cutters? The plant manager, hearing this account scoffed at the assertion and ran his hand and fingers over the moving conveyor in an attempt to demonstrate there were indeed no trapping points. Having read the report it suggested that the injury was sustained while removing swarf and, as there was no swarf on the top of the conveyor, the build-up must have been on the underside.

As we appeared to be going around in circles, I suggested to the manager we should be open-minded about this as opposed to adopting *them and us* attitude and I proceeded to ask the supervisor if there was a swarf problem. Before he answered, he looked at the manager and the manager nodded that he should answer. The foreman said it rarely happened but it could when the cutting lubricant applied was excessive, adding that was the machinist's fault, in an effort to please his manager. The manager, now exasperated, ploughed his hand again across the top of the conveyors in an attempt to show there were no dangerous parts then did likewise below the frame of the conveyor insofar as sweeping his hand along the underside of the track. With a scream, which I thought was a joke in poor taste, the manager whipped his bleeding hand away revealing a badly lacerated hand and fingers. Such was the manager's embarrassment, and obvious pain, he dashed away, instructing the foreman, "Get the…thing sorted." Obviously, we settled the claim with the employee but as I understood no such claim was submitted by the manager.

One other case that proved better than I expected was a business involved in boning and meat stripping from the heads of slaughtered cattle, with the meat being used in the production of beef burgers. The risk when first visited was being managed by a works manager who had progressed from a process worker to supervisor, to shift manager and then general manager. It was clear the individual had little to no idea about his responsibilities outside hiring, firing and productivity. Quality was also not high on this individual's list of priorities, as it was one of the untidiest locations I had seen, where offal, bone, wrapping, crates and plastic stillages were in an unholy mess; in fact, the place was a shambles. There was little wonder in my mind that there had been serious injuries amongst the labour force. The reason for the survey was that the existing insurer, understandably due to the business's employer's liability loss ratio, were not offering renewal terms; therefore, we were invited to quote understanding the terms and conditions would be subject to a survey within three months of inception.

As needs must, of course, the insured and their brokers reluctantly agreed to the conditions being imposed by the underwriter, as was made clear at the time of the proposed visit. So, having read the claims experience and heard of the management's and broker's reluctance regarding the survey I felt that I had a good feel for the risk, albeit without any preconceived ideas about how to tackle it. One thing I was sure of, in the broker and the insured's eyes, a surveyor wearing a pinstripe suit would be nothing to get too concerned about given that this was a messy risk, one that could be considered the least attractive of all the butchery processes. Attending any risk survey, you have to fight your corner to one degree or another, but there are others where they are simply a waste of energy, as you will never bring about an acceptable level of change. This was one such case where the manager, suspecting I was unimpressed, asked me if I had ever been in such a business before. I responded by citing several competitors and said that I had not seen their like, though, as it was so messy, a word that only tells half the story. In fact, it presented itself as a substandard risk, particularly given they were in effect food processors. Fortunately, I thought we are not providing public or products cover.

The survey got underway and, as anticipated, it was possible to find something seriously wrong within the first three steps into the boning section: a lack of safety apparel, knives left lying on the workbenches, no scabbards for the boners' knives when not in use, careless disposal of bones with other waste littering all surfaces, the latter problem I deduced being due to the offal skips being filled to overflowing. Where skull and legs had been stripped of the meat the boners simply threw the bone into the bins, most of which missed as the distances were five or six metres away. To cut to the chase, I informed the broker and the manager that it was, to us, an unacceptable risk as presented and I would be astounded if the underwriter decided to ignore my opinion. This resulted in the broker, momentarily taking his leave, making a call that it turned out was to a director whose family were cattle farm owners in Eire and Northern Ireland. Following that brief call, the broker persuaded me to be patient and not to leave for the airport given that my flight was not due yet for a few hours, as the director was on route and wished to speak with me. Having agreed I sat waiting patiently in an unoccupied office for about 20 minutes or so until I was ushered into what turned out to be the managing director's office.

Already seated in the office was a youngish lady, who was a family member and director of the farming operations, who warmly greeted me, welcoming me to Eire. Taking one of the office easy chairs the lady politely requested to learn about my findings which I listed in terms of severity and what would need to be done, so as not to give a totally negative response. Surprisingly, she requested that I provide handwritten recommendations and she would see to them immediately, not wanting to wait for my report when I returned to London. The lady took her leave, informing me she had other matters to attend to, and that it would give me time to put my thoughts in writing. Following my observations, in terms of priorities, I handed the director my findings and recommendations. Following this and asking about my flight details she suggested we had plenty of time to have lunch, after which she would drive me to the airport.

At the airport, the director assured me those matters highlighted would not only be implemented but maintained. Not being too swayed by the director's promises or courtesies I did relate to the underwriters the business dealings and my impressions. They were not too enamoured, nor I, but it was decided that we should at least appear as though we were interested as it was a London Market broker. So the decision was holding cover until the resurvey was completed. The following week, I was informed that the insured had complied with our requirements and would like me back to see the results at any time; the anytime invitation was a little unusual given the broker's original stance regarding policy conditions and resurvey. Previously I had informed the director of our policy of unannounced visits which she obviously had recalled.

In less than three weeks she met me off my flight and conveyed me to the factory, where I was taken aback by what I saw. The external areas were free of rubbish, heaps of broken timber pallets that had been there previously now no longer existed, with only neatly stacked, serviceable pallets, waste bins and skips were hardly filled so the impressions were positive. Upon entering the factory, I was left wondering if I was in the same place where everything was organised and employees suitably dressed in chain mail aprons, armlets, gloves, and scabbards; in fact, the workplace looked ready for a safety training film. There are times when, following a survey of a substandard business the insured will pull out all the stops to put things right, but even after a week or so there would be evidence to suggest that some of the old habits were creeping back in, so I was not totally sold.

Here, things looked wonderful after three weeks, but there is inevitably a downside. This new look had been embraced by all except one: the general manager, who was seen boning without any item of safety wear about his person. Back now within the office, I informed the director of my impressions from the very first visit and congratulated her and her management on achieving a 99% improvement from the gated entrance to the factory to the office so my recommendation was that we provide employers liability cover. Her response came as a bit of a shock when she repeated "99%? Why?"

I told her one of her employees was setting a bad example by being the only one not complying with the new safety directives, ignoring their safety posters about the factory concerning safety apparel, housekeeping, etc. The director now had lost her cool somewhat and requested I inform her who was not complying with her instructions. I responded by saying, "If your general manager flaunts the safety codes how could he ever be in a position to enforce them? Further, he is setting a bad example." Without a word the director got up and walked out of the office, leaving an eerie silence. I sat alone for a good ten minutes until the director at last returned. She smiled, sat down and simply said, "100%."

The lady apologised for not being available to return me to the airport but assigned one of the drivers, using her vehicle. On my way back to the airport, the driver congratulated me on stirring things up and the reason for the director not driving me was down to two things: firstly, the manager, who had flouted her safety directives had been fired on the spot and, secondly, following lunch break she planned on conducting a safety session followed by appointing a new manager. Unbeknown to me, following my previous visit, every employee was lectured regarding the way things were going to be, and the director had added that those who didn't like it could have their cards immediately. I know for a fact that we never received a claim in the following three years and it never came up again for a survey which was unusual and still remains in my mind as being an excellent illustration of good, positive management overcoming bad.

From Ireland to Borneo was all in a week's work schedule and the latter was one of the most adventurous locations I ever visited, where I was again looking into the activities of a highly respected Australian contractor with worldwide contracts. The site was the second largest open cast coal mine in the world, where the insured were assigned to provide the engineering facilities that embraced the maintenance of the services they had installed. To date, the insured had constructed a portal frame building that was a workshop complete with an office, a power generator building, water pumps and several kilometres of trough conveyor through the jungle to a pier that stretched out to sea half a kilometre to a loading jetty. The pier supported the continuance of the conveyor system so that the excavated coal was conveyed uninterrupted along the conveyors to the jetty, where it was loaded onto bulk ocean-going collier ships, principally bound for the US.

This was a mosquito-infested location with snakes, saltwater crocodiles, orang-utans, monkeys, sun bears and spiders and, because the living accommodations were primitive, to say the least, I and the insured's representative were housed in the Yacht Club Balikpapan. Here there was a bar, restaurant and 'safe' bathing area. 'Safe' was an important element because some weeks before our visit one of two of the club's kitchen staff, who were walking home along the only road through the mango area, was taken by a crocodile that launched itself at the man, taking him into the water on the other side of the road. This was not the first fatality and staff had been warned about this peril, which is why they tended to walk in pairs. After that, I never wandered outside and was forever on the lookout at the pier and pontoon. The next day was hectic, given what had occurred previously, but we had a schedule to keep to, so we started at the coal face, moving along the conveyor system and encountering orang-utans that were sitting by the roadside and on the verandas of some of the larger villas, seeking food as their habitat was being devastated by the mining activities.

Upon reaching the pontoon, where the lighters carrying fuel for the mobile plant and the generators were berthed, and discharging their flammable cargo into the pipeline that fed the mine, we encountered our first 'human' peril. There was a lighter connected up to the delivery pipe through which the crew were pumping fuel destined for the holding tanks at the mine face. On the pontoon were two welders, plus their supervisor, repairing impact damage to the edge of the metal platform and the handrail by way of electric arc welding. Needless to say, at the water's edge the wind was causing the sparks to fly in all directions, this in and about the lighter, yet nobody seemed to recognise the hazard even though there were prominent notices on the four handrails indicating 'no smoking'. My first comment was directed at our insured's representative, who had suddenly woken up to the situation. He instructed the supervisor to cease work until the lighter had finished discharging its cargo and moved off. The welding supervisor's reaction left me stunned; pointing to the signage he remarked, "But, boss, they are not smoking!" People's perception of risk was summed up perfectly by that supervisor's few chosen words.

During the time when we were recruiting specialist liability surveyors, we underwrote a drift mine in South Wales that had been bought by a private consortium and it fell upon me to conduct the liability survey. At that time, many mines had been closing down over the previous two decades mostly due to being unprofitable. However, there remained a local market for coal in the mining areas such as South Wales, where extracted coal would be sold to local power stations using fossil fuels, to coal merchant businesses and directly to households. The fossil fuel was traditionally extracted by hand as opposed to using modern methods of long and short wall ploughs that strip the seams mechanically, depositing the coal onto waiting trough conveyors, that in turn conveyed the coal to the surface to be washed and stockpiled. The drift mines that still operated involved miners on their hands and knees using pneumatic tools to chip away at the coal seams, then shovelling the coal into waiting tubs which, when full would be hauled mechanically up along the main road to the surface or, as at the mine surveyed, onto a trough conveyor. I was no stranger to mining, having been underground in Scotland, Nottingham, Yorkshire, along with other deep shaft mines in Australia and Africa that adopted modern methods of coal getting. Consequently, when arriving at a drift mine for the first time, which was a throwback to some forty-years ago, it came as a bit of a shock.

There were no niceties such as modern changing facilities, or the provision of suitable clothing other than traditional boiler suits, footwear, and the hard hat that I always carried, although my hard hat was not suitable as I needed the lamp and fittings that were offered, as were gloves and knee pads, the latter confusing me a little as they were not necessary at the other mines I had surveyed. Next was the trip to the coal face, which entailed at least a half-mile walk that felt more like a five-mile forced march over uneven ground, rivulets of water running down the almost 1 in 3.5 inclines, in semi-darkness and with few to no handholds available. The choice became worse later when I had to climb onto a running trough conveyor, alighting at the insured's representative's command, who incidentally was also the pit deputy.

Trying desperately not to be viewed as a novice I confess I had great difficulty trying to keep my balance, all the while admiring the agility of the deputy, who climbed on and off the conveyor like a ride in the park. At this point, the roof was lower, so that there was no upright walking, at which point I reflected stupidly on not taking up the deputy's offer of gloves and kneepads. This part of the journey was just about the worst I had ever experienced, with the deputy telling me to keep my head down as he could constantly hear my hard hat coming into contact with the roof due to the ever-decreasing headroom until I finally managed to hit the roof so hard the hat came off. From that point after, scrambling about in the dark to find it, I decided to progress even lower and slower.

A little while later we were literally walking like apes on all fours, with my neck being uncomfortably craned. Eventually, we reached a point when the deputy called out a worker's name and from the darkness a voice replied. Every now and then these colliers could be observed by virtue of the whiteness of their teeth and their eyes. There were, in fact, two miners sitting on the floor drinking liquid from their flasks. Exchanging a few pleasantries, the deputy explained who I was and the purpose of the visit. We heard noises from further down the roadway towards the coalface and so, out of curiosity, I asked what it was. One of the coal-blackened colliers explained that a work colleague was shoring up the tunnel ahead before they could get access to the face and I should take a look as this was a common task.

We found the noise source, locating another miner squatting cross-legged, in semidarkness, cutting a pine timber shore with a bow saw, with no such niceties like a power saw. When the worker had finished, he twisted the cut shore into the upright position and hammered it into place. Being a precision engineer in an earlier life I was in awe of the man's accuracy, as he appeared not to have a tape measure or any other measuring aid but it still appeared to fit perfectly without the use of wedges, simply a slightly angled cut and a sledgehammer. The working conditions were, to my mind, Dickensian; therefore, all credit to these miners as they appeared to be taking it all in their stride.

I had seen enough and finding out that the second route out was still being maintained, as required in a drift mine for safety reasons, I told them I wanted to get back to the surface. If I thought the walk and ride back would be easier, I was sadly mistaken. Combatting the climb back I was just tired out, at the same time wondering what those miners felt like after a full shift. Stumbling back into the daylight I was one relieved surveyor and decided that my priority was not getting the report written up, but the recruitment of a mining surveyor. I returned to the showers and changing room and try as I might, getting the coal dust off and out of me was a daunting task. Just when I thought I was clean my perspiration was again black and so were the courtesy towels provided. Eventually, after some thirty or so minutes, I emerged from the changing room and was dressed in my own clothes. At that juncture, I recalled my childhood, when every summer the family would make its way from London down to Swansea to visit my father's family. On one occasion my uncle, Thomas, covered from head to toe in coal dust, called in at my grandparents' home on his way back from a shift at the colliery to say hello as if he were on his way back from the office.

Now back in the colliery manager's office, I asked about the history of the mine and was surprised to learn of its age when the name of the mine triggered a thought. I asked about the accident history before it became a private concern and was informed of the collapse of the roof and a gas explosion during the days under the National Coal Board. I enquired how long the manager had been associated with the mine, which he informed me was way, way back under the NCB.

"So you were here when the roof collapsed and members of mines rescue service were killed?" I remarked without a second thought. Somewhat taken aback he told me he was and that it was not only mines rescue service people who were lost. He then commented on how well informed we insurers were given it was some 29 years before.

"Not really," I replied. "My cousin, Donald, was one of the mines rescue services who died and my father's large family are still living in and about the area with other family members being former miners."

I added that my elder sister and brother were born less than ten miles away from here. The mine deputy and manager were stunned. You simply cannot invent such a story and to think I walked the same route as my cousin Donald gave me a strange feeling.

Of all the nerviest, strangest and somewhat amusing events loosely associated with a survey, there are three that stand out in my mind, with the first taking place during my risk surveying of Stadium Australia, prior to its 2003 reconfiguration following the 2000 Olympic Games. Our insured, Multiplex, undertook the reconfiguration of Stadium Australia, also known as ANZ Stadium, a multipurpose development located in the Sydney Olympic Park precinct of Homebush Bay. The Olympic Stadium was initially completed in March 1999, at a cost of $690 million, and was used as the host stadium for the 2000 Summer Olympics. It was originally built to hold 110,000 spectators, making it the largest Olympic Stadium ever built and the largest stadium in Australia. However, after the conclusion of the games, the stadium required reconfiguration in order to make it more functional for a variety of popular sporting events, including rugby and other sports requiring the use of an oval field, such as cricket and Australian Rules football. Multiplex undertook the reconfiguration in 2001, which included the shortening of the north and south wings and the introduction of a movable seating section. Awnings were also added over the north and south stands, offering patrons undercover seating, all of which I was there to assess.

I checked into the Hilton hotel in George Street and had the concierge arrange a taxi to take me to Homebush at 7 a.m. the following morning, as I was flying out again that night. A city taxi driver was waiting for me when I arrived at the hotel reception the next morning, as planned. I jumped into the taxi, assuming that the concierge had informed the driver of my destination, so I sat back reading up the underwriter's notes when in broken English with a heavy east European accent the driver asked me where to? Surprised I asked hadn't the concierge told him to which he replied they had but he didn't understand. Now bemused I told him that I needed to go to ANZ Stadium Australia and again to my surprised he asked where that was? I told him to head to Homebush and on the Parramatta Bridge, he would see it as I had been there previously when the complex was under construction some years before. On Concord Road, with the Parramatta below, the driver suddenly became the all-knowing tourist guide, informing me that the large building down to our left was where up until recently he had been employed, adding that the hospital had a mental health wing.

Imagining the driver to have been a ward orderly, janitor or something of that nature, I casually asked if he missed working there. The story now started to unfold when he told me that he had been struck off and was waiting for his case to be reopened on appeal. The term 'struck off' sunk in and I asked what his job was, in answer to which he told me he was a doctor! Now I was paying less attention to my notes and more to what this Hungarian 'struck off' doctor cum taxi driver was talking about. Putting it politely, I asked why he had been disciplined and struck off, bearing in mind his English was not so good. My thoughts were perhaps a misunderstanding, incorrect diagnosis, falsified qualifications or documents and so on. "For having sex with a patient," came the laid back but a startling response.

"For what?" I asked as I was unsure what he said so he repeated what I had heard the first time. Now somewhat shocked I told him where professional improprieties were concerned his chances of appealing successfully were almost nil unless he could present the panel with irrefutable evidence.

At that juncture, I had heard enough but he continued and there was yet another twist in the account which was even more alarming when he said the sex took place with his wife, who was an inpatient. I didn't bother to ask for repetition as he had my fullest attention at this point. I asked him what his wife had to say and that this may have some bearing on his case but he said that was no good because she was dead! I was now anxious for Homebush to arrive when he continued with the saga adding that they were going to exhume her body as her death was now viewed as suspicious, which he welcomed as he knew they would find that he did not have a case to answer. I now had serious doubts about this person's mental health, concluding that he probably was in fact a patient or an ex-patient and was 'out on licence'. Now thankfully at Homebush, he asked if he should wait for me to return to the city but I declined, saying I would be here for hours and wished him good luck with both his hearing and finding his way around. A simple taxi ride turned out, on reflection, to have been most amusing, and to think I travelled down to the other side of the world to experience it. I later wondered how things had turned out; however, in spite of scouring the web, I found nothing remotely connected to the events described to me by the taxi driver. As for the survey, well it paled when compared to the journey, and in fact I cannot remember it.

Two other experiences merit a mention at this juncture in my story, both a little unnerving, that were faced while travelling to and from appointed surveys. These incidents involved not only an element of danger that some workers covered by our liability insurance face every working day, but also me intent on assessing those workers' exposures. The surprising thing about these incidents was all about the modes of transport and not the job of work or the process itself. Travelling to survey to major contract sites these modes of transport entailed two helicopter flights conveying me to offshore locations: one fixed location, the other floating. Both were perilous situations, one man-made the other natural, were equally high risk, which is ironic given the purpose of my journeys was to establish the quality, in loss control terms, of our insured's activities and exposures. What it certainly enabled me to appreciate and report on were those hazards that are by and large considered peripheral or incidental to the work processes.

The first of the two incidents involved No Man's Land, a Napoleonic fort sited at the mouth of the Solent where it meets the English Channel, directly between Gosport and Ryde, on the Isle of Wight. These forts were originally designed and strategically sited to repel any Napoleonic French naval threat and were re-armed twice since that period, during both WW1 and WW2. In more recent times, these forts passed into private ownership and were being converted into leisure and sports facilities and domestic housing. The external walls, roof areas, including the core structure, comprised reinforced mass concrete of over one metre in density. The work entailed the centre core roof being demolished and the level reduced to accommodate a centre courtyard, a swimming pool and gardens, while at the same time the remainder of the structures were to be converted into luxury living accommodations. The reasons the underwriters required a survey were that firstly the contract was technically offshore and secondly it involved heavy demolitions.

The labour force was accommodated in the fort during the weekdays and then shipped back to the mainland, when the sea was moderate, at the cessation of work on a Friday. Nonetheless, I did my homework regarding checking the BBC weather forecast for the date of the intended visit, for both the Solent and Christchurch Bay. The most favourable sea forecast was moderate to rough so I imagined the crossing would be just that given that the workboats were small. Unbeknown to me at the time the insured had also been researching the weather forecast and suggested given the time constraints that it would best that I make the short journey using his own helicopter. This a much-preferred option to a sea crossing where on occasions landing at the fort could be treacherous and had on occasions resulted in workers being dragged from the sea. A member of the construction team referred to the waves being about two metres from trough to crest, so getting off the small workboat could be 'tricky' sometimes. Regardless the flying appealed to me as time was of the essence to provide adequate liability coverage, even though the contract was estimated to involve approximately twelve months, weather permitting.

As arranged, I made my way to Goodwood aerodrome to pick up my flight early one November morning. It was overcast and windy, and I never had the opportunity to look at the weather forecast before I left home as I had no such access. We took off in gusty conditions and the pilot suggested that the forecast was OK, not favourable, but OK. I could feel the buffeting as soon as we hit height, and it got worse as we were following the direction of the Solent below. The pilot pointed out the fort in the murky distance as the rain suddenly was upon us. It has to be appreciated that the top of the fort is approximately fifty feet above sea level. At the time there was only one helipad in use so the pilot told me he would drop me off and then return once I was clear, as he felt that with the now high wind, of about force six or seven, the helicopter would need facing into the wind and lashing. All very dramatic, I thought at the time.

This opinion changed very quickly as I had a second thought before being instructed to unbuckle, open the door and drop onto the pad, where I was met by a wet and windswept site agent. The agent ushered me to a covered area with me watching the helicopter take off, turn around and make its way back in the direction we came, commenting that he was surprised given the weather that we made it. I was believing that this would be the last I would see of the insured as the weather showed no signs of improvement. The agent in the site office showed me the three-day forecast, which showed wind speeds and gusts of 29/30 knots and forces with the sea 'rough', whatever that meant in the context of the fort. We did the tour of what was nothing more than an enlarged restoration project in the middle of the ocean. The greatest risk was the journey to and from the port and when working in such conditions as existed at the time of my survey the wind and surface conditions would be a risk when working at height or near the water's edge.

Following a few hours in and about the structure, the agent informed me that he had word that the helicopter was back and lashed; I would need to let the pilot know when I was ready to leave. Not wanting to stay the night, or possibly longer for that matter, my response was that I had finished and would be on my way. We climbed back to the helicopter deck and with me now smartly inside the aircraft and buckled up, the pilot signalled for the lashing to be removed. As soon as the ties were removed it was noticeable what a difference they made, where we slid on the water-soaked surface of the helipad, which resulted in some smart skills being shown by the pilot in getting the helicopter ready for take-off and airborne. Once in the air he turned and climbed away, back to over the water and then to the coast and the direction of the shoreline. He was speaking to me but I hadn't heard because in the rush to get airborne I failed to put on my headset and what is more I never realised how wet I was. Needless to say that the risk never came up for resurvey not least of all because I never recommended it.

The second incident was off the coast of Western Australia, where the insured was laying a liquefied natural gas pipeline on the seabed off Karratha, connecting to the three fields. The project visit was the first of the three. Arriving in

Karratha I was to be flown by helicopter to the pipe-laying vessel out in the Indian Ocean, almost an hour's flying time away. The journey out was really enthralling with light winds, great visibility and sunshine and a very smooth sea below. The pilot, being a jovial individual even took the time to fly really low above a school of whales swimming below, where my photographic skills proved a complete waste of effort. Once on the pipe-laying vessel, I proceeded with my survey, making the odd observation regarding some equipment in use, but nothing untoward. With the Australian management, we discussed the safety principles of offshore working, which the insured clearly took seriously. Little did I expect to experience the efficiency of every matter discussed.

On cessation of the visit I was escorted back to the helipad and got into the helicopter when suddenly a siren sounded and it was as if all hell had broken loose. I was ushered from the helicopter by the manager of the insured who almost propelled me across a deck that was covered in aviation fuel. I recognised the smell immediately and made haste in the direction of the catch net about the deck. I didn't reach the secure area before the foam pumps were up and operational though, covering almost everything within ten metres, so I took the first opportunity to stand in the first particle of foam that blew my way. We all cleared the deck except for the fire-suited team, who continued to operate the fire suppression systems with the siren still blasting out its warning. Work had ceased on the vessel as the crew and pipe team had evacuated to the farthest decks, remembering this was a very large ocean-going vessel. Some 30 minutes later the all-clear was announced and work resumed with me returning to the helicopter. Apparently, a fuel hose had split and with the injectors pumping, it had spewed out the liquid under pressure, quickly swamping the deck. However, as per the safety procedure, the dispatcher saw the fuel leak, raised the alarm and the fire crew was standing by to activate the pumps and sound the alarm. Flying back to Karratha the pilot suggested that it was orchestrated to demonstrate to me how efficient their safety teams were. My response was that if that was the case, they should all be up for nomination in the next round of the Oscars!

It is inevitable, I suppose, at some point in time during my surveying days that I was able to contribute to our insured's business by way of me drawing on past development engineering experiences or work situations that were to all intents and purposes initially at least unconnected to the risk survey. As happened with the major labour intensive insured's attendance bonus scheme strategy being updated, resulting in improving significantly employee attendance. This turnaround was achieved by me suggesting they adopt a tried and tested attendance strategy of another of our insured who themselves had experienced a similar problem. Likewise, on another occasion the insured first considering and then embracing my suggestion of a method to safely move a mammoth piling rig from one point to another within the confines of Barry Docks.

Probably the occasion that does stand out in my mind above all others where cooperation between the insured and the insurer and was for me the best example of *added value* that took place in Yemen at Al Anad. The insured were so enamoured with us as insurers we were subsequently requested to write the country's two principle cement-manufacturing plants. The saga began with a simple survey request citing the construction of a new cement works at Al Anad midpoint between Sanaa and Aden. Here the project involved the opening of a limestone and shale quarries and the construction nearby of a cement processing plant all of which was to be self-sufficient in terms of power and water.

My journey took me from Dubai to Khormaksar Airport, Aden where I was to be met by the broker who would be accompanying me during the survey. Ironic that I landed at RAF Khormaksar in 1960 almost 50-years ago as an 18-year-old soldier experiencing my first overseas posting. The journey from the airport by road to the site was uneventful save the odd military road checkpoint and search however, these were once again trouble time in Yemen. At the site, I met up with all the construction heads including the project engineer who was an extremely quiet friendly man with had an excellent command of English so there were no communication problems. There was a military presence around the site due to the quarrying operations having the usual supply of registered explosives for mining processes.

At the initial meeting, the project and progress were made known which then included the setting up of the generator house where five of these large items of plant, absolutely essential to meet the demands of the cement works, were to be installed. I expressed concern about the arrangements due to the fuel storage tank adjacent not being bunded and the fact that the ground fall was from this extremely large fuel tank directly to the generator house. I suggested that a spill or a fire would engulf the site's only means of power if the storage remained without a bund. Almost before I had finished speaking the engineer in Arabic was relaying my concerns to two other members of the party who appeared stunned momentarily until one walked swiftly away.

Moving into the generator house, minus the roof now, the large diesel-powered generators were being installed by the suppliers of the plant judging by their smart logo overalls. I casually asked about fire protections which the engineer suggested would be something to consider but would welcome my suggestions. I explained that once installed their problem could be accommodating something to suppress a fire and that if the passive protection did fail, they could lose all five generators. Understanding the concern, the engineer asked what they could do at this point in time to avert such a disaster as he put it. I suggested that they should construct a simple firewall between each generator while the roof was off as constructing them later could prove difficult. Adding that having to move any other services would prove costly. Speaking of passive fire protections, I suggested the installation of five ceiling mounted extinguishers, with their automatic detection and activation features to prevent such an occurrence which along with the firewall protection were standard insurance requirements or recommendations. Such situations were not unusual and therefore to be expected where active and passive fire protections were involved.

Moving on and noting the terrain, I asked the insured about rainfall as they were virtually under the mountainside that soared way above the plant that was interrupted with *wadis* along the adjacent range. The engineer had held talks with some geological consultancy, who mysteriously had never visited the site, suggested that during heavy rainfall it would be impossible to predict which area would be affected by a flood. Looking over the site and the location of the main cement processing plant I was of the opinion that provided the insured diverted any water away immediately from the end of the large *wadi* directly adjacent their plant it would be advisable, this based on our experiences in Oman. With the insured's engineer, I climbed up the mountainside about two-hundred feet where we were able to see the route of the *wadi* and therefore what appeared to me at least the likely route of any water. Continuing the debate in the site offices it was suggested that they should anchor the loose rocks from about one-hundred feet and lay concrete in the surfaces of the *wadi* wall and the base thereby effectively constructing a huge sluice.

Following two full days of constructive talks, I returned to Dubai which is when I received word that the insured were requesting I survey their cement works up in Sanaa and then revisit their site at Al Anad to check on their progress regarding my observations. It was at this juncture things became somewhat complicated as our intrusions were proving to be the least of the insured's concerns. The resurvey was arranged attached to it some urgency requested by the insured. At the cement works there was according to the engineer some good and bad news however, the news was particularly good for us the insurer but not so for the insured due to a road traffic incident. The insured showed me around the site once again starting at the generator building where their progress since my last visit extended to the fuel storage tank which had since been re-sited and bunded in a depression that further reduced the risk of an uncontainable fuel spillage. In the generator house, the five generators were segregated by way of firewalls extending approximately one metre above the now completed roof with each generator having an Inergen pod positioned above it.

I expressed my surprise that they had completed the work so quickly and that given their responses so far I was convinced that the work to resolve the *wadi* and flood issue would soon follow. Moving out of the generator house the engineer requested I follow him up the mountain where I would be able to see the progress made regarding the anti-flood arrangements. At about 100-feet I could see the work had in fact been completed as the engineer had previously suggested with the *wadi* now resembling a 10-metre wide sluice approximately four metres deep. There was a line on the wall of the *wadi* which the engineer went onto explain that it was not man-made but had been made by the gushing water. Now at a loss, as to describe my bewilderment at this project, the insured went on to explain that they commenced work on the *wadi* the week following my visit and no sooner had they completed it than the rains as expected came. The water cascaded down the mountain via as was predicted the identified *wadi* and was running at one time over two metres deep with the fear the walls would collapse. The watermark on the wall was higher than expected but true to form the insured built the wall allowing for the unexpected. Nonetheless, their design and workmanship withstood the water pressure and assured loose rocks tumbling and by having extended the sluice they diverted the water to deep depression on the other side of the site adjacent the main highway.

Due to water being required for the process and domestic use the insured had already commenced excavating a lagoon to capture as much rainwater as was possible during the following rainy season. So all appeared well albeit the engineer had not revealed their bad news so I enquired. Walking to the new process plant the insured pointed to the large cylindrical kiln, measuring about 30 metres long and about 3 metres in diameter appearing to be ready to set between the twin sets of rollers located at each end of the newly fabricated steel and concrete frame. The engineer informed me that the truck conveying the kiln section, loaded at the docks in Aden, was making the journey to the plant when the articulated transport encountered an acute camber in the road resulting in the vehicle complete with kiln toppling over. When the load was reloaded and reached the site, they discovered that one end had been distorted therefore it would have to be returned to India to either be repaired or a new section manufactured consequently production was being put back another three months.

Purely out of curiosity as we were not involved in this obvious claim, I asked for details of the buckle imagining it to be so severe they were having to ship it back to India. As it turned out the distortion was only at one end of this very large steel cylinder, therefore, I suggested that the manufacturers would surely conduct a repair and not fabricate another. I then went onto to learn that the distortion was about eight or so centimetres and only at the extreme end half metre from the bearing which prompted me to suggest that they should carry out the repair themselves. Now back in the meeting room, I went on to explain the theory behind my observations where I explained at Ford, air gauges were used to check the roundness of pistons where these gauges would, when applied, reveal any degree of ovality. I was convinced by this time judging by the look on the faces of those present that I had somehow lost it. I went on to explain that occasionally a heavy-handed quality control inspector inflicted impact damage on these sensitive gauges consequently they were sent to the gauge cribs for repair and recertification.

What we would do in the gauge crib was to insert a round, hydraulic plug in the ring gauge, apply heat to the gauge and increase the pressure of the hydraulic plug until the gauge was perfectly cylindrical once again. This technique I went onto suggest they could try it as the kiln was only out of roundness at one end where the strength was limited, hence the only part of the kiln to suffer damage when it fell off the truck. Now the room was silent until one of the other engineers pointed out the diameter of the kiln and where could they find hydraulic equipment of that size. I suggested that they forget the hydraulic ring but commence the repair by applying heat by way of oxyacetylene torches to the distorted areas and when sufficiently heated simply insert standard hydraulic jacks, these mounted on chocks, into the kiln and apply the pressure to the distorted area, simply measuring any movement by way of a precision fabricated calliper gauge. There was again a period of silence until the proposition was fully realised with the engineer suggesting they would surely give it a try. On returning to Dubai a week or so later the broker asked me to call the engineer giving me his number. However, before I made the call I received an email with a photograph showing the kiln in operation with a short note saying that the Indian fabricators had sent a representative to assess the damage and that they conducted a successful repair along the lines I had suggested.

Routine Surveying with a Twist

Just occasionally, an insured got found out by the efforts of the surveyor conducting a post-loss survey, who was there for no other reason than to prevent a recurrence. There was no ulterior motive other than to get the measure of the insured by conducting a routine survey, at the same time understanding that hopefully the circumstances leading up to the loss had been rectified. Nonetheless, some insured overlooked the most obvious and basic of security or safety measures involved in their undertakings, and consequently acted against them resulting in claims situations. Alternatively, where perhaps an injured employee was concerned, his account, occasionally backed by the supervisor, duped the insured's hierarchy into believing that the accident was in some way unavoidable and difficult to explain.

In my experience, post-loss surveying more often than not revealed a flaw in the working practices, lack of suitable protections, inappropriate or defective equipment, much of which came about through poor management. Having worked in a pressure cooker like Ford, in an effort to get the job done, both employees and management were prone to take the odd chance; some succeeded, while others failed miserably to their cost. In the final analysis, where there had been a disaster, it was generally found that the rules, established policies and procedure were not followed or were ignored.

Just when things technically were progressing so well there were instances that I still get very embarrassed about and involved insureds you would least wish for. The first was at an engineering concern where I met up with a co-director, one of the nicest and accommodating people you could ever wish to meet. The task was a simple routine liability survey, for an insured with a no claims history, that I had received instructions on a month or so before I got around to fitting the risk survey in. This was located in the vicinity of another insured who represented exactly the opposite: claims in abundance and one on the verge of renewal terms not being invited unless there was a complete change in their obviously cavalier approach. I attended the first risk and it was a disaster, so when arriving at the second location and finding it so good it made my day, momentarily at least.

At this second appointment, the insured's director ushered me into his small office, invited me to have tea and asked about my time in insurance, background and other pleasantries. We eventually got around to him answering some general questions about the business, so generally, I suggested we simply have a walk through the plant as so many of the blanks in my report would be completed once

I viewed the workplace and activities. As predicted, the tour went very smoothly, with just the odd observation made, which the director agreed they would deal with. Back in the office, we dealt with the debrief. I was about to take my leave when another gentleman, the other co-director, entered the office and introduced himself. He was interested as his partner enlightened him on a few issues that they should deal with but said all else was fine. Well, not exactly as the new arrival suddenly stopped in his tracks and turning to me said quizzically, "Cornhill Insurance?"

"Yes, Cornhill," I responded. "But we changed insurers over three months ago. But thanks very much for the free risk assessment!" I showed the gentleman the policy document but he told me that was the case up until recently but that they never renewed the liabilities. I've been embarrassed before, but not professionally, and I let the underwriter know how I felt and what sort of impression it left the ex-insured with. So for as long as I could recall I double-checked any survey instruction following that howler.

I had instances where I was sent to the wrong address to conduct a survey, while the one above was the correct address but the business had been moved to another insurer; however, a building contractor commencing a contract on the wrong building is altogether another matter. The contractor, our insured, dispatched a small team of five tradespeople to knock down a double garage, clearing the ground ready to build a new structure, all while the clients were away on holiday for three weeks. As the scope of the works was innocuous it was another risk survey classed as routine and therefore a site to be surveyed when in the area within the contract period. Calling the insured, I was provided with the address, the name of the client who would not be in residence, the name of the foreman on site and a brief description of the works, duration and contract price, all very much as to be expected.

Arriving on the site two days later I came upon a new exclusive development of four medium-sized detached houses and one larger house, four of the properties with attached garages and the largest property adjacent to a paddock with a small thatched barn and a now very recently vacant plot where obviously another structure had stood. Clearly, these residences were not all sold as two had 'for sale' boards posted. The foreman showed me around and informed me where another detached building had stood and been demolished without incident, it being the proposed site of the new double garage at the end of a short driveway from the new private roadway serving all the properties. The former building had been demolished with the only evidence remaining being a pile of timber joists, large timber double doors, some box stall half doors and some feeding troughs. My thoughts were that they were materials for later use as they were clearly very old, perhaps dating back to the 1800s. The contact yet to be completed was at the stage where the excavations for the new garage block strip foundations and the electrical trench for future supply were being dug by hand. The reason given for the manual labour was that there were some unidentified underground services in the vicinity.

Moving to the small portacabin I found the site drawings on a large drawing board and the site plan for the new garage and contract specifications, so nothing of note and nothing to be concerned about. On one of the site plans there were some heavily weighted lines around the buildings and service road, which I was informed were not involved in the contract works and were therefore not to be disturbed which included a new drive as previously there was simply a short, 15 or so metre unmade track. Informing me of the client's instructions, in letter form, the old barn to the southwest, was to be the site of the new garage, as clearly shown on the architectural drawings. I enquired if the foreman had met the client, which he stated he had not as they had departed on holiday the day before and up until now he had been on another contract. What made me a little uneasy was the question of, if the client was intent on utilising the stabling, why have it closer to the house than the new garaging?

My misgivings were made known to the foreman purely based on what I saw as it being illogical; still, the client probably had other plans we were not privy to. The foreman had been quiet during my deliberations and went really quiet, losing a lot of the confidence I had already come to expect from him in my short time on site. He asked if I would excuse him for a short while as he needed to make a phone call.

After a while, in surveying, you know when you have hit the proverbial nerve so I sat patiently waiting in the portacabin for his return. After what seemed an age the foreman returned and simply told me that there had been miscommunications between the architect and his office, with the result that they misinterpreted the client's instructions. What it had amounted to was that they had based their instructions from the client on some dated drawings obtained from the local authority planners, where the 'barn' was shown as being the only structure apart from the original house.

The upshot was that work was suspended, waiting on the client's return, with our claims people suggesting negligence on our insured's part and professional negligence on the part of the architects. Fortunately for all concerned demolition of a building is generally not classed as 'development' and therefore planning permission was not needed. Further, the demolition did not require approval as it was not in a conservation area. It would have been interesting had the case come to trial regarding apportioning blame but I was informed that we and the insurers of the architects met most of the costs with this funding a new contract involving two new buildings: stabling and garage.

Just occasionally there were times where the underwriter admitted he feared the worst when he was requested by a broker to consider a piece of business; just by looking at the business description it sent warning signals shooting into the sky. With the first case, the underwriter was having me survey the business simply as a favour to one of our regional inspectors, whose wife was employed by this particular broker. The trade description was a 45-gallon drum restorer where the business collected these large drums and where possible salvaged them for resale. The underwriter also told me that he didn't want to write the business, irrespective of the no claims history, because the trade was just one step up from scrap metal merchants, whose reputation went before them in terms of pollution, third party and workers' injury claims. Putting the information to the back of my mind I agreed with the broker to collect the inspector's wife at the broker's offices and she would direct me to the site. I collected the lady, and the first thing I couldn't have failed to notice was the way she was turned out, which was not in the slightest conducive to visiting an oil drum restoration business.

Not wishing to give the impression that the risk we were about to see was dirty and unattractive, from a liability viewpoint, I held my peace about her attire and talked about her husband who I had known a long time, and her experiences in broking, in short, small talk. Arriving at the site which was at the end of a run-down industrial estate it had all the appearances of the scrap metal merchants I still had in my mind's eye. The perimeter fence comprised a high corrugated steel fence over three metres high so that from the outside nothing was visible within. At the open main gates was a retractable traffic barrier that the gateman raised upon recognising the lady to let us through, indicating the reserved parking areas near the offices. My first thoughts were *where are the scrap drums and processes* as all I saw were some large corrugated metal sheds. To say I was disappointed would have been an understatement because quite simply there was nothing to see until a truck entered the yard area stacked with all manner of damaged drums, which had me believing that I was in the right place.

We got out of the car and the first thing that struck me was the noise from the sheds, comprising compressed air and hammering, so I imagined what was going on. Now inside the offices, we were met by the managing director, who surprisingly was really well turned out, and therefore clearly not involved in the reclamation of these containers. We sat in his office and after he had chatted to the broker, he asked me what information I required and what I wished to see. I completed the formalities concerning the business: health and safety, accidents, numbers employed, etc., which all seemed perfectly in order, and then he offered me a recent letter from an EHO. The EHO had inspected the site, which was something to be boasted about as the official couldn't have been more impressed and complimentary; it was as if the managing director had written the letter himself.

We both left the offices and went through the entire work processes, from start to finish, which was totally out of step with other similar risks I had surveyed. Almost every drum contained liquids; therefore, these were put through the decontamination shed, where the contents were checked. Anything suspect was sampled and analysed by their on-site laboratory while the remainder were pressure steam washed, emptying the contents into an underground holding tank. The remainder of the work involved repair work, with the final processes being the painting of both the interior and exterior surfaces. When complete, these drums would have been difficult to tell from new ones.

When finished with the processes we walked back across the yard to the office where I admitted to the MD that I was surprised by the business being so well managed and that I had no adverse remarks to make. Having departed the scene, I dropped the lady back at her office and returned to London. I prepared my report for the underwriter and some eight years later the same underwriter related, at his retirement dinner, my written risk assessment: 'After completing the survey we returned to my car and I couldn't help but notice that the broker's shoes were completely free of any contamination, dirt, grease or oil thus leaving my car's carpets as clean as when she first got in!'

Another yet not so dramatic case involved a hotel group where a very famous movie star had allegedly slipped on the water that had splashed from a water feature in his hotel room, fracturing his hip so that filming on his latest project had to be delayed for several months. For reasons of confidentiality I am unable to name names but spaghetti westerns were all the rage at the time. I was conducting a post-loss survey and the underwriters were keen to get this claim, if one came in, off the books as soon as possible. I was introduced to both the new head of personnel and the general manager, the latter of whom was withdrawn during the survey for fear I believe of committing himself to anything. This was not the only loss at the hotel, but the second, where another claim was being intimated, following a claims notification from a foreign holidaymaker.

Concentrating on the celebrity I saw the room and the water feature, which was switched off and asked to see the manager's accident report. There was silence as there was no real accident report, simply because of who they claimed the individual was. I remarked that it does not matter who is involved; an accident is an accident and if we do not want a repeat, we take corrective action now, not later, and to do that we need to be fully aware of the circumstances. The head of personnel cut in, suggesting that they had flown the injured person out by ambulance helicopter immediately and following treatment and hospitalisation for a short while the movie star had flown back to the US to recuperate.

Now looking at the scene I noted it was, for the most part, carpeted so I posed the question of the situation at the time? Apparently, nothing had changed, and they had not let the suite since the accident as it was paid for a fixed period. I asked about the footwear or anything else that could have caused the fall because I said, "You do not *slip* on a carpet if it is fitted as well as clearly, this is. Perhaps you could trip if it is rucked or badly worn, but in this case, neither condition exists. So what about the footwear, was the person intoxicated, what time was it, dusk, night, early morning that could have affected his vision and balance?"

I was losing the battle as the manager said they were more concerned about the wellbeing of the guest than looking for what may have caused the accident. My response was that the status of the guest where accidents or incidents are concerned is of little importance but the staff had an interest in protecting the good name of the hotel and the prevention of other accidents. There was little to be gained from talking further so I asked about the other incident.

Apparently, the other alleged accident involved a guest falling down a carpeted stair, but I again metaphorically speaking hit a wall where the investigation was concerned. The UK guest allegedly tripped on a rucked carpet and fell, hurting his back, which resulted in the hotel night manager simply offering to take him to hospital. The guest refused treatment, asking only that the incident be entered in the hotel's accident book. He had his young son and another guest witnessing the fall, although again the information was sketchy and no statement was forthcoming from any of those involved. I also learnt that the next day the guest checked out with his family and again no further details were available. I had to remind those present of the group's accident and incident procedures, none of which appeared to have been followed. Again, albeit probably too late, I requested the night manager's account of the incident, where it happened, photographs or anything, as I believed the hotel or we as the insurers hadn't heard the last of this.

Unfortunately, I had to turn off the charm when the personnel manager intervened, telling me that I should rest assured that she knew, as a qualified lawyer, and with the claims history in Portugal, that there would be no repercussions as this was not the UK or the US. Besides if there were to be a settlement it would be insignificant and hardly worth the effort as the courts here in Portugal would limit the size of the claim. Now being completely exasperated I asked just how long she had been working in the hotel and tourist industry, as I felt she was sadly out of touch. I then felt constrained to inform her that the likely booking was made through their agents in the UK and that they would be the first likely contact a claim would come through. However, I also reminded her that Portugal was now part of the EU and if I were to sue it would be through the European Courts so the hotel shouldn't get too complacent by living in Portugal's past.

Later I spoke with a senior director who happened to be visiting the hotel at the time, and who was alarmed to hear of the inactivity on the part of the management, but put it down to the fact that the hotel was, in fact, a very recent acquisition and they were still possibly working under previous policies. As a consequence of these two incidents, I was invited to address all managers at their next annual general conference, where this personnel lady was present. I couldn't resist informing the assembly of the incident at one of their hotels where it transpired that the injured party was a habitual claimant and we had to settle for a four-figure sum due to a distinct lack of information on the hotel's part. As for the movie star, there was no claim submitted as the hotel picked up the medical bills plus the helicopter ride.

Very rarely I came across a situation where an insured in managing his business came face to face with a set of circumstances never envisaged or encountered before, where the situation theoretically could not be improved on. As surveyors, we were expected to identify general shortcomings and, drawing on past experiences or by adopting standard practices, we arrive at a satisfactory conclusion. An example was where one highly rated HNW client had a problem meeting a policy condition that required a UL (Underwriter Laboratories) rated safe weighing over 100kgs, which we considered posed transportable obstacles, that had to locate it above ground floor level. The problem the client faced was that the safe couldn't be moved to an upper level, to satisfy policy conditions, due to the layout of the residence and their inability to introduce mechanical handling equipment. However, my contention was that the client had a basement and if the safe were lowered there it would meet the policy wording, requiring mechanical means to move it. Lateral thinking overcame perceived shortcomings regarding the portability of the safe through us being flexible and slightly amending the policy wordings. Following a management review, I was required to draw up a new standard which was adopted worldwide where UL rated safes were concerned.

So, moving to the general problems where our insured or their broker possibly had little to no previous experiences to draw on, which if not resolved could impact on the insured's claims history. One business was a corporate insured who was faced with an age-old industrial plight involving absenteeism on a Monday and to a lesser degree on a Tuesday. During a visit to the group's head office, the chairman was casually discussing general problems including speaking of the labour force that was without exception so depleted at the start of the week that they resorted to running shifts at the weekend involving premium rates of pay. It was as if there was a conspiracy amongst the predominantly unskilled workers employed on the packing lines, in a populated area where there was high employment; therefore, the insured dismissed the notion of additional labour almost as soon as it entered the debate. He and the board were designed to accept the situation until he mentioned it to me while discussing general problems. The reason for the exchange of views was that we, the insurers, had been largely instrumental in turning this risk around when it initially had a poor claims history to one worthy of praise in less than two periods of insurance.

Requesting my opinion, I enquired as to them having any notions of introducing an attendance bonus scheme which in truth had the other board members sitting bolt upright. I went on to mention one labour-intensive business who struggled until they too became resigned to three-shift working plus weekends, which dug deep into their 'bottom line'. I also mentioned that this same insured found that if the employee was carrying a slight injury they appeared to stretch the convalescence even though there were other light duties they could have performed. This business chose not to introduce a bonus attendance scheme, which meant that the board accepted the inevitability of increasing the headcount to overcome their problem. I also mentioned that the business's turnover of labour shot up, so there was pressure put on other departments such as accounts, personnel and training. The information provided seemed to have gripped the imagination of the chairman, who was prepared to try anything that would improve the profitability of the group by that point.

The bonus scheme was subsequently introduced and for a few months, things did improve, but it involved strict conditions regarding attendance where, if absent for a medical condition the employee was required to provide a medical certificate. As the weeks and months went by the absenteeism started to marginally climb again so that near the year-end those who qualified for the bonus did show a marked improvement in attendance naturally as did the turnaround of labour. Just prior to Christmas I was as usual invited to the board's Christmas lunch where again the chairman discussed business strategies and successes. The bonus issue was up again for debate, and my question was about the amount or the size of the bonus where the accountant revealed the six-figure sum of which 40 per cent had been paid out, with the residue going back into their accounts. I had no idea where the notion suddenly came from when I asked if they would have been happier to have paid out all of the allotted bonus or improve the absenteeism.

The chairman stepped in, commenting that they had calculated and allowed for the bonus fund and that absenteeism was the bugbear, as it simply cost them far more. So I asked that if that was the case why not inform the workforce that there was no fixed bonus payment, and just tell them that the allotted fund would be shared amongst those qualifying at the year-end? There was silence until the chairman after a few moments of thought said they would announce it after New Year. The upshot was that the business's absenteeism dropped like the proverbial stone and during my September meeting the absenteeism had reached the stage where there was no longer weekend production, except of course in engineering and maintenance. The insured was amazed and wanted to know where the idea came from. I had to inform him that we had a case where an employee was injured playing rugby and was signed off work by his doctor, but our CEO being unsympathetic, told him that he should forget his bonus the following year. The employee struggled into work on crutches for about five or so weeks, all the while regardless of holding a doctor's certificate excusing his work, and secured his bonus.

The most challenging loss control situation I encountered involved an insured piling contractor who had the most difficult of contracts where they were engaged to replace the timber piles with interlocking metal sheet piling around the water's edge and finger docks at Barry Docks, South Wales. The caterpillar-piling rig with metal tracking and percussion hammer weighed about 140-tons and had completed about 100 metres of quayside when I arrived on site. The insured were now faced with an access problem due to the dimensions of the dock entrance and service roads, which would restrict access to the low-loader articulated transport carrying the machine further. We were summoned as, following discussions regarding the access problems between our insured and the port authorities I learned that they believed there was just one solution as to how they could get this large item of the plant into operational positions amongst the six finger docks and quaysides.

Undoubtedly the problem our insured faced was that at the outset and while successfully tendering for the contract they did not take into account the restricted access within the dock. By all accounts, neither did their clients as they would never have been informed of the size and weight of the insured's piling rig believing such detail would have been taken into account at the tendering stage by the insured. These obstacles became all too apparent once the rig had completed piling the open-sided water's edge and was set to move between the finger docks. Now taking into account the challenges, they required further insurance and approval of what they arrived at as being an acceptable and satisfactory solution.

The insured's subsequent submission was to erect temporary steel bridges spanning each of the finger docks in turn that would enable their piling rig to be driven and manoeuvred about, not overlooking the fact that this rig had only been able to enter the dock by way of a sea-going barge, all due to the aforementioned restrictive access roads.

By the time I had arrived at the docks the insured and their engineers had brought onto site, also by way of barges, four very large, reinforced steel joists measuring approximately 35 metres in length. The intention was to cut recesses into the concrete apron that surrounded each of the finger docks on opposite sides and lay the two sets of RSJs into the newly created slots, forming a bridge. This is where the additional insurance cover was required, against property damage of the client and our insured's plant in a non-work-related activity. My first reaction took those present by surprise because I submitted that the metal-to-metal surface offered little to no traction or grip to the caterpillar's steel tracks which would surely be the case as the 120-ton rig, less the jib, would come to bear, particularly as it reached the centre of the temporary bridge, with deflection being a certainty. In engineering, deflection is the degree to which a structural element is displaced under a load. Coupled with vibrations the twin steels could conceivably twist resulting in the rig possibly sliding off the beams, into the water. The claim I could foresee involved damaged quayside, loss of plant and recovery costs and possibly business interruption of the port while repairs and recovery took place.

To avoid the pairs of RSJs' twisting, I asked why they were not welding them together when an engineer said they could not do so as the total weight of the pair would be restrictive. Exasperated, I asked why they could not be welded in-situ which at least had the engineer back on track. My next question was the level of deflection which alarmingly they confessed they did not know, but they planned a trial run beside the finger dock, by way of the twin beams being placed on two concrete blocks set the same distance apart as that of the finger dock. Then with the rig being driven on and parked in the centre of the twin beams, they could then measure the deflection. Obviously, I wasn't surprised by the lack of preparedness from those involved, as they were making it up as they went along. This is where I suggested a practical solution to both our problem, as the insurer, and their problem as the insured, wanting the safe completion of the contract.

My suggestion was that they did not need to conduct a deflection measurement at all by firstly placing the pairs of beams together across each finger dock and when in position weld them. They should then float a barge up under the beams strapping them to it and after mooring the barge, flood the dock or when at high tide up until the barge was taking the whole weight of the beams and the machine, which they could measure by viewing the Plimsoll Line on the barge. Not that they would observe any movement, as the standard barge is usually in the region of 60 metres long and ten metres wide, with a load capacity close to 1,500-tons. Adding a bit of humour to the obvious relief of those present, I said they should be grateful for the advice as if this master plan of mine were to fail because of unforeseen circumstances, the barge below it would catch the rig!

It was one of the most satisfactory responses I had ever experienced as a surveyor and engineer with the insured remarking how stupidly simple it all was now given that these barges are capable of carrying extraordinary loads, way more than their rig, in fact, to reiterate, it was the form of transport used to deliver the rig in the first place. We provided cover for the duration of the contract, on condition of adopting my recommendations, which the insured did with the entire contract completed without a claim.

From some poorly run pieces of business, I will move to the most desirable, with the pride of place regarding the very best risks ever surveyed going to two organisations: one a religious order and the other a sporting organisation. Little Sisters of the Poor was the former, while Marylebone Cricket Club, based at Lords Cricket Ground, was the latter. Where Little Sisters of the Poor were concerned the order took the health, safety and welfare of all to heart as it was fundamental to their faith. As for the MCC, their organisation were not only lawmakers for the game of cricket, but some of the committee members were influential figures from the upper and lower Houses of Parliament, police service, legal profession, medical profession, and so on. While each insured had different goals, they achieved them by adopting the highest principles. What I learnt was that while the average, law-abiding citizen, will act responsibly where the laws of the land are concerned those in such organisations set the standards above that by thinking and acting beyond the norm. As far as the holy order of the Sisters goes their duty is to God, where every person's wellbeing is their sole purpose in this life.

Little Sisters of the Poor is a Roman Catholic religious institute for women established to cater for the poor and aged. I was requested to survey two of their hospices: one in London the other in Brighton. Not being familiar with the order I read up on it before making the appointment because with care homes and hospitals we saw many claims for injuries such as assaults, trips, slips and falls, handling injuries, kitchen incidents, in fact, a diversity of injuries including stress. Expecting that it would be difficult as it was a charitable organisation, I believed that with funds being tight I would be looking at overworked sisters and helpers, rundown premises, in fact, honest hardworking people who for the most part were without financial rewards. Ironically I find myself back to vocations which I found amongst the ranks of the insured persons who embraced missions without the question of financial rewards.

My contact, as expected, was the mother superior, or Mother Mary as she was known and she had been waiting on my call. Arrangements were made as she wanted a particular sister to be present, as occupational health and safety was more Sister Marie's forte. I met the two nuns as arranged and as usual, requested tolerance regarding my questions but these when translated into layman's term would be understood by the underwriters. Touching upon how they were organised I got the impression straight away from their responses that I was speaking with two very knowledgeable people; particularly where statutory duties were concerned, they needed no prompting. Never once, during the forty minutes we spoke, did I catch either glancing at one another, as if looking for support, when answering a question. Every one of their answers was straight to the point and just occasionally elaborated on as if I understood only part of the message they were attempting to get across. So well was the meeting going that I had to take a reality check lest I was being cleverly side-tracked?

Deciding that I had sufficient information I requested some legal documentation such as their safety policy, accident records, inductions for new starters and their latest safety audits. Normally these take some retrieving particularly in less organised businesses, where they haven't been seen for ages. Well, those documents were all in binders and extremely well kept, save there was just the very odd entry in their accident book and their audit findings, completed just four weeks prior to the visit, which was yet to be completed. Being suspicious by nature when I see a business so well organised, I requested the audit for the previous 12 months, as I wished to see if there were any trends. The audit binder was produced and showed about four years of quarterly records with actions taken on the few defects listed. I was now beginning to feel embarrassed and asked exactly how and why they were so well informed and organised? Mother Mary was somewhat taken back but with tolerance explained that health, safety and welfare were fundamental to their beliefs whether that involved themselves, patients, me and anyone else for that matter.

Having now understood that I was in the presence of really caring and informed people I asked where they obtained their knowledge from as the statutes would not have formed part of their holy orders. Both sisters laughed and told me of their first night class at a local technical college where they had enrolled in the Health and Safety at Work classes. The class was made up of trade union members, managers from industry, building site supervisors, a haulage company manager, all male, who asked them if they were in the right class? Mother Superior asked those assembled, "Doesn't health and safety apply to everyone?"

I requested that we conduct a whistle stop tour and wish to visit a ward if possible, the laundry, kitchen and maintenance workshop. Every location was supervised by a knowledgeable sister and found to be without any problems, in fact, it was flawless, so I completed arguably the best survey of a risk I had ever had the privilege to visit.

The second site visit of the Sisters was near Brighton and comprised a multi-storey residential Victorian block with old sash windows and, as with London, was managed by sisters who were dedicated and knowledgeable, running what can only be described as a near-perfect setup. Before leaving, the sister who took me through everything and made a request concerning their contract window cleaners. The window cleaners, regardless of the height, were jumping from one exterior window ledge to the next without any harness. Ladders were often seen to be insecure so the sisters were concerned about workers falling from a height, from which they would surely die. They had mentioned it to the contractors but it fell upon deaf ears, with the response being for them not to worry. Obviously, as we carried the public liability for the order there could be claims arising from a fall; after all, I pointed out, the sisters controlled the premises and could be brought to book if a window ledge collapsed, or a person below was struck by a person falling or some debris. I informed her that I shared her concern so I would take the matter up with the contractors and keep her informed.

As promised I contacted the window cleaners' manager requesting I visit him as I had an urgent matter to discuss. The meeting took place in their Sussex offices where I informed him of our concern regarding liabilities. Having the manager's attention, I informed him that we would be withdrawing cover unless the holy order changed to more a safety-conscious contractor. As we insured this holy order worldwide it seemed likely that they would do so and consequently, I suggested he took our stance seriously as I would be putting the concerns in writing so that should there be an incident, we would release the information to the HSE. I was assured, by a very worried manager, that he would personally attend the hospice when next his men were there to ensure their own safe working practices were followed. Further, we decided that we would request the sisters include in their site audit the window cleaners' safety standards. The meeting was productive and we were subsequently informed of the total cooperation of the window-cleaning contractor. This, without a doubt, was the best of the best risks surveyed with the most satisfying of conclusions.

Lords cricket ground was another highly rated risk surveyed, only second to the Little Sisters of the Poor. Lords is home to Marylebone Cricket Club or the MCC. The organisation and the arrangements were such that it could neither be faulted nor criticised in any way, as the safety and health of staff, members and the public were at the top of the committee's priorities. Long before the Safety at Sports Ground Act became law, the committee had already implemented and maintained safety standards that had subsequently become law in the UK. Of course we, as the insurers, should have anticipated a proactive insured given the guidance and advice within their committee, but also the awareness that they had of the need to be seen to be above criticism. From the Nursery Cricket School to safety standards within the stadium during the likes of test and county matches the controls and stewarding were excellent.

My reason for favouring The Sisters risk above Lords was simply down to the fact that they were starting with a clean piece of paper, with no experts to call upon, and no guidance save that which their representatives learned at night school, whereas, with Lords, the committee had amongst its number those who were probably involved in the drafting of the Act; consequently, I would have expected no less.

Both risks rated 'exceptional' and were a pleasure to survey. Finally, I want to turn to the question of when a survey is not a survey; a question that revealed unwittingly the extent and level of a lateral thinking surveyor's investigatory skills. This came about as a result of attempting to arrange a routine liability survey and ultimately led to opening a proverbial can of worms. Survey requests were sent as hard copy to the survey team and placed in order of priority: post-loss, new business and routine. When arranging a priority survey, we attempted to organise a less urgent survey nearby, thus reducing time and travel. With one such risk, I tried unsuccessfully to arrange a routine visit, only to experience continual resistance from the broker who was the initial contact. The broker claimed that his client was difficult to tie down due to his extensive business travel. Consequently, as the risk survey was routine, with no major losses reported, the survey request was returned to the waiting list until, as was the practice and now at this late juncture, with renewal being imminent, it was cancelled.

Unbeknown at the time this alleged insured ran a number of spurious companies in the area, covered by the unsuspecting branch and obtaining insurances mainly for employer's and public liabilities. The business premiums were modest and for at least three years had operated without losses or claims. However, in the fourth year, a few minor unrelated claims were submitted that due to the size of the losses the local branch manager had the authority to settle.

An unrelated routine survey request was received and arranged for a business where the address submitted was on the very same industrial estate as the one risk I had in the preceding year made several unsuccessful attempts to survey. Arriving on the estate I looked up the business details of the troublesome insured and thought I might take a look while in the area, time permitting. Following the completion of the arranged survey, I asked the insured's manager if he knew of the elusive insured, quoting the name of the business. I enquired because their business had been on the estate for many years; surprisingly, though, they had never heard of them. Now intrigued, I decided to drive around, as time permitted it, looking for the address. That proved to be fruitless as I found nothing at all along the named service road. The only thing I established was a vacant plot, by virtue of the numbering of the units either side of the vacant plot being consecutive.

Considering the situation now to be completely bizarre I made enquiries at the reception of the two immediate neighbours, either side of the vacant plot, with the first telling me that they had only been in their unit two years so they couldn't help. I had more fortune at the other, whose manager told me of a fire that had all but destroyed the building and business next door, resulting in the structure being subsequently demolished and the site cleared. What happened to the occupier, the proprietor of the business did not know. What I did learn was that the name of the former occupier resembled the name of our insured, save for one discrepancy: one was a limited company and the other not.

Returning to the office I reported my findings back to the underwriters who, in turn, contacted the branch learning that no representative had ever visited the site and neither had the broker, allegedly. An enquiry was set up with the book of business involving the broker being closely examined, where it was established that the minor loss totals had exceeded the premiums received by a considerable margin. The deception was successful due to each of the losses being settled below the level that would have drawn attention negatively, involving all the six fictitious insured. Although never proved or externally investigated, a senior branch member subsequently resigned from the company, although there was suspected collusion between a possible third party and the broker. The matter was hushed up and quickly closed, with no credit given for my efforts, as it was an embarrassment to the company, not least of all both internal and external auditors.

Up Market Surveying

Years passed with me conducting commercial business surveys. However, during my later years in Dubai, I was requested to move into the personal lines as International Head of Risk Management, Private Client Group. Here, the role entailed dealing with high net worth clients in the Middle East, India, Turkey and Greece and overseeing the Australian and UK risk management teams. Then, as opposed to drinking tea out of a mug in a manager's or works director's office I was sitting in a mansion, drinking Darjeeling tea out of a bone China tea cup. The workload hadn't decreased; in fact, such was the demand, it involved on occasions weekends and the odd evening, daylight hours permitting. Being prepared was the policy as I was literally at each client's beck and call. It was the first time in my career I was not conscious of the number of appraisals I conducted, because in many cases there was more than one visit due to certain information not being available as the client was travelling or the same having more than one home.

In many cases with these clients they owned and occupied more than one property and in more than one country so as and to be expected befitting my job title and status the client would request I undertake a second visit at another of their properties outside of my region. This, of course, did not just involve residences but the likes of classic cars, artwork, stamps, artefacts and other collections. As happened on three occasions whole families embarked on overseas travels to attend the likes of weddings; chartering a commercial airliner to do so, such was the size of the party. All the while, these clients were carrying family heirlooms of considerable value. One final matter that merits mention is that with all HNW clients I encountered they were poles apart from the many commercial clients I came across, just perhaps because these insured more often than not were revealing personal details, including family relationships, that we all share and can sympathise with; consequently, the relationship becomes very personal.

Assessing is not quite like normal surveying, since, having made their fortune the insured wanted it secure and for a small percentage of the value they could, with our assurances, rest easy. I cannot recall ever having to make a recommendation that entailed a mind-shattering sum. In fact, in one case, I was happy not to recommend that a prestigious insured add contents insurance on top of his property cover as he felt he didn't need it. His property was estimated to have a rebuild cost of about US$2.5million. When talking with his mother and father, during their assessment the same day, they asked whether their son's cover was adequate. Guardedly, I told them that both their own and their son's rebuild values were wholly adequate. The mother, a very perceptive lady, asked me about her son's watches and some antique furnishings; these were family heirlooms, which tactfully I tried to avoid answering. Obviously, knowing her son as only a mother might, and not waiting for a response, she picked up the phone and made a call. After a brief conversation conducted in both Arabic and English, she hung up and then asked me to revisit her 'short-sighted boy' as she so eloquently described him, to provide full contents cover.

Called upon to assess two of India's wealthiest people, a brother and sister who were seemingly at odds with each other, we at least had them talking again through their insurance dealings with us. The brother and sister had separate business interests and homes and apparently different lives, sharing little for some unexplained reasons. During the assessment of the sister's property the subject of thermal imagery came up, a modern technique using infrared cameras to identify suspect electrical services. This immediately caught the sister's imagination and attention.

As both brother and sister had industrial premises, I casually mentioned thermal imagery as a useful aid, with all the benefits and advantages, which they could also put to use periodically in their homes. Plus, if so inclined, why not purchase one camera and share it with the brother for conducting routine inspections in their homes and business premises alike? Off the record, before I flew back to Dubai, I was invited to one of the lady's factories where all three of us, brother and sister, along with their respective technical managers, met up for informal discussions regarding the cameras. I later heard that obviously sold on the idea, they had a demonstration, made a purchase of a camera and suddenly they were back in each other's good books again or at the very least sharing something to both of their benefits.

Out of the very large number of appraisals, I conducted some of the most memorable were anything but straightforward like the owner occupier of a large, beautiful property on the Palm Jumeirah, Dubai, where we insured both house and contents. The property owner was a gemologist and so was looking to us to provide high net worth cover, which of course entails a free assessment regarding fire, theft and other perils for the like of domestic staff. I received the instructions on a standard form that listed contact details and address; the address was vital given what was insured, and contents including the likes of gems and jewellery. I was responsible for making my own appointments, usually directly with the insured, so it provided me with the opportunity to exchange niceties before the assessment. The time and date were set and I arrived outside the address a full fifteen minutes before the appointed time and sat in my car until five minutes beforehand, got out and made my way up the front path. I rang the multi-chime doorbell, which was immediately answered by a uniformed housemaid.

"Good morning," I said, handing over my business card. "I am here to conduct an assessment and I have an appointment at nine."

The maid looked bemused and quietly said, "Sorry sir, nobody told me to expect anyone and there is only me and two other servants here." After an awkward pause, the maid added, "I suppose you had better come in then."

Seeing her discomfort and the fact it was my policy only to enter a property when the visit was confirmed, I said, "No, sorry, I can't do that. I shall go back to my car and call my office for them to confer with the owner." I thanked the lady and wandered back to my car to make the call. Getting back to my car, I immediately called the office for them to speak with the owner and let me know what was happening because even though I was invited I was not going into the house, as I could be anyone. I only had to wait a few minutes before my phone rang and the underwriter told me that Nyrindha, the insured, had forgotten, she apologised and would be there in fifteen minutes. Further, I should go back to the house and get the maid to make me a cup of tea or coffee.

Now confirmed I decided to return to the house explaining the situation to the maid informing her that the insured, her employer, had forgotten and would be back shortly, and in the meantime, she should make me a cup of tea or coffee. "Don't worry," I said after a moment's thought, "forget the tea or coffee, I need some photos so I shall take some external views of the property until your mistress arrives home," I said leaving, the maid and entering the rear garden area. I took about half dozen external views of the property after which I made my way back into the lounge, to find the maid speaking on the telephone, as it turned out, talking with the owner.

While in deep conversation on the phone the maid was looking oddly at me as if things were not right; not reading too much into this I casually sat down and made some notes, during which time the maid hung up the phone and said, "Sir, Mr Al Karma didn't know about you coming?"

I said, "No, well he probably wouldn't have as I made the appointment with Aparna Nyrindha."

"Ms Aparna Nyrindha?" "But Ms Aparna lives next door, number PJ21!"

I couldn't believe what I was hearing, for my instructions were clearly 'PJ19' and here I was in PJ19, but Aparna was nowhere to be seen. Probably by this time the client was waiting patiently for me next door. For the second time in my career I was totally embarrassed at being in the wrong house but right address, according to my instructions, that is. I said to the maid, "Apologise to Abdul Al Karma for me please and should he wish to contact me or my company you have my business card." I even took time to point out to the maid the address on my PCG (Private Client Group) instructions, hopefully leaving the maid in little doubt about the genuine error, and left.

I was at a loss as to how I should deal with it, as it certainly would reflect on both me and the company, for this was not a commercial bit of business but a high net worth policyholder. After all, I reasoned, the client would assume that, if the insurer cannot get the correct address, what else can we get wrong? I decided to drive up to the end of the frond away from the properties, planning to drive back when I got my thinking straight. Consequently, I drove up to the end of the frond, which of course was a cul-de-sac, returning outside the insured's house number PJ21. I parked up at the end of the insured's drive, got to the front door and was about to ring the doorbell when it was opened by Aparna.

"Hello, Stuart! I thought you were already here in my house?"

"Well," I said, "I thought I would give you a chance to get home and organised before I called so I drove up to the end of the front," I replied.

Aparna laughed and with a smirk said, "Come on in and sit down. You must be exhausted," she added with a hint of sarcasm. "All that driving and you preferring Abdul's coffee to mine!" So the news travelled fast.

"It's not funny Ms Aparna when your insurer can't even get the address of an important client right," I replied, offering it up as a weak form of excuse. Albeit that was the second most embarrassing situation I found myself in but the insured took a liking to us and ironically not only did I end up assessing the neighbour Mr Abdul Al Karma's property within the month but also another client directly opposite even though I suspected I was the butt of those three insured's humour during the following years.

Nonetheless, the worst was to come, and here I could not blame the broker, underwriter or administration staff because the next farcical occurrence was all down to me. Our insured, a Middle East Emir, was a patron of African and Arabic art and possessed a multimillion-dollar collection. He required that when not on display, this highly valuable collection of art was secured against accidental damage, theft, fire and the environment. I was requested to oversee that the proposed storage arrangements were adequate, so I worked closely with the Sheikh's Art Manager and their appointed contractors to convert one of the Sheikh's owned industrial units into what was effectively a strong room. Visiting the facility for the first time I found that the unit needed a refit as it had a wet sprinkler system. Leaking water systems are a serious threat, and it had roof voids and too many points of entry; consequently, some major changes were required and these suggested improvements were presented to the insured via the broker and art manager.

Following the first visit, the insured made the necessary improvements, never cutting corners and introducing even the smallest suggested improvement. Regardless of the insured's efforts, I was requested to visit the facility again to view the progress made, plus the insured had considered another improvement by not having security on site but in an alternative location nearby, yet overlooking the storage facility. Yet again, as requested, I returned to the facility, finding both my own and the insured's suggested improvements had been introduced, including the night security man being relocated and that the insured having installed an infrared CCTV camera linked to an alarm connected to the police. It was a perfect set up so I informed the brokers that the insured should be congratulated on their efforts and I would be highly commending the insured to the underwriter.

Believing this was the end of the matter I was in India when I received a call from the HNW underwriter, passing on a message from the insured, that as everything was now fully operational at the storage facility, it would be appreciated if I could just cast my eye over it one final time just in case they had missed something? This was a major client and the head of an Arabic State, so who was I to refuse? Arriving back from India I called the art manager and made an appointment a few days hence to call at their offices to collect her and then drive to the unit together, as it was in a difficult location. Arriving at the registered business address, a modern multi-storey block, I was perusing the business notice guide in the lobby when a tall, dapper Arabic gentleman asked if he could be of assistance. "Yes, I am looking for the Art Manager's office but I confess I can see *arts and crafts* but no names."

"Come on, I will show you," the gentleman replied. We got into the lift without another word and he pressed a button, presumably for the appropriate floor. "I suppose you've come to see the art store?" he asked.

"Yes," I said, "but you know they have done such a fantastic job I really don't know what I am doing back here; it seems to be a flag-waving exercise if you ask me." Waving an imaginary flag.

The lift arrived at the desired floor, we alighted and at the first corner and in the first office my guide put his head around the door and simply said, "Stuart's here."

Without so much as a glance or acknowledgement to the gentleman, the art manager said, "Hi, Stuart. I will be with you in a second, just let me finish this." The Arabic gentleman walked off, and as I said, "*Shukran*," virtually the limit of my Arabic, he simply put his hand to his chest and disappeared down the corridor. We drove to the site, talking idly about the business and the sheikh's passion for art, and as anticipated found everything in order at the storage facility, so I drove back to the art manager's office and then following dropping her off and exchanging a few pleasantries I headed on back to Dubai.

Back in Dubai after an hour's drive, I pulled into my parking spot just when my phone rang with the HNW underwriter excitedly asked, "What was he like?"

Puzzled, I replied, "What was who like?"

"The sheikh," replied the underwriter.

"How the hell would I know?" I responded.

"Well, you ought to, after all, he was in the lift with you!" came the response!

Given the art manager's off-hand response when the sheikh told her my name and that I had arrived, it never occurred to me that we were both in the presence of the head of state. The sheikh, knowing me by name, suddenly sunk in and how embarrassing that was, given my attempt to be flippant about the survey. How was I ever going to live this down, I wondered. Well, I didn't have long to wait because within that same week my presence was requested at the sheikh's main art gallery where I was requested to survey it and make my recommendations, as the sheikh wanted this included on the schedule. *Obviously, I got away with it as his art manager later said that the impression created, was one of being highly professional yet open, which left the insured with a lasting impression, more than likely of me being lucky,* I thought.

When the police ask the victim of theft if they are insured then close the file if the response is positive then, as insurers, you have one or two issues to ponder. In the case, I was to become involved with I concluded that the police wanted to keep the crime rate down or the crime rate was higher than the police authority wanted to admit. What this did was to force me to write and have an article published in a Middle East journal where I opined that the police's actions would only encourage the criminal elements. Further, if they continued to adopt such a policy of advertising a low crime rate, this could give rise to people getting blasé with their personal possessions. From an insurer's standpoint, particularly where high net worth clients are concerned, and where the asset values are considerable, it could escalate matters, as criminals will resort to violence. The journal received many reader comments, but not one complaint or counter-opinion was offered.

What led me to such an opinion regarding almost lackadaisical policing came about following a post-loss survey for a PCG policyholder where a valuable item of jewellery had been stolen from the insured's home. Arriving at the house in the UAE I met the wife of the insured, who told me that their maid unbeknown to them had been deceptive and calculating by having a paste jewel inserted in one of her diamond earrings, the value of the three-carat diamond being a little less than US$15,000. Before the loss was discovered the maid resigned, telling the lady that she had to return home to the Philippines due to a family bereavement, this after a year of satisfactory service. All appeared normal until the teenage daughter of the family arrived home from school in the UK for the summer. Sitting in their lounge the daughter told her mother to stop rubbing her ear, a habit of many years, as it was making the diamond stud dull.

During the following week, the daughter suggested that they return to the jewellers who made the earrings and have them cleaned and polished. Returning to the jewellers the lady removed the earrings placing them on the counter in front of the salesman. Immediately the salesman stood back and looked directly into the CCTV unit covering the counter, establishing that it was functioning. With his hands in full view and away from the counter, he informed the lady that one was not a diamond. The lady shocked told the shop assistant that she had purchased them from the jewellers, which he affirmed was true, saying he remembered her but repeated that one was not a diamond. He then called over the other shop assistant and pointed to the bogus item and the other salesman made the same comment that his colleague had made insofar as one was not a diamond. Now totally perplexed the lady called the police on her cell phone and refused to leave the shop, with the items still resting on the counter, exactly where she had placed them, and with the salesmen still standing clear.

The police arrived and both the lady, the daughter and the salespeople gave statements, with the salesmen sensibly suggesting the police look at the footage on the digital CCTV monitor if they in any way doubted the sales staff's version of events. The police took the earrings away, during which time they were assessed by an independent valuation service, who confirmed that one diamond was as per the original sale but not the other, as this was not genuine. The claim inspectors viewed the claim and agreed to settle for the full amount as the items were itemised on the policy.

My involvement, other than with the police, was to establish the exposure if the insured was so careless about such valuable items as they had an approved safe. Clearly, though, it was not used as much as the insured would have had us believe. The reason being I was in possession of the schedule and requested to be shown a selected number of items including an extremely valuable dress ring, a solitaire diamond ring of some five carats, a lady's gold and a diamond Omega watch. The lady pointed out the watch in a winder on the dressing table and in fact, the items not in the safe or on the person amounted to approximately US$120,000, as per the previous valuation.

Clearly, the lady was lackadaisical about her jewellery and tended to take it off and leave the items on the dressing table where the now recently departed maid would put them in a drawer, out of sight. When the lady wanted an item of jewellery, she would pick the nearest available so this practice was not unknown to the maid; therefore, she would have had time to visit a jeweller and have a pair of earrings made, retaining the genuine diamond. Other people including domestic staff and friends of the maid later reported that the maid gambled heavily and that probably led her to make the switch and then fly back home to the Philippines before the loss was noticed. It was clear that the UAE Police would never seek extradition and there were no criminal charges, leaving this maid's passport clean. For my part, I suggested that for all the police knew this maid could now be working somewhere else in the Middle East with the same thing about to happen again. In fact, I added that she has been making good out of the crimes committed, and all the while the UAE crime rate remained static.

Being general insurers, we were requested by a high net worth insured, again residing in the Middle East, to provide goods-in-transit cover for a very valuable work of art they had purchased at world-renowned auctioneers in London. The value of the purchase was in the vicinity US$1.8-million and would increase the insured's assets by approximately a further six per cent. My task was to assess the transit arrangements, including vetting the carrier's capabilities from the auctioneers through to the customer, at our insured's residence.

Naturally, as commercial and personal lines insurers we were extremely well-informed regarding shipping and storage inefficiencies in general, and this was not an appraisal to be taken lightly given a large single item of considerable value. The plain facts are that where fine art and other antiquities are concerned, they are more secure when in an occupied location than when being shipped from one place to another. To understand the concern, the art world's losses per annum range between US$6 and US$8 billion, with most of those losses occurring during transportation as a direct result of theft, damage or simply loss. Consequently, our underwriters were not prepared to include the newly acquired addition on the schedule up until the time the piece was secured in the residence that I had previously appraised.

My survey was thus more of an assessment, commencing in the Middle East where the international carrier would be delivering the artwork into the hands of an allegedly reputable local carrier who had transport and secure warehousing at both Dubai Free Zone and Jebel Ali port. At either of their locations, the local carrier would inspect the item to verify that it was undamaged, repack it and then transport it to the insured's residence. Following discussions with the underwriters, the suggestion was, as a matter of policy, for me to check out their locations, as opposed to just their operations that the artwork was thought likely to handle the piece plus importantly the carrier's available modes of road transport. The reason behind checking all locations was to establish the carrier's management standards and controls across the whole organisation, as opposed to just inspecting the most prestigious of their locations, which we gathered was at Dubai International airport.

At Dubai Free Zone, a stone's throw from the airside of Dubai International Airport, the selected local carrier had impressive offices some 30 metres or so from a detached modern unit that was their warehouse, and which backed onto the airport's perimeter fence. The designated carrier's building housed the inspection, storage and packing activities of the business. The entrance to the Free Zone had gated security checking in and out for all visitor transport while those tenants occupying premises simply displayed passes in the windscreens of their vehicles. For private vehicles, such as my own, there was only a cursory glance from security when I drove through the gate to a visitors' designated parking areas. As for the proposed carrier's transport, they were, in the main, common or garden rigid binned trucks and vans displaying stickers in the windscreen and of course the sides bearing the business's name. None of the vehicles were fitted with GPS, nor were there any specific security features, even though a van would have been suitable for some smaller pieces of artwork given their vehicles dimensions and axle weight. Another major negative was that these vans were general purpose, therefore lacking racking or security fixings to hold securely the packed artwork during the journey. Plus, I could not establish if the business ever conveyed mixed cargos, which I took as a 'yes' as the manager's response was evasive.

As for the warehouse, this comprised a portal framed building, with profile steel cladding to both roof and elevations. Access was via either a steel roller shutter door or a mantrap pedestrian door. Inside the roller shutter door, there was a security screen to prevent the interior of the warehouse being viewed from outside when the roller shutter was up. The exterior of the building was fitted with security lighting during the hours of darkness, essential as the facility operated around the clock, and a digital CCTV system. Consequently, all the arrangements were as to be expected with a facility handling high value items. Leaving the office building with a manager, we approached the warehouse and this is where the problems began because the roller shutter door was half raised and the security screen wide open, permitting a full, uninterrupted view of the workings and larger contents inside the building.

Not mentioning this obviously lackadaisical approach to the manager, we continued. One of the staff upon seeing our approach from inside the unit jumped up and sped towards the roller shutter door control panel. However; my direction was towards the mantrap because I could see both doors were open which indicated that the interlock was not functioning. Now inside, the embarrassed employee, who was a supervisor tried to explain that the mantrap was malfunctioning and they were waiting for an electrician. My question to the manager was how long had the system been out of order and why? He turned to the supervisor looking for a response that clearly wasn't forthcoming, so I pursued the situation concerning both the roller shutter door and security screen to which the manager offered a lame excuse of just having taken a delivery.

Turning to the manager I asked what the custom and practice was insofar as where did the delivery vehicle stand to enable loading and unloading? Again, they suggested that they would conduct loading inside the unit whenever possible so why had I asked? Wasn't that the case of the delivery just received? My questions were extremely probing and the manager struggled, often turning to the supervisor for a satisfactory response. While they were never made aware of values I asked what were the ranges and types of consignments handled to which I got the first positive reply insofar as they handled bullion and precious stones daily. Adding all of which were secured in a very large, freestanding Chubb safe and the facility had PIR linked to the police centre at the airport, a few minutes away. The supervisor also pointed out that the only entry and egress was through a manned security gate, as the airport security fencing shut off any other possible route. This was fast becoming a battle with an organisation that clearly was out of touch with the level of intellect modern thieves possess. So I suggested that my assessment was in the main about the handling and ferrying of the piece of fine art and as for the safe, as large as it was, I submitted that the artwork in question would simply not fit in it.

My feelings were that I was in consultation with an organisation lacking awareness in current events and developments so I set about explaining my concerns as the insurer. Firstly, the lack of maintaining a high level of security once the carrier took possession of the piece. Next, I needed to be aware of their transport's route to our insured's residence, because I explained if I were contemplating theft it would be on the route, adding that if they loaded with the security screen and roller shutter door open their security arrangements were nullified. Further, from what I had just witnessed this wasn't the first time the activities inside were open to the world. So given that the security people agreed a delivery time and date with the client, this information would give any criminal element interested in the piece vital information. At this suggestion the supervisor who was obviously struggling to maintain credibility submitted that the situation observed and the mantrap problem would be immediately resolved.

Being extremely cynical at times I asked whom the forklift truck seen parked alongside the building belonged to. I was informed it belonged to the storage business in the neighbouring unit. So why, I asked, was it parked outside their building if it was their neighbour's truck? Again, without thinking, the supervisor told me that from time to time they borrowed it for some of their freight that was too weighty to manhandle. Now constrained I informed those in attendance that forklift trucks are a means of forced entry and that their roller shutter door would offer only token resistance, as the airport security fence, should the perpetrators elect to use that route. I added that with or without the key being in the power panel on the truck, they were offering a useful tool and that I was surprised given the Wafi Mall ram raid 18 months ago, involving US$10-million of diamonds. There, the perpetrators simply used a car to successfully carry out the crime, which compared to a forklift truck is but a toy. I had given up, as had the carrier's representative's attempts to present an acceptable face so I suggested I needed to look at the Jebel Ali facility resulting in the manager providing me with site contact there and directions.

At the entrance to Jebel Ali port, there were manned security gates of far superior quality than at Dubai Free Zone, where the carriers occupied an extremely large warehouse with finger docks and roller shutter doors along three sides. Internally, there were forklift truck operations loading and unloading general goods from parked up commercial vehicles and in and out of the high racking throughout the warehouse. The 'art store', as it was referred to, was a walled section provided with a steel door, secured with a good quality lock and with the key in kept in the key cabinet within the manager's office. As the art store was in the centre of the warehouse where access would be difficult, this seemed that it would have been a far more fitting location for the artwork until I entered the store.

Within the art store, I found many items of artwork standing directly on the concrete floor, without racking, thus leaning on other items. Some were in crates, while others were simply wrapped in cardboard and bubble wrap. My count was just under fifty pieces, some of which had clearly been there for some time as some wrapping had fallen or been knocked away. Thus, the scenes at both locations made it impossible to provide cover for such a valuable item of art. The insured was informed of our findings and, being an avid collector, was positive in his response even though the carrier had been recommended to him. The matter fell silent for a few weeks until the underwriter was informed that the piece was now at the insured's residence unscathed and was about to be fitted with both a motion sensor and environmental tags prior to then being professionally hung. The insured was now seeking our opinion regarding the additional security features that I had discussed with them when I conducted the previous appraisal. We were intrigued as to who conveyed the piece to his residence, so when I put the question to the insured, he replied that it fitted nicely in his Range Rover!

Probably the one type of appraisal I never was comfortable with, because just occasionally it resulted in adverse comments, concerned HNW clients with extremely valuable collections of art. There were insured who left me wondering just why they possessed their collections; was it as an avid supporter and connoisseur of art, simply as a matter of investment or a combination of the two? Regardless, given my way of thinking, surely those clients recognised the importance of securing these valuable assets, otherwise, why seek insurance coverage? Alternatively, was acquiring insurance coverage their idea of risk managing? It was difficult to conclude otherwise in some circumstances.

This is where the problem lay for me as an appraiser. Had these art collectors been like another insured it might have been more understandable. Mr Khan our insured fully understanding his take on financial matters, had secured within his home vault £9 million of gold ingots, commenting to me that he didn't trust banks and that gold was the only sensible option, not least by virtue of being very transportable. What motivated the art collectors was extremely important from an insurer's standpoint as their motivation could have huge effects on the care they took with their possessions. In some cases, the extremes of their preservation levels knew no bounds consequently the steps taken by two Middle East emirs and a Turkish collector were substantial, while in contrast a Greek and an Emirati collectors' approach could be summed as simply lackadaisical.

On an occasion in Greece, I was requested to appraise a collector where surprisingly the vast majority of the collection was on display or in storage at the head office of one of the insured's companies. Arriving on site I was shown around by the administration manager who provided me on arrival with the latest schedule of the collection present in the offices, which amounted to some US$8 million. Decision making regarding the location of some of these pieces was apparently left to the discretion of the manager, who used in-house maintenance operatives to hang the paintings and sketches where appropriate. To compound matters in the decision making regarding the siting, hanging or storage of a newly acquired piece, the office manager openly admitted he had little to no idea what the value of the newly acquired piece was. I did sympathise with the manager, suggesting that I was sure he would exercise far more care knowingly handling a painting valued in excess of €1 million compared to another valued at €7,500. This, I attempted to explain was as much a dilemma for me as an appraiser as it was to him, like the cover, albeit made up of mixed sums, was for the entire collection.

The theoretical survey niceties over, the tour of the offices commenced, of all places, in the main stationary stockroom, located on the ground floor. Within the room the manager had stored five large paintings, with each observed resting directly on the concrete floor and against one another. I explained the basic precautions necessary: spacers, off floor storing and covers in the main, particularly in this case, because of the installed wet sprinkler systems, which were prone to leak occasionally. Attempting to defend his decision-making, the manager explained that there was no other room large enough on the upper floors to store these five pieces. Ironically in the adjacent corridor, there was an even larger piece resting against the wall, a recent purchase, and compounding the situation at the far end of this passageway a janitor was using a wet floor scrubber.

At this juncture, I was left in little doubt that the items were all vulnerable to loss, either through theft or accidental damage. The accidental damage seemed particularly likely to come by way of impact, water and sunlight. My next line of enquiry centred on the number of staff present, their working hours, site security and visitor controls. The responses were, to say the least, negative; in fact, it was as if some of these issues were looked upon as being of little to no consequence, which was highlighted by the unprofessional location and hanging. To illustrate the location and hanging issues, on a stair adjacent to a large window there was a military scene of Napoleon's retreat from Moscow, a large piece within a gilded frame, that was suspended by two small brass mirror brackets and in direct sunlight at certain periods of the day. The value of the assets, including those in the stockroom, I assessed as vulnerable to damage exceeded US$766,000.

As a consequence the aforementioned situations were wholly unacceptable, while in terms of fire and theft the total loss could be as much as US$4 million. Unfortunately for the client, it left me with an easy decision from an insurer's standpoint, as the exposures were simply not acceptable. What was so frustrating in the decision making regarding the final and overall assessment was the fact that I could not communicate directly with the insured. Having only the administration manager to deal with, who clearly had little to no idea regarding values or loss prevention initiatives, meant taking a hard line. It was highly unlikely I reasoned that the manager could have explained the storage shortcomings to his employer that would have brought about acceptable changes to the satisfaction of our underwriters, hence the decision to decline the risk.

Once again in the Middle East, I found myself conducting an appraisal of another valuable art collection that was found within a large occupied two-storey mansion. The walled property was provided with both passive and active fire and security protections plus attended by manned security staff at all hours. I was being shown around the property by the broker who had visited the home when first occupied by their client some three months before. The residence had been totally refurbished and the client's artwork had lately arrived on site so that insurance cover was now required. The artwork within the home had been professionally handled regarding locations, hanging and each piece being fitted with movement sensors. Sitting down with the broker I studied the contents schedule, which included the artwork, that amounted to something in the order of US$15 million.

After perusing the schedule, I assumed by what I had seen it had to include the like of jewellery or artefacts because the artwork figures were simply not adding up. I was nonetheless assured that the figure was principally down to one of the art pieces so I suggested another walkthrough to establish values. The broker, with very little HNW experience, was a little put-out, so I requested that he should use his calculator and prove me wrong, explaining that to under insure was critical in the event of a major fire and to over insure was costly. We started the walkthrough again and towards its conclusion, the broker was at a loss to explain the values on the schedule and the figure now displayed on his phone calculator. As the insured was not present, I asked the housekeeper if there was any other place further artwork could be sited or perhaps there was some not yet on site. The lady told us that there were some paintings in a portable, demountable and temporary cabin, out near the security lodge, and she would have the security man open it up for us.

The portacabin interior was found fitted with some steel racking with timber inserts and this racking was crammed on either side with a great deal of artwork. The first thing that struck me was the value of the pieces there, as over half of the art was within this temporary building with some pieces found to have been loosely stored and leaning against others, while the windows at the rear had the security grilles and shading removed, resulting in the potential for forced entry and strong sunlight passing into the interior. To compound matters was how some of the pieces have been stored and secured which entailed some being literally nailed to the timber inserts in the steel framework with the nails used passing through the frames into other artwork stored immediately behind. It went without saying there was one embarrassed broker and an insured who subsequently requested our presence again to discuss the issues as he was totally unaware of the situations we had come upon. As far-fetched as it may seem regarding this surplus part of the collection the security staff were instructed to store these pieces and they were the ones who chose to do it in a Neanderthal manner in the portacabin near their lodge.

Just when you believe you have seen it all in survey work, regarding particularly blasé high net worth policyholders' risk-taking, there are always exceptions. Occasionally, there is a policyholder so inventive you are forced to stand back and admire their vivid imagination. Added to this, the situation would leave you just like the unsuspecting would-be thief, both extremely embarrassed and certainly frustrated. My planned appraisal was of an HNW policyholder in Arabian Ranches, Dubai, a very wealthy area where most properties were more than several million US$. Security by way of manned gated entry points along each service route, with excellent levels of street lighting, mobile security patrols and most of the properties being continually occupied by domestic staff although they were not resident in the main house but usually housed in an annexe. The property was one such place where the policyholder's business took her frequently out of the country travelling to conduct her business dealings in the likes of London, New York, Rome and Hong Kong. The appraisal was a necessity as the lady's jewellery was valued at more than the beautiful detached house and its general contents, so the underwriter required me to establish the level and suitability of the security.

Following my general lines of enquiry in the presence of the insured, we got to speak of both passive and active security arrangements within her home, and I asked if she believed the level of her security was sufficient given the values spoken of. My very first observations always without fail entailed viewing any items of jewellery being worn, particularly if they were extremely high value pieces. As with all insurers, we experienced our share of losses where the wearer either lost, damaged or had stolen items outside of the home; therefore, it followed that habits were given every consideration. My first recollection of the lady was that the jewellery she was wearing was very modest compared to the values indicated on the schedule so I concluded that the rest was kept within a safe, and was consequently something I would need to see at some point during the appraisal. The jewellery listed was for the most part family heirlooms, including a dress ring, matching tiara and a necklace alone valued over US$3 million.

Eventually, we started our tour of the home and learning the whereabouts of the safe we entered the lady's bedroom and located an average-sized freestanding safe in the walk-in wardrobe. It was at this point, for the first time, that my hopes for reporting positively were sunk, despite the intruder alarm, lighting and locks; windows and doors, being impressive. Looking at this modest safe I commented that given the sum insured, where the jewellery was concerned, the safe would not meet our requirements. I asked if this was the only safe she possessed, as hopefully perhaps there was another elsewhere? At this point, the lady's smile got bigger but purposely ignoring my question she asked what was wrong with the safe in front of me? I explained that it was not fixed and was probably located in the first place a thief would look, adding that her domestic staff knew the whereabouts and it was likely that other tradespeople visiting would too.

To offer an answer to the insured's question regarding the safe's suitability I estimated it would take less than 30 minutes to breach and given its portability could be taken off site within minutes to a place where the thieves could work on it at their leisure.

"That would be nice," the lady remarked. "As we would soon find it." Now clearly our minds were not running along the same lines as her remarks had me bemused. All the while detecting she was enjoying the moment I asked how so? Again, ignoring the point, she answered, "If you are insisting, I will have the safe anchored so it is not so portable; is that OK?"

I still had her comment regarding the safe being found in the back of my mind, so I assumed that there was an electronic tracker installed somewhere. Sensing the lady read my mind, yet again, I asked her again how so. She insisted on opening the safe up and I could see for myself. The lady's adopted attitude was commonplace with many HNW clients which was why it made the task of appraising for the most part so pleasant.

Now I knew that I was being fed a story so I asked about another safe again only for the lady to ignore my question by continuing to open the safe, by way of producing a key, inserting it in the keyhole which allowed a keypad to pop out of the safe door.

At that point, I asked permission to step out of the wardrobe before she entered the key code but she simply said, "Close your eyes, if you must." Now the safe was unlocked and she invited me to swing the door open, which I refused saying it was best she did that. The great surprise was yet to come insofar as the safe was empty save an envelope adhered to the single shelf inside. Written in English on the envelope were the words; *Sorry, waiting on lottery win.*

The lady, on seeing the look on my grinning face, commented, "I read somewhere once that a locked portable bogus safe is an irresistible attraction particularly one where there are activated intruder alarms. Is that true?"

I replied, "Don't ask, just look at my face." The lady obviously enjoyed the moment and said any thieves who saw that inside would probably dump the safe out of shame, hence it being quickly found! With the safe still, open the insured invited me into the en-suite bathroom where set on the marble tiling was a small toiletries cabinet that she swivelled permitting her to access a single 60 x 60 cm ceramic floor tile, that when she pressed her hand lightly on one corner, the tile tilted permitting the lady to it slide it to one side. I had seen such arrangements before but not with a swivel cabinet and a removable tile so I complimented her on her imagination. Once the tile was now out of the way it exposed the top of a very large UL-rated floor safe, clearly presenting a formidable challenge. The great thing about floor safes is that you never know just how deep they are sunk and, without protruding surfaces or edges, it is difficult to attack. Again, on this occasion, a thumbprint was required plus a combination, impossible to read, she opened up the safe, inviting me to view the contents.

Secured there within this safe, neatly stored in velvet-lined trays, were a few rings, earrings, bracelets, two ladies watches, and on the lower shelves documents and binders including passports for her and the family. My first impression was that this jewellery, albeit valuable, was not close to that cited in the schedule.

Where, I wondered, were the ring, tiara and necklace set? Putting my thoughts to the lady she said, "Oh, those are in the bank's safety deposit boxes and haven't seen the light of day for a long time. They're far too valuable to be kept at home and too showy for everyday use."

I was forced to ask if she enjoyed dragging me about by the nose knowing all the while the real valuables were tucked away in some bank's vault. Before I left the insured, wholly satisfied with what I had seen and the precautions taken, she asked me if I liked her envelope message. I said, "For an eminent orthopaedic surgeon, I just wonder from whom you inherited your sense of humour as I would wager you are a barrel of laughs and have your patients in stitches in the operating theatre."

"The word Stuart is sutures, sutures," the insured replied obviously with the intent of having the final word. So ended the very last and one of the most satisfactory high net worth appraisals I ever had the good fortune to assess.

State Securities and Enforcement

Whilst travelling throughout the world conducting surveys there were a number of notable events that I never envisaged as they were only marginally connected with risk surveying. In most cases where the unexpected turned up during a survey, I felt confident enough to know that I was capable of handling the matter satisfactorily. There were trickier situations too, though. There are tales to be told at the borders of some countries, and within those borders, that I was simply not prepared for as no one person ever told me that travel would be a problem; jet lag yes, passport or visa issues yes, but me being seen as a security risk, definitely not. Yet it is this that took the job to a whole new level when national security staff started to take an interest in me.

To be expected there were in the UK inevitably brushes with security forces, as I visited some sensitive establishments and that required me to sign the Official Secrets Act, after of course being vetted. The list of encounters outside of the UK is short but they were not without incident, principally because of the two passports that I needed to carry, flying in from a country where I was not resident, visiting sensitive areas, or simply being open with my responses to security questioning. Regarding the passports, certain countries were rather tetchy about seeing stamps of entry and exit from countries where their relationships were anything other than cordial. For example, both India and Pakistan and Israel and some Middle East countries made me selective regarding the passport I was to travel on. Once though, renewing my Pakistani visa, the wrong passport, with an India visa in was inadvertently sent to their consulate by our administration staff. It was returned with a single-entry visa even though I had visited the country on many occasions and we had offices there.

The one occasion that definitely took me back somewhat was where I was unaware that the proposed survey entailed me entering a region of frequent terrorist activities. Unlike my visits to Iraq and Kabul, where the populated areas were totally occupied by armed services both national and foreign, in this case, there was much less protection. The perceived risk just resulted in me being briefed and counselled by our own in-house security, based on information provided by the media, possibly the local staff and just occasionally by the insured, before I set out. However, the proposed survey to an insured located in the Pakistani border region with Afghanistan was only made known to me upon arriving there and then made more obvious by prearranged security measures. The local office staff and insured of course were fully aware of the problems however they lived with it day in and day out so to them it simply became a way of life.

I arrived in Karachi from Dubai with the intention of surveying an insured located in a rural area north of Sukkur, in the Pakistan/Afghanistan border region. The journey entailed an internal flight to Sukkur then heading north by road transport to a small industrial development, ten or so miles from the international border. I was to be accompanied by Khalid, our senior underwriter based in Karachi, who I knew very well, so I never gave the proposed trip another thought, leaving me only to focus on the insured: an international foodstuff manufacturer.

We made the internal flight and upon arriving at Sukkur we were met by a small party and waltzed through airport security out to the air terminal forecourt. Parked up on the forecourt were two armoured vehicles, one occupied by fully armed paramilitary police in their blue fatigues and one with obviously army personnel in their distinctive khaki uniforms. I had been to several cities in Pakistan from Lahore, Islamabad and of course Karachi so the picture was not unusual. However, I concluded that this was an airport and therefore high-profile security would be provided for a sensitive facility. I did nonetheless comment to our underwriter that it looked as though they were expecting someone of importance.

"Yes, they were waiting for you." Ignoring the response as an attempt at humour we were ushered to a waiting car and set off without me not once looking behind to see who those security arrangements were really for. During the journey, we chatted about Dubai and other personal matters and all the time I heard this whining which appeared distant so I thought perhaps one of the wheel bearings on the car required grease. We passed through some remote townships, which appeared occupied by only men, traditionally dressed, with no western clothes and a considerable number of camels. It didn't register at the time but we were clearly the centre of attention, probably because of the defective bearing? We finally reached our destination: a walled compound where following us being checked, a soldier ordered the gates open. Within the compound, there was a two-storey building and a guard room and to my great surprise a line of six armed police and soldiers. Now confused I looked out of the rear window and both the armoured cars had come to a halt. Once we were secure inside the gate both the armoured vehicles sped off with me commenting, "You were not kidding then?"

"But surely you heard the siren?" replied Khalid.

"No, I thought we had a defective wheel bearing!" I felt stupid, although Khalid thought now that I was now joking.

During the entire visit inside the compound, those police and soldiers were patrolling, which I learnt was the routine twenty-four seven. The surprise was yet to come as, when speaking with a member of the staff I learnt that a French diplomat had stayed in my allotted room two days before and the facility was described as being something akin to a safe house. Speaking with one of the armed police that evening, whilst strolling around the grounds, I enquired why there were both police and army present. His response took me a bit by surprise when he replied, "We don't trust them and they don't trust us." During the survey when the insured learnt I was, in fact, British and not American, the escort disappeared. Further, the insured even drove us back to the airport, taking in Sukkur, the Lloyd Barrage across the Indus River and museum, and even had the curator open up the museum for a special guest, on the way.

As strange as it may seem though the first encounters where I experienced security problems were in Northern Ireland at the height of the troubles and ironically involved both the British Army and the Garda. The superintendent from our Belfast office and I were looking for a factory in Armagh, one of the places of high tension, when we seemed to be going around in circles looking for the premises. As we entered a road, that crossed a river or canal, we were suddenly brought to a halt by a roadblock and were clearly targeted as the traffic in front had been whisked through, leaving us isolated. The roadblock comprised two armoured cars positioned across the road, bringing us to a halt. A police officer armed with a semi-automatic machine pistol, pointing the weapon straight at the windscreen of our car, approached while I was sifting through the survey papers simply looking for the address as I felt this officer would be able to direct us to our desired location. My colleague wound down the window as the officer crouched down now with only his head showing above the door and asked where we were going?

I knew the drill and being unperturbed I continued still looking through the papers for the address when the officer asked what I was doing as I barely acknowledged his presence or the implications of the roadblock. I told him we were looking for the address of a business in the city, at which point I am convinced that my English accent sunk in. He asked if I was English what were we doing driving around the city given that it was unwise to venture into certain areas. I informed him that I had come from London to complete a survey for my employer, at the same time handing him my business card, and quite simply we couldn't find the address.

At that juncture, the police officer stood up then and waved to the armoured cars where unnoticed, certainly by me, a soldier had mounted a medium machine gun that was pointing directly at us. I had served in Northern Ireland so I knew the procedure and asked the officer light-heartedly if he wouldn't mind ensuring the safety was on, nodding in the direction of the soldier! He laughed and asked the address we were looking for which, it turned out, was about half a mile away, and still being a policeman, asked my colleague what was the insured's business? He told him it was a bakery and that the same company had other facilities in Belfast, Derry and Cookstown which we also had to visit, all of which seemed to satisfy his somewhat suspicious mind. The policeman holding up the traffic both ways, as the armoured cars had reverted back to the kerbsides, turned us around and wished us well on our way. My colleague said he was pleased that my accent paid off as they would have completed a full check of him, the vehicle and so on otherwise.

A little later I was again surveying the Gaelic Athletic Association (GAA) following a claim and loss at Croke Park in Dublin. I had completed the surveys south of the border in the Republic and was at Casement Park, Belfast not long after the murder of two British Soldiers there. Needless to say, the tension was at its height, with troops everywhere, foot patrols, roadblocks and helicopter activity. I was with the county secretary of the insured and arrived at Casement Park with the same superintendent underwriter who was with me when in Armagh. The roads were busy around the sports ground and, while driving into the entrance, we were stopped by a foot patrol of a British Army regiment.

The patrol I found were quite aggressive and were running a check on our vehicle, all while we were literally being held at gunpoint. One of the soldiers looked at me and spat on the floor beside the car which incensed me as it was an act of pure disrespect for a legitimate business group. I wound down my window and looking directly at the soldier said, 'Its people like you in making those types of gesture that give us a bad name; what if children saw you acting like that?' He replied in words I cannot repeat including telling me to go home and enjoy my home comforts. Incensed I simply quoted my army service number, adding that I had years' service with the colours that included two tours of active service plus one tour in the province, suggesting that he should show me more respect. As a serving soldier, you never forget your service number so my response took him aback somewhat and he replied, "Sorry, Sir," and turned away.

Once inside the gate and moving on foot to the centre of the playing area I was looking back at the stands and spectator standing areas; all the while we were being, what I can only be described as, 'buzzed' by a very low flying military helicopter who hovered directly above us, so much so it was difficult to talk. It certainly got to the GAA's secretary who commented on the provocative nature of the army's presence. I suggested we move to the building where we resumed our conversation to complete the survey. As a side issue, the very reason for me not bringing my own vehicle over on the ferry to the province was because of the UK number plate, which I was informed was unwise, unlike in Eire where I drove untroubled on many an occasion surveying in my own UK registered vehicle.

The third action-packed visit involved a joint survey with my colleague, the head of the property survey team. The business was new and was an innocuous chicken processor located on the West side of Lough Neagh, easily found along the road skirting the loch, we were informed. We had pre-ordered a small hire car from Belfast City Airport and planned on using this to carry us around as the visit entailed several locations principally located in rural areas. When we arrived at the arranged car hire desk where we were informed that the car we chose had been taken and that we were being upgraded for the same price. The car offered was a black Ford Scorpio with tinted windows and was impressive so they got no argument from us. This, however, was where the problems started as both my colleague Roy and I were dressed in dark suits, Roy's shoes were always highly polished and he simply looked immaculately groomed, almost military like! Roy was about 1.70 metres, short hair, upright with a barrel chest, looking anything but a property surveyor and adding to his appearance, he wore metal framed spectacles that had tinted lenses.

Sticking to the directions provided by the insured, we travelled up and down the roads around the west side of the loch without success. In the end, I suggested to Roy that we find a local shop or somewhere where we could get directions. Eventually, we stopped at a post office where we walked in and both the counter staff and the customers stood back when Roy asked for this factory's location in a very English accent. The lady at the counter informed us it was back up the road we had just travelled along, "At least four times?" the lady remarked.

Roy being Roy, asked if the lady was sure and she almost apologetically assured him that she was. So we thanked the lady and got back in the car, driving back from where we came. As there was only one business, a fishery company, along that stretch of road, we decided to enquire at one of the big waterside houses along the route. A lady playing with a youngster in the garden grabbed the child when we drove up the drive and asked shakily what we wanted? I apologised for startling her, this big black car arriving up her drive hadn't helped, telling her we were desperately trying to find this company, chicken processors, we had come to insure, reportedly along this road.

With a smile of relief, she informed us the factory was less than 200 metres away from where we were, with a fishery sign at the entrance of the lane! We must have travelled past that sign at least half a dozen times by this time and simply you cannot mistake a chicken processor for a fishery company. Returning back down the drive we were quickly at the fishery sign as was suggested. We turned into the lane and entered the car park directly in front of the factory with both of us noticing the many faces peering at us through the windows of what was clearly the office, unaware that they had been informed of our presence and our tour! We got out of the car and with just our clipboards we walked up to the factory door. We were met at the door by a lady asking us if she could be of service. I asked if she would be Ms Raffety and she shakily stated she was. I took out my business card and handed it to her and when she read it with much relief said, "Jesus, we thought you were special branch cruising around, looking at your motor car and the way you are dressed. It's all around the villages that you were on the prowl," she added. That explained why we saw so few people. The survey turned out to be a non-event but the positive was our period of infamy for a few hours.

We had to extend our period in the province for another day as this corporate risk, operating as chicken processors, had catchers who only operated at night to collect the birds from rearing farms when the birds were quiet. Chicks were placed in rearing houses, fed and watered for about three months and then captured and transported to the factory, where they were killed. The catching process needed to be conducted during the hours of darkness and the catchers used subdued lighting, entering the rearing houses and thus causing a minimum disturbance. If the birds were spooked, they would rush away from the catcher, crushing other birds in the process. Travelling at night in the province's countryside was described as dangerous with the police, army and activists about so my colleague told me that I should find these catchers alone. After persuasion, he agreed to accompany me just for the very last time.

The insured informed me of the route these catchers would take, going from one rearing farm to another. The workers' activities and working conditions were to be observed which would have been reasonably free of hazards during daylight but problematical in poor visibility. Essentially there was hand catching, crating up the birds, forklift loading and driving. For my colleague and I, we had to be aware of the external risks in the form of activists and the authorities. It was just our luck that we were caught up with a police night patrol at one of the rearing house, who were familiar with the catchers. The catchers explained our role, so the police warned us about driving during the small hours and that we should return to our hotel on a route suggested by them, which we did without further incident. It was the night porter who summed up our night's work when upon entering the hotel. Getting our room keys, he asked where we had been as it was about 3 a.m. We told him and he listened to all the while open-mouthed finally uttering the words, "You must be mad, how much do your bosses pay you?"

The story doesn't quite end there because the following morning at breakfast we were chatting about the risk when Roy mentioned he felt that someone had been in his room while we were out last night. Suddenly it became clear because last night we wore casual clothing and when we returned I went to the wardrobe where I noted that the flap on my jacket pocket was tucked in. Being meticulous about those sorts of habits, they never die, so maybe I thought I was slipping until, more notably, my Knights of St Columba pin was not behind my jacket lapel but in the breast pocket. KSC is a Catholic fraternal service organisation, which is why in the province I kept the pin out of sight. Convinced now we had been subject to a visit I suggested we have a word with reception.

At reception we asked for the manager and informed him of our concern, although nothing we were at least aware of had been taken. His response came as a bit of a surprise, "I am sure your rooms have been subject to an unofficial search but by whom, the Provos or the Garda, who knows? Maybe both?"

My response was, "How could that be, we are guests here and I am surprised."

"I cannot control what I cannot see," replied the manager.

"We are living in trouble times and while I can vouch for my staff's honesty, where their loyalties and interests lie, and for that matter any guests such as yourselves, well that is another matter." The manager's frank responses left us with little doubt that these were indeed trouble times.

Whilst surveying in Israel, the reason for me being there was that US-based surveyors were refusing to fly over because it was considered too dangerous! It was OK for those in Dubai as they were used to it, was the reply to my question to the head of security about the dangers. The survey programme included the largest building in Tel Aviv, a very large shopping mall on the West Bank, and a kibbutz down in the Gaza Strip. Security was the purpose of the visit, as two of the places were in reasonably active areas for hostilities. As there were no direct flights from the UAE we flew in via Jordon, transferring to another flight that took us to Tel Aviv. Passing through immigration I found myself quizzed regarding purpose and duration, what was I doing in Dubai and other questions regarding where I was going after and all this regardless of me carrying an invitation letter from our office in Tel Aviv.

I was quite surprised at the lack of cooperation by the head of engineering in the Azrieli Centre, which was to be the first of my three visits. The engineer simply told me that he was far too busy to spend any time with me. Left with the little option, I told him, "Your principals I assume arranged the survey, through our New York office, but as they didn't realise you were so busy, I shall take my leave and fly back to Dubai." The engineer's bravado seemed to suddenly disappear as I was walking out of his office door without waiting for his reply. He was now asking me to wait a moment to see what could be arranged. To rub salt in the wound I replied, "You do realise that there is possibly only one other insurer that has the capacity and appetite for a risk of this size?"

"Look we probably got off on the wrong foot so tell me what you want, what you need to know and where you want to go?" asked the engineer sheepishly.

The building was the tallest in Israel and comprised three towers reaching out of an extremely tall podium so I told him that as we would be concerned about terrorism, perhaps being accompanied by a security member would be beneficial. Manned security and passive and active fire protections were top rates and as for the risk of fire, it would be restricted due to compartmentation within the structures. So the risk survey ultimately was completed save one detail and that, as usual, concerned building contractors who were present working on the third tower. Going through every item of security included labour vetting including nationalities, work experience on sensitive projects, plus vehicles, plant and equipment registration, which was all very impressive yet surprisingly one area of security seemed to be overlooked. Apologising I told those present that I had no wish to rain on their parade but had they thought about it?

I explained the scenario which had occurred at a highly sensitive government facility in Northern Ireland, where the building was targeted by the IRA in a way which almost succeeded. I was not surprised that they were unaware of the flaw in their security, as the breach of security in the province was only discovered by accident. A site-building worker made the find when searching for some of his work equipment and came upon some other unidentified items, that after security had been informed, turned out to be explosive. Some of them had been systematically lodged in certain parts of the equipment. For obvious reasons, I cannot relate the method or the extent of the security breach but suffice it to say it was very simple yet it could have proved a disaster. However, as good fortune would have it a mishap caused the plot to be discovered and the threat nullified. Full credit to the Azrieli Centre's security, they took the matter very seriously and I learned later that their checks proved fruitless, but the method and potential had been duly noted.

Back at the airport, preparing to fly outbound for Dubai via Jordon I felt the full weight of Israeli security services. A simple question as to where I had been for whatever reason aroused their suspicions when those places included Gaza, the Azrieli Centre and the West Bank and of course where I came from and where

I was bound for next also proved problematic. The next lines of enquiry involved who I had visited, which by chance included mainly the country's largest agricultural chemical plants, another shopping mall on the West Bank and a kibbutz in Gaza. To me, the agricultural plants involved products liability, but to the security services, they probably suggested explosive potential, which resulted in obviously a more technically minded security person being called for.

With my notes, I was quizzed on why the layout of the plants and surrounding areas were listed. Where were my photographs? When I informed him I had for security reasons not taken any photographs and that the plans were to help explain environmental exposures it seemed to satisfy the enquirer. Regarding the security notes, I explained that the property, as with any other site was of importance, due to fire and perils risks. The enquirer departed after a few other questions which I never understood the importance of, regarding me being a loss control engineer with mechanical qualifications, so why was I visiting chemical plants? My explanation was that product and quality related details were of the utmost importance rather than the formulae of those products, which is where the interview closed.

Now with the two original security officers back in the room, I was asked to explain what I had seen or noted while I was down in Gaza, in yet another line of enquiries. One point I remembered was that my driver and I had been stopped at one point, giving way to a column of battle tanks crossing our road down in Gaza, a stone's throw from the kibbutz subject to survey. The tanks numbering about four squadrons, possible as many as fifty were settling in an olive grove with the crews immediately embarking on camouflaging up the vehicles which in all must have taken at least 15-minutes, regardless of the armour count being sizeable. So, when asked, I remarked that I hadn't seen that much armour since my days in Yemen and Germany. It has to be appreciated that I wasn't au fait with my driver at all as he was employed by the company, so I saw no point in not revealing what I had seen. In fact, I recalled asking the driver if this was the norm when seeing the tanks, in answer to which he guardedly told me he had served in another branch of the armed services.

Next, I was asked why I seemed so well informed; in response, I sarcastically asked if they would like my army number, rank and details of my service record? Without waiting for a response, I summarised my military service adding that while it was a long time ago, some things you simply never forget. As for me learning all this, I did not understand what would have been gained by me witnessing that which is blasted all over the news in the West almost every day. This seemed to stump these security people and, changing the subject, asked me if I had been given anything by anyone during my visit?

Not believing things could get even more involved I informed them that the management of the agrochemical business after two fruitful days of surveying presented me with a gift pen set. Revealing this, the whole thing started over again with these individuals asking where the gift was. Informing them it was in my luggage they asked for this to be bought into the room. Another person was now in attendance and I was told to open my case and then they began carefully sifting through my personal possessions. Not finding what they were looking for I suggested looking in my shoe bag. Carefully removing the pen set, they placed it on the table and began swiping it with a laced swab stick. All the time I was laid back, not even curious, as I knew that it was genuine because I had tried both the fountain pen and biro. Their subsequent search, as anticipated, proved futile; consequently, two people left the room with the other two remaining and inviting me to repack my case. Finally and at long last, I received a friendly remark when the remaining security officer said, "I see you are ex-military in your packing; have a good flight." The officer then turned and left the room which I took as a signal for me to return to check-in. Just another day in the life of an insurance surveyor, I concluded.

The most involved situation has to have been in Yemen where, regardless of travelling with a well-respected businessman, I was treated very harshly by Yemeni soldiers on the routes between Al Anad, Aden and Sanaa. If anything, my British passport seemed to bring out the worst in the soldiers and given army roadblocks could be just about anywhere in two trips we were stopped three times. Searching the contents of my briefcase, which included a camera you would think of as being of no interest, I was forced to delete any photographs taken of the cement works in Al Anad and other photos of the cement works up in Sanaa, plus some that were not even taken in Yemen, but in Abu Dhabi. I reasoned and asked sarcastically if the dunes and palm trees were a security risk.

Once, in Cyprus, I was there to survey the docks in Limassol and Larnaca where I was being shown around the dock viewing the activities, plant and equipment. Following a tour of the container park, I moved on to the warehousing and following consultations with the port authority I was about to depart when I was approached by the Port of Larnaca security who drove up in an SUV with blue lights flashing. The port security was there to quiz me about who I was and if I had permission to take photographs inside the port. The plant manager, who was inside the building walked out and confronted the security, who immediately recognised him. He explained that I was from the insurers and was with him. Also, he had permitted me to use the camera. I interrupted at that juncture as I thought security was being a touch overzealous, asking why a few photos of the container park and warehouses were so sensitive, as these could be seen from the public road and the sea.

"What about the Royal Navy's warship over there?" the security officer asked gesturing with his hand. I looked in the direction he was indicating and saw the vessel, which up to that point in time I had ignored, as it wasn't the only warship berthed. "It's not me who is concerned," said the security man, "but the officer of the watch." It turned out that he had been watching me from the ship, seeing me moving around the dock taking photos. Royal Navy ships were apparently frequently in the port and this being one of their latest vessels they wanted to know who was taking photos of them and why. I admit I did laugh and mentioned that the vessel was paid for out of my taxes and urged that he should look at my photographs and remove those that were possibly sensitive to ease the concern of the officer of the watch. He did go through my shots and found not one anywhere near where the destroyer was berthed and apologised. For good measure, tongue in cheek, I suggested he hand one of my business cards to the RN officer informing him that we provided excellent rates for service personnel.

One of those days that you have occasions where nothing seems to go as planned happened on the border between Macedonia and Albania following the conflict between the insurgents and the Macedonian army a year earlier. Travelling from Dubai to Skopje I was required to fly via Milan, which at the time didn't concern me too much, as I had experienced problems travelling between Pakistan and India, PRC and Taiwan, and of course into Libya. The reason for being in Macedonia was to look at some hotels' security and a large civil engineering project in Skopje, while in Albania it was to survey the Hilton Hotel in Tirana and the national sports stadium in the same area. The necessity of the flight into Skopje from Milan intrigued me a little as the business was raised through our Greek office and to me going via Milan seemed an odd way round, but I just put it down to the relationship between the two countries and the greater awareness of the branch personnel.

Once I had completed the surveys in Skopje the Athens office had arranged a private taxi to take me all the way to Tirana, a journey of about three hours involving 150 kilometres. We set off and progressed steadily for about an hour until we came to the border with Albania. The road was closed and armed personnel were holding the traffic up, searching each vehicle and checking documents. I sat patiently until an armed officer finally approached our vehicle, directing the driver to park and saying he should follow him to the border office, never giving me so much as a glance. The driver was gone for about twenty minutes when he returned with the same officer. The officer then requested my passport, asking where I was going and the purpose of my visit and following my response, he told me to remain in the vehicle. All the while the Skopje driver was leaning nonchalantly against the taxi, smoking. The officer returned after a few minutes and handed me back my documents with a courteous salute, informing me that I was welcome to Albania but with menace turned to the driver informing me that neither he nor his vehicle were going anywhere thus informing me they were being turned back.

So I found myself an hour's drive from Skopje with my baggage at a roadside on a border where there was only a solitary office building, pillboxes spread along both sides of the road and some military vehicles. Politely, I enquired of the Albanian officer what I should do now I had lost my taxi. He simply replied I should use an Albanian taxi. Stepping into the discussion the Macedonian taxi driver told me to be a little patient as a replacement taxi was on its way. I imagined that it was coming from Skopje therefore, I would be here an age. However, in less than ten minutes this private car arrived and without so much as a word the driver put my luggage in the vehicle, ushered me in the back and drove off through the zigzag barrier with a wave to an armed soldier. We sped off in the direction, I suppose, of Tirana. I guessed that there was still tension in the air.

A survey programme for a prestigious hotel chain turned up the most involved entry into a country I have ever faced, not so much through the risk itself but the circumstances that caused me to be there. The Corinthia Bab Hotel in Tripoli was possibly the jewel in our insured's crown, a magnificent piece of architecture boasting a five-star rating and probably one of the very best hotels I ever had the privilege to stay in. Flying from Dubai, I made my way to Malta to meet up with my contact there: the group's insurance manager. Arriving in Valletta I caught up with the directors and some of their management team, only to learn that my usual contact had flown off urgently to their hotel in St Petersburg, Russia, leaving me to conduct the survey of the Bab in Libya alone. Usually, the insurance manager used my visit as his excuse to get to see the hotels through another's eyes.

I took the scheduled flight to Tripoli and upon arriving I was not expecting a reception committee, just the courtesy car to take me to the hotel to conduct a routine survey, an overnight stay and then to fly back to Malta some 20 or so hours later. As I was walking up the companionway though, along with the other passengers from the flight, a tall, officious Libyan singled me out and demanded my passport. The official was dressed in a long black leather coat almost down to his feet and buttoned up to the neck. It was, as expected, warm to say the least so his perspiration didn't suggest nerves but he did look out of place in his attire. The person who had demanded my passport looked me up and down without so much as giving it a glance and began slapping my as yet unopened travel document on his sleeve. All the while my fellow passengers were passing us by so they couldn't help but suspect that the individual was an official and me possibly in trouble as his posturing was anything but friendly.

The man finally began flipping through my passport, several times from back to front, and then finally got to ask me what my business was here in Libya. I told him that I was to conduct a risk survey of a hotel and would be flying out again the next day. He seemed to ignore my answer and asked me who I was working for. I believe because I hesitated, wondering whether I should say the hotel or my employer, he seemed to think he had stumbled on something significant. I told him I was here to inspect a risk for my employers, AIG, but also for the Corinthia Group who were our insured. He asked who AIG was, struggling with the 'AIG' by saying 'AGG' so, repeating AIG I enlightened him by spelling out 'American International Group'. With that, he immediately picked up on the 'American' part and straight away said, "We don't like your type here so you are not welcome."

"For the record, I am not American and I would remind you that you are holding my British passport." Almost ignoring my responses, he asked me what the real purpose for my visit was and if I was genuine, why not fly direct from Dubai where he said he had noted my residency visa, this as to opposed flying through a European country? Not looking to antagonise the official I told him that Corinthia's offices, who partly own the hotel, were based in Malta and that I had flown there to meet up with their representative with the purpose being to conduct a joint visit here in Tripoli.

"Well, where is their representative?"

"He was called away on important business to Russia; therefore, I came on alone," I answered.

"How convenient," was the official's reply.

"Look, clearly you have a problem with me, so why not let me return to the departures lounge and I will fly straight back out?" I replied to his attempted sarcasm.

"That would seem to be a sensible course of action don't you think?" By this time, I was exasperated and requested his name so that I could at least inform my superiors and the part-owner of the hotel exactly who was responsible for turning me back.

"My name is of no importance to you but my state security role is in Libya's national interest, not yours," he replied.

"Well, I am sure your job is very important but so is mine so unless I get to see the facility neither Muammar Gaddafi or the Corinthia Hotel Group will not have adequate property insurances in place."

"Who did you say?"

I repeated, "Muammar and Corinthia."

"You mean President Gaddafi?"

I said, "Please understand the insurance policy document doesn't deal in titles but names and yes the insured's name on the policy is Muammar Gaddafi, as he is a joint owner of the hotel."

Without another word, other than that I should follow him, he marched briskly up the companionway with me at a fast walk behind him. We went straight into the immigration hall, past all the long queues, to a VIP desk where speaking in Arabic to the immigration officer and nodding in my direction I was once again the subject of attention from my fellow passengers, all of whom had passed me by some 20 or so minutes earlier. My passport was quickly stamped and ushering me through the antagonistic official handed my document back and disappeared without another word. Name dropper I thought and was about to walk to the line of representatives behind a barrier when a uniformed driver enquired, "Mr Stuart?" Taking my small case, the driver ushered me to the courtesy car. Once settled inside, he said, "That was quick. You must have been first through."

"You had better believe it," was my response.

Related Challenges

More often than not many surveyors are looking for issues, negative as opposed to positive, to report back to their underwriters on. Fear is probably the principal reason for this approach as in almost every loss case there will be questions asked as to why the risk was underwritten in the first place. Inevitably, the underwriter will then refer to a survey report, should one exist, and will be hopeful that overall the risk surveyed favourably. Alternatively, if not, they will ask what action was taken to avoid losses and if the surveyor made recommendations were these introduced? Consequently, following audits, I was required by senior management to write a complete synopsis on the challenges that both insurers' and surveyors' face.

While holding the utmost respect for many, many brokers I met during my time *they* posed the biggest challenge. Even when wrong they would inevitably side with the insured, their client, without accepting and recognising that their short-sightedness could adversely affect the very interests of those they were attempting to support. The biggest culprits I found were inevitably the international brokers where they would have account handlers, akin to salespeople, looking after their client's interests by ensuring they were adequately protected by their policies. This was as opposed to providing technically proficient staff acting professionally and providing added value by ensuring suitable arrangements were in place to prevent losses.

While appreciating that my employers had my complete trust regarding acting in their interest, there were times where my morals were put to the test in ways that financially acted against the very organisation that paid my salary. During my time in Ford loss control, I have to confess I never lost compassion where genuine accidents were concerned regardless of who was at fault; however, I did draw a line if it shifted the responsibility away from the guilty party, regardless of any pending claim. Indeed, insurers frequently come across habitual claimants who will do all they can to dupe their employers and also the insurers. However, as the investigating engineer, I took exception to the tactics of some insurance claims managers where there was a genuine case for compensation.

One situation involved a not so educated and unaware employee who suffered serious injuries while carrying out his normal duties and the claims manager attempted to buy the individual off with some cheap offerings. The employee, being a family man with five children was some five weeks away from taking his family off on a camper van trip to the Lake District and was in the hospital recovering when he was visited on more than one occasion by Ford's insurer's claims manager.

The circumstances involved a forklift truck carrying some large cages of automotive parts down a slope to the rear of my office. The noise became a distraction so I visited the area and discovered that a small hole had appeared in the concrete surface which was causing the solid tyre trucks to bounce a little, hence the cages they were carrying rattled. I spoke with the supervisor for the area and suggested that he place a metal plate over the ever-worsening hole, as a short-term measure, and have plant maintenance make the necessary repairs during the weekend, on the next day when production was almost non-existent. The metal plate was placed over the hole and a speed restriction on the slope posted. I believed that to be the end of the matter until the weekend when the defect would be attended to.

Arriving back in my office on Monday morning I found an accident report that said an employee pallet checker had over the weekend been accompanying a loaded forklift truck to the pallet bay when the load toppled off the truck onto the employee fracturing his leg, as it turned out, in three places. I did a double-take when I read of the location as it was adjacent to my office, on the slope providing access to the pallet compound. I contacted the supervisor who I had spoken to only 60 hours before and sheepishly he said the large hole had caused the problem! My response was to ask about the repairs and the whereabouts of the temporary metal plate which had since gone missing, although the danger signage was still posted. The plate had been removed by persons unknown and as a consequence, with the volume of traffic, the hole grew ever bigger and deeper due to maintenance inactivity.

The employee was taken to the local A & E department and was admitted suffering a fracture to his femur, tibia and fibula resulting in hospitalisation for at least one month, after which he would require months of physiotherapy. I knew the employee very well, as some years before I had been his supervisor, so immediately felt a lot of sympathy for him as he was a diligent and cooperative worker, albeit a little slow thinking sometimes. Being aware of his family I drew comfort in the fact that Ford's welfare and the unions would ensure his interests would be looked after. I took on the investigation as it was me who initiated the first steps to eliminate the hazard. Interviewing the truck driver, he reported that as the lighting wasn't good, and he was driving backwards, as required, he just didn't notice the plate was missing, as it had been present at the start of the shift the day before. He even suspected the repair would have been completed. He suddenly hit the hole, the truck lurched and his load toppled off onto the checker. Following matters up, the maintenance log was checked and showed no entry regarding a floor repair, so the supervisor had lied. The situation smacked of inefficiency and indiscipline and I was thankful that things were not worse and as far as the supervisor's involvement there was a plant enquiry and rightly so disciplinary proceedings.

Speaking with employee welfare during the next week's enquiry about how the employee was coping I learned that the claims manager had even visited him in hospital. That evening, being suspicious by nature, I visited the checker in hospital and was impressed by the number of visitors who had attended plus the cards, flowers and the like and I spoke with his wife who I had met before. Speaking to Ted, the injured worker, he told me of the kindness of all who had taken time to visit him and also that the claims manager had discussed his proposed family holiday and how it would now have to be cancelled as he could no longer drive but for the insurance manager's kind offer. Apparently, the claims manager told him not to worry as he would provide a driver and car to take on the driving to their required destination and back. Ted also intimated that the claims manager had mentioned funds to cover his loss of income from projected overtime which was about one hundred pounds. I was speechless as Ted said he would not be pursuing a further claim for compensation. So the claims manager had got to the worker without union representation or legal advice, which, given Ted's limited take on worldly matters, seemed morally inexcusable.

Before I left the hospital, I asked both Ted and his wife not to sign or agree to anything before first of all the long-term prognosis was established and secondly, safety engineering had investigated the accident fully. I mentioned his union representative but Ted asked that they should not become involved, yet another inexcusable tactic from the claims manager, I surmised. Returning to the plant the very next day I spoke with the insurer's claims manager and asked him about the visit as he had never bothered before when an employee was injured. The claims manager seemed pleased that he had dangled an offer and the employee had accepted and all this without any prognosis regarding the injury, future earnings potential, or long-term disability. I ran into Ted some months later while conducting an audit and he was still walking with a stick and a pronounced limp. Meeting up with the claims manager at a later date I expressed my disappointment at his tactics and, in his own defence, he cited so many spurious claims involving clear collusion and misrepresentation that he felt it balanced things up purely from a business point of view. In turn, I suggested that while I knew that there had been such cases during my time as a loss control engineer, I also liked to think that we in our department were both swift in our responses and thorough in our investigations, so that our efforts had narrowed these spurious claims down considerably.

The outcome of one of the most remarkable and memorable loss control solutions devised and offered by the underwriters and myself took place at the scene of a major Korean motor car manufacturing plant in Turkey, where we had recently paid out a large claim for hailstone damage to the bodywork and windscreens of a number of new cars, fresh from the production line. There is a history of major losses where hailstorms are concerned from locations as far apart as India, South Africa and the United States. The damage can be severe but it can be limited, even prevented, where large stocks of vehicles are kept in the open, for as little US$ 20 per vehicle. Following the survey, it intrigued me that given this was a natural hazard why manufacturers did not introduce removable snoods to protect a product that had taken time and money to produce and that many customers were waiting to take delivery of. During discussions my mind raced back to my Ford and Cornhill days where, while not protecting vehicles from the likes of hail, there were instances where vehicle body protection was devised and implemented.

At the Ford plant at Dagenham, there was a location named Frog Island where the company stockpiled new vehicles waiting to be collected by main dealerships. A delivery took place once and the dealership noted that bodywork on some vehicles was slightly pitted. These vehicles were reworked and the body restored but Ford still set up an investigation which resulted in the foreign bodies being identified as under burnt ash from our very own furnaces. This resulted in research as to why we hadn't experienced it before. We had some other fallout issues but they emanated from local resident complaints involving their washing lines of freshly laundered pieces being speckled with small metallic particles and what appeared to be ash, with some of the clothing not capable of being restored. Safety engineering who were responsible for environmental issues concluded that the strength and direction of the wind were responsible which turned out to be the case. Following that, the opening of the furnace hoods was then governed by the strength and direction of the wind.

The second case was a painting contractor insured by Cornhill where we had on the books a number of individual claims from paint splash and wet concrete splash where there were no contracting operations taking place? Thinking of the height and the wind direction and the Ford experience I suggested that we look further afield which we did and located the source. There, working on two high-rise office blocks, were contractors, some three-hundred yards away and out of our eye line, conducting some spray concrete facia and painting work. Samples were taken of the splashes and analysed by the local authority, resulting in our insured being identified as the source of contamination with Cornhill meeting the claims to restore the affected paintwork. The solution at Ford was to reiterate restrict the furnaces being opened and temporary covers provided for long-term parked vehicles while Cornhill adopted painting exclusions during certain weather conditions. In addition, where high-rise painting contracts were notified, we conducted liability surveys.

Armed with those experiences I recommended a practical solution to the hail threat in Turkey by the insured introducing removable snoods as at any one time they could have an estimated 1000 cars uncovered in the open. This was opposed to the adopted policy of some motor manufacturers who adhere a disposable protective cover to the roof and bonnet on some of their more expensive models, particularly those that are due to be transported and possibly stored externally. However, I considered this a costly, impractical exercise where our insured's large, run of the mill, stocks were concerned. Thus, in keeping with my role as a loss control engineer, I came up with an adaptable and reusable snood that could be strapped to a new vehicle while placed in the open and removed just as quickly, within two minutes. As car manufacturers change models quite frequently, the idea was to make a standard size as most popular vehicles are similar in height and width, therefore only the length required flexibility. Given that the bonnet, roof and windscreen suffered most damaged it would simply involve providing an adequate number for the manufacturer's most popular models. All this was discussed with the insured at the time of the visit and they seemed extremely keen on the idea; so much so that I informed them I would investigate.

In an effort to meet the insured's requirement my research took me from India and the Far East to seek out a business who could develop the design I had prepared. With the cost factor being so important and an order likely to be over US$20,000, the manufacturers of the prototype couldn't have been more accommodating. However, the insured and we as the insurers baulked even though this was a one-off price for a product that would have a life expectancy of at least a decade and could be used on several models, within reason. In loss terms, the claims we paid in repairs were more than the quoted cost of a consignment of snoods, and year on year there continue to be many, many losses, where the loss figures are no longer calculable. We patented the snood as a result of the time and effort spent and the half interest expressed by other concerns made us realise that it was a perfectly viable product and that we needed to protect our investment. Since that period there have been numerous claims for hail storm damage yet still both insurers and vehicle manufacturers continue to do little to nothing to minimise losses that have long since run into millions of dollars.

Legacies

When you or your employer decides to call it a day on your career there is inevitably the nagging thought as to whether or not you have in some small way left a little of you behind. During the normal course of a career there inevitably will be the ups and downs, successes and failures alternatively a passing that goes totally unnoticed. Recalling one such parting where it wasn't until the individual went into early retirement that those very people who decided on the employee's fate never appreciated until too late the extent of the employee's contribution to the business. As a claims manager, the person was a quiet unassuming employee who went about his task of assessing and settling claims without either *making waves* or in any way being a burden. By all accounts, his efforts went unnoticed therefore appeared to those in high places a run of the mill individual who while on a good salary would certainly not be missed. During a review of the claims department, it was decided to offer the manager an early retirement package thus allowing the board to promote one of the supposedly rising stars of the claims department to embrace the challenges of a relatively new aggressive and progressive insurance group.

Accepting the package on offer the very senior claims head without so much as a word of discontent walked off into the sunset and by all accounts not once looked back such was his disposition. The manager was to the lesser employees a very knowledgeable and helpful individual who certainly to me was always ready with words of wisdom consequently when conferring with others all agreed he would be sadly missed. The claims department had moved on but now led by a well-qualified manager who unfortunately while possessing the professional qualifications had limited claims experience for the top position. This questionable inexperience gave rise to tougher policies in respect to settlements and reserving, the latter being too low, which began to show a marked decline in performance when compared the predecessor's management that caused those in the higher echelons to look once again at the claims department. Following a thorough examination, it was decided to approach the retired former head of claims with an offer of reinstatement with added incentives which was accepted and within a short space of time, the results began to improve. The upshot was to appoint on this occasion a deputy manager who would shadow her superior until she was ready to assume on merit the position, ironically that date more or less coincided with the claims manager's originally planned date of retirement some two-years later.

The legacy of this manager became all too clear to see results in the group claims being back yet again on a stable footing with the newly appointed head living on the legacy of her former boss, a tribute to the individual. So these events got me wondering following forty or more years in the profession whether or not I made an impact or lasting impression with my former employers or in my chosen occupation. This curiosity not borne from any egotistical viewpoint as there were countless risk recommendations, requirements, guidance or observations made whilst surveying where one or more might just have avoided crippling injuries, the loss of lives or major losses involving property. Of course, we will never know but what I do know is that within the industry there still exists original loss control and loss prevention guidance concerning injuries, disease, environmental, fire and security that will stand the test of time. Well, certainly what I am aware of is that those hazard guidance notes compiled and written by me over the final two decades of my career are still in use in two major insurance groups.

While with AIG, one incident that stands out which I took exception too was where Paul Jewell and I compiled and revamped my hazard guidance notes written while at Independent Insurance that was subject to copyright and subsequently sold to a competitor. As I maintained intellectual copyright with Paul concentrating on the underwriting input, I wrote a fresh collection expanding other trade hazards. Having spent the best part of three years putting this work together that including breaking new ground for other business lines a whole new series was issued. This came to the notice of the Senior Vice President of commercial lines who posed the question as to where this revolutionary piece of work came from. One of his subordinates replied informing him that it was the collective efforts of the engineers that included extracts from a well-known US loss control publication, the latter to me suggested plagiarism. Never one to bite my tongue I wrote to the SVP, copying in the involved AVP that he was incorrect insofar as the work was mine alone, no plagiarism, no extracts or reference from other works and the underwriting section from Paul Jewell, his very own head of SME. Further, my response that before making such statements individuals should conduct their own research first, obviously there was no response from either party or in fact any other person copied on the original email which didn't surprise me at all.

The point being that there will always be those that follow and by adopting such a policy they do very little to advance the business whereas by being a little inventive and brave the business has every chance to thrive. What I found during my time was that the insurance industry is exciting with ample latitude for the creative individual to express themselves. Unfortunately, many stereotypes in the industry view radical thinkers as enigmas, in short, require keeping on a tight leash. Fortunately, I worked for some very senior people who were themselves innovative therefore valued forward-thinking people such as those at Independent and PCG at AIG.

At Independent and later at AIG the aim primarily was to educate both the insured and our own staff as to where risks or hazards existed. Consequently, I set about compiling those loss control manuals or as they were commonly known at Independent Insurance, trade hazard guidance notes, which was my first attempt at putting my knowledge in writing, all based on experience so that it could be used in the future. Previously for the British Home Parks Association, I wrote a specific safety manual for them which was widely sought after so at least we were aware of something that worked. My belief has always been that risk or loss control is not high on the insured's list of priorities as they inevitably have other pressing matters to attend to such as productivity, quality, taxes, labour and staff matters, which all affect profitability. Consequently, the information contained within any manual had to be relevant, clear, easily digested and user-friendly. Looking at similar guides I found them to be the exact opposite and unless the reader is loss control trained and informed plus has plenty of time to absorb the detail, I found them anything other than practical.

An underwriter has a proposal landing on his desk and is being pressed to provide a quotation but is not familiar with the trade. At Independent Insurance the underwriter simply electronically accessed the relevant trade, on a single page, which included at least one photograph, all of which could be digested in a matter of minutes and decide on the information provided whether or not they had an appetite for what was being proposed. Likewise for surveyors, wherever they were, car or office, electronically they could call up the same information where the related trade or occupancy hazards were listed, even rated, so the surveyor who may have never visited such a trade before knew where to pitch their questions and concentrate while on site. We later made this electronic guidance available to both our insured and brokers such was its merits.

As with any project that appears to work the demand within the company grew so I set about adding to the number of trades already covered. This demand increased by virtue of the head of SME requesting that the distribution be widened and following consultations with the regional managers recommended that the number of trades and occupancies should also be increased. The temptation was to follow the better-known publications where they certainly listed the trade hazards but also included numerous general perils such as electricity regardless of the energy source not being directly used in the process. By avoiding technical detail and in layman terms the intent being to ensure that the reader was not being side-tracked by the likes of technical specifics or jargon.

Not for one moment claiming credit, for what many thought, made these guidance notes unique and creditable was the underwriting footnote on each trade that was written and devised by a highly qualified commercial underwriter Paul Jewell who amongst his other qualities had excelled as a senior property surveyor for almost a decade. Shortly after these notes were placed on the server, we were made aware of some brokerages copying the details and making them available to potential clients. Just how these notes were received is best illustrated when I received a call from the US where a major insurer requested permission to copy the pollution sections from the now expanded trades' guidance. At that time the number of guidance notes had reached a total of 106 with another ten general hazard guidance notes to cover electricity, manual handling, mechanical handling plant, working at height, trips, slips and falls, personal protective equipment and so on. As to my legacy regarding my contributions when the manual was finally completed, including copyright, it was purchased by another major insurer for a five-figure sum and some fifteen years later I have received word that it is still in everyday use.

Setting aside the manuals the issue that stands out in my mind is that credit is rarely if ever given for the efforts of engineers and surveyors in the wider scheme of things. Every once in a while, the insurance industry gets hit by a spate of property-related claims from conditions they never had an inkling of previously. Of course, what these losses trigger is an inevitable rise in premiums to balance the book where such conditions are found to exist. Of course, such a market reaction doesn't just apply to property but also personal lines, liabilities, motor and so on. Example here being where burglary, in a certain area, suddenly become commonplace so home contents premiums rise and tougher conditions imposed. Those employees in high-risk occupations such as asbestos resulted in higher rates or the trade even considered taboo by some insurers. However, to simply believe the trade process alone gives rise to the insurers taking appropriate measures would be incorrect. Measuring the insurance industry's response in the late to mid-90s stress-related claims became high profile and as liability surveyors, we began investing survey time looking into stress management. Early in my career stress management was never given more than a cursory glance until claims were exceeding £250,000 emanating from the likes of social services, national health service and management.

Independent Insurance contributed a great deal in pursuing loss avoidance policies and were without doubt pioneers where combustible panels and surface coatings were found present in buildings. They achieved this by being the first insurer during my time to sponsor a PhD in fire engineering where such materials and conditions existed which is where my involvement is about to be concluded. What Independent set out to do was to gain a better understanding of the subject and while we had our own in-house, extremely experienced, fire surveyors they were not experts in all manner of materials that were being widely developed and continually introduced into buildings endlessly, many labelled *fire-resistant* or even *fire-proof*. Through personal connections, I was aware of the work going on at Leeds University and contacted the head of faculty for an opinion on the possibility of sponsoring an engineer. We identified an engineer who had already received two known offers from the US and persuaded him to take up a post with Independent as a fire surveyor while at the same time beginning and completing his doctorate. The research that went into this specialist area exposed some other conditions that could exacerbate a fire situation not previously recognised, for example, the volatiles that exists in other materials. It should be understood, as it was eloquently put to me, that is the whole point of a PhD: to contribute to the scientific community by discovering something which involves identifying gaps in existing knowledge.

Our engineer's research identified that work undertaken by some at Exova Fire and at Maryland University in the US had made assumptions and therefore was incomplete. What took many by surprise, including us at Independent, was the effect of materials such as metals, paints, adhesives and so on has in conjunction with the likes of EPS (Expanded Polystyrene).These materials increase the heat giving rise to the release of volatile gases and it is the release of those gases that contribute to conflagration making effective firefighting all but a token gesture in some conditions. So now the study took an additional turn for the worse as we, like so many others never recognised the added risk, while our PhD fire engineer did. Consequently, as insurers now better informed, we began widening the net during survey work looking at such as issues, not so much solely the fire load but the types of materials that had previously, in the grand scheme of things, been considered inconsequential.

The reason why in many cases this initiative has not gained the recognition it merited is that there are so many so-called experts in the field who are simply working without real substance, using past discoveries made by the real experts such as Dr Ryan McCreadie and others at the faculty of engineering at Leeds University. Even those in positions of responsibility are still playing catch up and in the interest of maintaining any credibility, the rhetoric is simply the work of others that commenced over three decades ago. During a Dubai seminar, I submitted that not only were the building designers and developers behind the times but the fire services were saddled with an impossible task in the event of a fire on high-rise structures. Why I was so aware was because our sponsored fire engineer worked alongside the property surveyors at Independent continually updating us on his research. Ironically this same source suggested to me at one point early on that I should investigate the efforts of the Australians who had at that time began introducing fire breaks in those high-rise buildings to stem the fire spreading upward where combustible panels were installed.

As with any hazard, the issue is that many are simply analysing the losses as opposed to identifying the root causes, because only then can they take appropriate measures that will have a lasting impact. To illustrate the extent of the expertise in the firefighting echelons a fire officer responding to the most recent tower fire in Dubai citing that a discarded cigarette possibly being the cause of the fire while another more realistic officer suggested a cigarette could have but that it probably ignited rubbish. During our research many years prior to this, we applied a burning cigarette directly to a panel in an attempt to ignite it but it failed simply leaving a scorch mark on the material. Of course, a cigarette could ignite other combustibles but the inference was, according to one fire officer, the cigarette alone was responsible, which only made the statement less credible as the fire started externally on an upper floor where no waste or other combustibles existed.

What gave cause to Independent becoming so proactive in our research was following on from a total loss of a business where the fire spread so quickly the fire service's efforts had little to no impact. This regardless of them being on site so quickly and with less than eighty-five per cent of the structure unaffected, and with little to no combustible materials within their efforts proved futile. Having little to no impact the fire officer decided that they should concentrate their firefighting efforts on the neighbouring premises. There were other losses of a similar nature consequently as insurers we applied stricter conditions and all such properties where similar materials were present so that they were insured at a higher rate with conditions not then heard of being applied.

Of course, we have to accept that there are considerable commercial considerations as these materials are inexpensive to produce, lightweight and therefore easy to install with excellent insulation qualities. However, there still remains those manufacturers who while promoting their products claim better fire-resistant qualities. It was in fact during a luncheon meeting with the financial director of a leading European expanded polystyrene producer, claimed his products were fireproof. Without so much as looking up from his lunch Dr Ryan, who was present, articulated, *Everything burns*.

There the story ends insofar as my legacy goes; through Independent Insurance, fire research into plastic-based materials was advanced from the mid-1990s to early 2000 in the UK. Alas though just to show how little effect it had on these materials' usage, in property development in UAE, during the late 1990s and into the early 2000s developers were permitted to construct over 600 high-rise structures using plastic-based insulation materials, resulting in some of the largest fire losses recorded in three skyscraper buildings. At the time it struck me as astonishing that there were still people present who believed they could extinguish an external fire on a high-rise building over 150 metres above ground and that such a fire could alone be caused by a carelessly discarded cigarette. I added facetiously that as there were two external fires in the same building was this down to more heavy smokers in residence? I also posed the question that, as there were another 597 high-rise buildings in Dubai, similarly clad, and there had been no fire incidents, could it be assumed smokers in those buildings were more responsible?

The evidence simply just did not support the fire department's claims as the fire disintegrated the panelling and any other materials, so citing the cigarette was simply clutching straws. Based on our UK and Greek fire losses it was established that there was a clear misunderstanding of the dangers where heat sources were concerned, including faulty electrical services, lightning, welding, sparks, barbecues and ovens. I did anticipate that my presentation might be contentious; however, to the contrary, I received no less than one dozen requests for a copy of my presentation which suggested to me that some of the detail was an eye-opener to a number of people in responsible positions.

Taking My Leave

There obviously comes a time when either you or your employer decides to call time on your career and at that time for me I didn't give it too much thought either way because of my circumstances. Financially, due in the main to a prudent wife, we were extremely comfortable and as for my physical condition, I could cope with the demands of conducting high net worth assessments without any problem. It wasn't like that some two or three years earlier when I was asking myself what on earth I was doing at this time in my life, some 100 feet above the ground on a narrow gantry that gave access to a salt silo in wet blustery conditions in the North-West of England? I wasn't sure whether I was just being foolhardy believing that at 70 years of age I could still physically cope, but at the same time I knew the job so well, so why should I stop?

Nonetheless, the opportunity to finish my career in PCG assessing high net worth insured was such a blessing as it was a delight. The reason being that for the most part, while not in those insured's financial positions, I was still a policyholder with assets, and thus with the very same concerns. Being a kindred spirit, as it were, tended to make my role as an assessor easier plus being as most insured were middle-aged or elderly there was a sense of affinity. Imagine conducting an assessment where the house and contents exceeded US$50 million and then following the visit being invited to dinner with the family or a round of golf; well, that happened to me on a few occasions.

Without a doubt, the greatest satisfaction I experienced was in the conversion of a commercial risk where regardless of my input it could not have been achieved without a deal of teamwork. While the underwriter is most certainly the decision maker where an insured is concerned the surveyor is surely the field guardian of the account. The underwriter will measure the performance of the policyholder by way of profitability but not necessarily being wholly influenced initially by the bottom line alone. Other significant factors that a site survey is expected to reveal entails the insured's management attitude and control or commitment which are critical going forward, not just in the existing period of insurance but possibly years hence.

In keeping the very best example of teamwork that I can recall involved a declined risk that was offered to our underwriters that read like a horror show. This in the main entailed the liability claims experience of the proposer while being insured with two other general insurers involved a string of negative results over a number of preceding years. During the first year with our underwriters, the trend appeared set to continue with the insured's loss ratio nearing a colossal

200%, at which point many right-minded insurers would have walked away; this certainly being the business decision of the previous two insurers. The initial liability survey, the first ironically this insured had ever experienced, put a different complexion on matters by way of sensing there was enough commitment at the very top that the malady that affected the insured would be ruthlessly tackled with the plea being a short period of grace. This as the result of a single heart to heart discussions with the insured's principle, a survey programme put into place, all recommendations made to be agreed and tackled within a defined timeframe, specific loss control guidance provided and finally a quarterly review.

The positives regarding this piece of business were laid out and in loss control terms rated favourably, a brave stance given the claims history. However, the underwriter was not present on site consequently never witnessed the managing director's mood or commitment therefore put trust in the field operative with surprising results. In the first period of insurance, the loss ratio fell by half; regardless of this Herculean effort the M/D of the insured showed no signs of letting up during the subsequent survey programme. What was so laudable was that the claims culture prevalent in the risk was the first casualty insofar as being tackled by way of the one-month probationary period being extended to six-months. It was not uncommon when reviewing the claims file to notice the number of trivial innocuous incidents that resulted in an extended period of absence and therefore inevitably a claim would follow for pain and suffering and a loss of earnings. As with some of my experiences at Ford, the word gets out resulting in a tried and tested process to achieve even minor settlements.

The insured's course of action where any employee was found to have been involved in malpractice or working ignoring safety rules was disciplined by way of the probationary period where pertinent being extended, secondly suspension and last but not least dismissal. Pre-employment medicals became very much order of the day resulting in the insured being far more selective at the recruitment stage. Medical records were constantly being reviewed as were employee absenteeism with the latter always requiring doctor certification. Regarding medical certification, there was a requirement imposed regarding sign-off by the respective medical practitioner which surprisingly went some considerable way to reducing long-term absenteeism or employees returning unfit. These simple but effective measures resulted in a remarkable turn round wherein the third year the risk's loss ratio fell to 60% followed a year later by a further 18% drop all due to the combined efforts on the part of the underwriter, the insured and the 'field guardian'. It stands out as being the very best example of teamwork in over forty-years of surveying.

Finally there is one thing to be recognised for your efforts or indeed your occupancy status within the industry but to have your presence being noted from an external organisation is quite another matter. During the time when surveying began taking me overseas out of the blue I was the recipient of a mail the source of which was all too obvious as the contents intimated it involved the French expression 'raison of d'Etat', 'reason of the state'. Briefly I was being requested to consider work in the interest of a HM Ministry while traveling and completing my employer's tasks wherever. I cannot recall the exact wordings now but following iterating my loyalties I destroyed the correspondence while not fully understanding what the requirements of the role involved albeit I had previously read and signed the Official Secrets Act 1911, needless to comment before the Act was amended in 1989. Subsequently I revealed at the point of signing only that detail to my employer because on certain occasions, my duties involved me surveying insured who were themselves bound by the Act. These surveys entailed visiting sites involved in sensitive development and manufacture of munitions, a whole range of fighting equipment or visiting ministerial sites where our insured were regular approved contractors for without such clearance neither they or I could ever have gained access.

Surprisingly there were some establishments where I was unaware of my security status having been examined before being granted access such as the survey at the research establishment at Aldermaston, the construction of the new GCHQ establishment, a US airbase, two Royal Navy dockyards and other what I considered lesser military or sensitive sites. It was as if my status was of no concern, which in reality was most certainly not the case. On a number of occasions, the insured's initial contact was not one of the same with the representative I met at the business address who by and large was the person who usually managed the day to day operations involving the likes of security, labour, manufacturing and quality. I can without fear of contradiction state unequivocally that a broker never accompanied me on those visits or was involved in making the survey arrangements hence accepting their none security standing.

Regardless of the occupancy my policy was to introduce myself and inform the representative regarding the aims and objectives of the visit and the type of information I would be seeking, never once mentioning security other than day to day preventative arrangements concerning the likes of fire and theft. During one such visit the insured's representative was so obviously unaware of my security standing when whilst touring the modern highly mechanised and equipped machine shop I commented on some machined parts idly enquiring what the dimensional tolerances were. At the same time identifying exactly what the metallic items being machined were to the astonishment of the representative who subsequently enquired, 'who exactly are you Mr McCreadie?' These cylindrical turnings were quite simply in the initial stages of manufacture to be used in HE munitions. It did cause the manager to enquire why given the stage of manufacture and me being an insurance surveyor and all how I managed to identify the size and more importantly the type of shell/projectile. While these items were in the early phases of manufacture the site operations to me were low key so in an attempt to side-track and to allay the representative's obvious anxiety, I took time to explain that access to these products final destination would rightly be nigh impossible.

At another UK site the insured, employing a team of highly qualified technicians, were engaged in the further development of current and obsolete military equipment which I found absolutely fascinating as I had served with fighting units equipped with some of those items. The reasons for being on site was again two-fold; the workers including management were regardless of being civil servants were statutorily covered under an EL policy while the processes involved treated parts and materials from a specific insured covered by our Products Liability policy. Further it was not unusual for such insured requiring the standard liability insurances for employees where often their duties and activities took them overseas. Regarding my involvement overseas it has to remain guarded albeit the subsequent insurance reports and appraisals were in a few cases of a more delicate nature yet at least to the uninitiated standard with some subtle detail that was peripheral to a particular insured or proposer.

As I recall the most in depth report I produced did not directly involve an insured albeit it was obviously of some interest and value as was my analysis and assessments centred about certain emerging markets. In such cases some detail concerned work processes, machining techniques and local produced equipment for the home market that I identified as certainly being patented in the West. One of the most intriguing meetings I had whilst in the Far East entailed being less than subtly quizzed about material used in the manufacture of caterpillar tracks fitted to armoured fighting vehicles. Sounds all very intriguing but in that particular case, as I took the time to explain I was not a metallurgist and besides there probably existed sufficient technical information in the public domain to have provided the enquiring party with the depth and level of information I certainly didn't possess or was privy to. One thing for certain like a number of the larger businesses we insured oversea it was possible to establish that with a little research or the odd slip of the tongue by an interpreter to learned some had separate and wider interests than that on offer.

What came as the biggest surprise was that the interested party clearly was aware of my employment history where details such as whilst serving as an armament artificer I would most certainly have been involved in the field where certain equipment was concerned? It should be borne in mind some insured and brokers required a sighting of my CV before me being cleared to conduct a survey that could have been viewed in a number of ways. It would have been nigh impossible not to have disclosed almost ten years work history from the age of fifteen, all of which was detailed in my service record on discharge. On reflection with my curriculum vitae revealing military college, indentures, trade summary and regular army service home and overseas so I thought little more about it. Of course not overlooking the fact that all of that was some twenty years before where the likes of the Conqueror, Centurion and Chieftain battle tanks were obsolete in the UK albeit the latter was still at the time in service in a number of Middle Eastern countries. Of course British armoured fighting vehicles are arguably amongst the very best, if not the best in the world consequently foreign designers and producers as expected will always be actively engaged in catch up.

It would really be amiss of me not to refer back and provide details concerning one visit involving a government official, at an insured, as a consequence leaving others to determine the justification for my reservations regarding her attendance. Very occasionally when I was about to head out overseas I was made aware, by a source, that an insured selected for survey was a subsidiary of a larger organisation consequently where other businesses making up the group had wider and more diverse interests that would not be obvious at the risk to be assessed. Very much in keeping with some UK groups, or indeed other countries or states, with a diversity of business interests not covered by our policy. One very good example of this being my account of the PRC baby product manufacturer where one official attending was obviously working to a different agenda hence duties, responsibilities and therefore reporting lines not being quite as narrow as first intimated, in fact the lady admitted she had attended university in the UK, hence her flawless English further openly admitted not to have been in the employ of the insured at all due to her being a direct PRC report.

All the while believing that I was free to go wherever, to enable me to view and assess the manufacturing processes, was not strictly accurate as was the question of photography that was certainly not permitted. Further the Taiwanese brokers and I were accompanied and directed for the entire five to six-hours while on site and always with the same PRC representative present. The site itself was considerable where I estimated that it would not have been possible to have visited all the areas making this judgement based on the size of the workforce and the buildings on the site plan. At lunch time while crossing the yard adjacent the four large canteens there were disciplined queues of workers, some five to six deep, stretching back fifty metres or so. With the most obvious being that a large number of employees were wearing heavier work apparel than those others whose lightweight overalls carried the insured's logo. What really struck me was firstly the unquestionable status of the PRC official and second the high levels of security that was way over and above that expected on a site seemingly involved in the manufacture of baby products. In fact, what confirmed my suspicions regarding the extent of the activities on the major of two sites was that while surveying the Shanghai factory it was the exact opposite with no PRC representative present and security almost non-existent.

This small matter of opting out of the visit to the Shanghai site flew in the face of the lady's assertion that she was simply an observer and to a lesser degree an arbiter insofar as them wanting me to gain a favourable impression of the PRC's efforts where product quality was concerned. Given the baby feeding products manufactured in Shanghai involved the most critical processes, due to having to achieve and maintain extremely high hygiene standards, I would have expected her to have been present there rather than at any of the other manufacturing locations, yet surprisingly she decided against the visit. This decision arousing my initial scepticism that her role was considerably more than just a 'flag waving' exercise. To further confirm my suspicions following some off-hand comments, earlier in the day, regarding ISO the responses gained revealed she possessed little to no knowledge insofar as being unaware of the insured's QA accreditation where design was concerned or indeed the difference between ISO 9000 and 9001.

Having cited both good and bad memories, it must lead ultimately to me reaching a point where I conclude, either through rose-tinted glasses or in the cold light of day, whether my career had been a success or not. Obviously, I measured the problems and mistakes made against the successes or at least those cases involving nothing too disastrous in trying to arrive at a fair conclusion. The only verdict that I arrived at was that I should let others be the judge and in doing so, to avoid possible bias, I should exclude the opinions of friends and ex-work colleagues. Having considered all, I felt that my career was nothing better than average, at least up until it became known that I was leaving loss control and going into retirement. Just before I was about to clear up my desk, I received four offers of employment, full or part-time, but preferably full-time, from corporate clients: two international and one UK. The fourth offer came as a real surprise from a US insurance competitor of my, about to be ex-employer, based in the US requiring me to relocate to take up a senior role all irrespective of my age.

So all it leaves is for me to say that there were many individuals who I owe a great deal for their support throughout my career namely, Alan Steer, Keith Cheshire and Jim Fage at Ford Motor Company; Geoff Ratcliffe and Richard Nicholls both at Cornhill/Allianz Insurance; Michael Bright, Keith Rutter, Robert McCracken, Mike Watts and John Monroe at Independent Insurance and not overlooking Paul Jewell, David Cook and Anne Owen at AIG. I had other matters to reflect on when attempting to reach the conclusion, since at least three suiters held me in high regard even though the business connection initially involved me, an intrusive insurance surveyor, arriving on their doorstep and taking up their precious time. Consequently, I think that those were the best judges of my accomplishments, which suggests I couldn't have been that bad an insurance representative and just maybe a credit to my profession.